Southwest Virginia
and
Shenandoah Valley

Thomas Bruce

HERITAGE BOOKS
2012

HERITAGE BOOKS
AN IMPRINT OF HERITAGE BOOKS, INC.

Books, CDs, and more—Worldwide

For our listing of thousands of titles see our website
at
www.HeritageBooks.com

A Facsimile Reprint
Published 2012 by
HERITAGE BOOKS, INC.
Publishing Division
100 Railroad Ave. #104
Westminster, Maryland 21157

Originally published 1891

Copyright © 1997 Heritage Books, Inc.

— Publisher's Notice —
In reprints such as this, it is often not possible to remove blemishes from the original. We feel the contents of this book warrant its reissue despite these blemishes and hope you will agree and read it with pleasure.

International Standard Book Numbers
Paperbound: 978-0-7884-0765-9
Clothbound: 978-0-7884-9309-6

CONTENTS.

PART I.

DEDICATION.

PREFACE.

INTRODUCTION.

                                                                                            PAGE

CHAPTER I—ORIGINAL SETTLERS 1

    Country west of the Blue Ridge, and the first settlers of Southwest Virginia — Their troubles with the Indians—Frontier warfare— Gradual formation of the counties until 1861—Primitive life of the early settlers : their laws, morals, etc.

CHAPTER II—TERRITORY OF SOUTHWEST VIRGINIA 23

    The great valley—Southwest Virginia a part of it—Territorial limits of Southwest Virginia—Its geological formation—Its scenery, climate, agricultural and mineral resources—Its advantages as a manufacturing centre.

CHAPTER III—SLAVERY 44

    Slavery : Its effect upon the country, upon the people owning slaves, and upon the slaves themselves — Abolition of slavery one of the causes of the progress of Southwest Virginia.

CHAPTER IV—NEW RIVER RAILROAD 53

    The New River branch of the Norfolk and Western Railroad Company—Part played by the New River railroad in the development of Southwest Virginia — Its inception and beginning — Its original charter—General G. C. Wharton—Dr. John B. Radford—First organization—Meeting at Eggleston's Springs—Resolutions of incorporators—Richard B. Roane, Thomas Graham, J. D. Sergeant, and Walter Wood — Governor Gilbert C. Walker — Options and coal lands, and the manner in which the road was captured from the original incorporators—Country which was opened up by this railroad—Pocahontas and the Flat Top coal regions.

IV INDEX:

                                                                                                PAGE

CHAPTER V—NORFOLK AND WESTERN RAILROAD 76

    The Norfolk and Western Railroad Company: Its inception and beginning—The Norfolk and Petersburg Railroad Company—The Southside railroad—The Virginia and Tennessee railroad—The Virginia and Kentucky railroad—The New River branch—Creation of the extension mortgage—The Cripple Creek extension—The Norfolk Terminal Company—The Bluestone extensions—The Clinch Valley extension—The Elk Horn extension to Ironton, Ohio—The Scioto Valley railroad—The Southeastern extension into North Carolina—The Shenandoah Valley division—Increase in mileage of the Norfolk and Western railroad for the past ten years—Increase in passenger and freight traffic—Increase of its rolling stock—Its financial advance.

CHAPTER VI—NORFOLK AND WESTERN RAILROAD—CONTINUED . . . 99

    Norfolk and Western Railroad Company (continued)—Policy of the company—Its equipment, service, and regulations—Its adjuncts (the Roanoke Machine Works, the Virginia Company, and real estate operations of the latter)—Speculations of the Norfolk and Western Railroad Company through the Virginia Company—Statutory regulations regarding railroads holding real estate—Commissioner of Railways of the State of Virginia the proper governing authority in these cases—General remarks on this company as a railroad corporation.

CHAPTER VII—JOINT-STOCK LAND COMPANIES 110

    The joint-stock land improvement companies—Their origin, formation, and mode of government—Their effect upon Southwest Virginia—These companies the means of manufactures and enterprises being brought in—The general results of their efforts—Speculation in connection with them—Its effects—Various opinions concerning the same—Lieutenant-Governor Tyler, James S. Simmons, L. S. Powell, L. S. Calfee, A. M. Bowman, E. S. Stuart, J. Lawrence Radford.

CHAPTER VIII—LYNCHBURG 120

    Lynchburg—Gateway to the Valley of Southwest Virginia—Something of its earlier history—Gradual growth of the town from antebellum days until the present—Its commercial and manufacturing interests—Its capital—Its business progress—Its climate—Its religious privileges, educational facilities, and social status—General remarks concerning Lynchburg.

CHAPTER IX—ROANOKE 132

    Roanoke—Derivation of the name—Big Lick—Its inception—Original owners of the soil—Its inhabitants—Its sudden progress—Change of name to Roanoke in 1882—Roanoke's rapid growth—The causes of it—The Roanoke Machine Works—Incorporation of the place as a city in 1884—Its manufacturing industries, commercial enterprises, and joint-stock land companies—The peculiar patriotic spirit of its inhabitants—Their pluck and energy in a material way—The laboring population—Strikes—Present number of people—Capital and financial condition of the city—Its churches, schools, and journals—Some general remarks about the city—Its probable future.

INDEX. V

PAGE

CHAPTER X—SALEM 149

Salem—Its name—Surrounding country, scenery, and climate—A summer resort—The seat of learning, refinement, and culture—Manners and character of the people—The land companies—D. B. Strouse, A. M. Bowman, J. W. F. Allemong, J. T. Crabtree, Dr. Dreher, George Allen, William M. Nelson—Industries and manufactories—Mineral resources and F. J. Chapman—Wonderful growth—Number of inhabitants—Financial status—Religious, educational, and social features of the place—Something concerning its future.

CHAPTER XI—RADFORD 160

Radford—Situation of the town—Formerly known as Central—Original owners of the soil—Inception of the place—Its gradual growth until construction of the New River Railroad—Incorporation of the place as Central in 1887—Purchase of the Wharton and Radford farms by the Radford Land and Improvement Company—West Radford—Development of the same—Its enterprises and industries—The Radford Development Company—Growth of East Radford—Spirit between East and West Radford—Resources of the town—Its financial status—Its population, schools, churches, and hotels—The Radford "Enterprise"—Future of the town as an iron centre.

CHAPTER XII—PULASKI CITY 171

West of New river—Stock-grazing section—New river plateau—Pulaski County — New river-Cripple creek mineral region — Cripple Creek extension of the Norfolk and Western Railroad Company—Martin's Tank—Beginning of its development—Growth of the place, and change of name to Pulaski City—Bertha Zinc Works—George T.Mills—L. S. Calfee—The furnaces and other industries and enterprises—Population, churches, schools, and social state of the town—Pulaski City as an iron centre—Probable future of the place.

CHAPTER XIII—WYTHE 179

Wythe County—Max Meadows—Wytheville—Crockett and Rural Retreat—Washington county—Glade Springs—Saltville—Future of the cities and towns of Southwest Virginia.

PART II.

INTRODUCTION.

PAGE

CHAPTER I—SHENANDOAH VALLEY 195

Territory traversed by the Shenandoah Valley railroad—Early settlers of this country—Indian warfare—Peace—The growth of the country—The Civil war—This country part of the battle-field during the war—Climate, scenery, agricultural and mineral resources—Manufacture and cost of making iron—These natural advantages original cause of the development of the country.

CHAPTER II—SHENANDOAH VALLEY RAILROAD 208

Shenandoah Valley railroad—Organized in 1867—Dates of construction of the various parts of the road—Completion to Waynesboro Junction—Tripartite agreement between the Shenandoah Valley railroad, the Norfolk and Western railroad, and the East Tennessee, Virginia and Georgia, which constituted the Virginia, Tennessee and Georgia Air Line—Issue of new mortgage by the Shenandoah Valley Railroad Company—Interest of the Norfolk and Western in this company—Receiver appointed—Purchase of the road by the Norfolk and Western Railroad Company—Some general remarks as to the effect of this purchase upon Shenandoah Valley.

CHAPTER III—LURAY 215

Effect of the wonderful Caverns of Luray upon Shenandoah Valley—Luray—Derivation of its name—Its gradual growth—Discovery of the caverns by B. P. Stebbins, Andrew J. Campbell, and W. B. Campbell—Purchase of Cave Hill by these parties—Litigation over the same—Decision of the supreme court against the purchasers—Sale of the property to a Northern syndicate—Description of the caverns—Advent of Shenandoah Valley railroad—The Defored tannery—Rapid growth of Luray—The Valley Land and Improvement Company—Manufactories and industries of the town—Population, schools, and churches—Luray Inn—General remarks upon the place.

CHAPTER IV—SHENANDOAH—GROTTOES 224

Shenandoah—Formerly Milnes—Centre of a mineral region—Some of its advantages—The railroad shops—An iron-manufacturing point—The furnaces—Its advantages as a divisional point—The Shenandoah Land and Improvement Company—Capitalists connected with it—Something as to the future of the place—The Grottoes of the Shenandoah—Weyer's Cave—Fountain's Cave—Madison's Cave—The place now called Shendun—The Grottoes Company—Jed. Hotchkiss—Improvements made there—Its future as a business centre and summer resort.

INDEX. VII
PAGE

CHAPTER V—BERRYVILLE............................. 234

Clarke county—Date of formation—Its resources—Population and class of people—Berryville, the county-seat (formerly known as Battletown)—Growth of the place since the advent of the Shenandoah Valley railroad—The inhabitants of the place—Churches, schools, and social status—Many facilities and advantages of the town—Formation of the Berryville Land and Improvement Company—Some general remarks upon the town.

CHAPTER VI—FRONT ROYAL........................... 239

Warren county—Formed in 1836—Character of its agricultural resources and mineral deposits—Front Royal, the county-seat—The twin cities, Front Royal and Riverton—Something of their past history—Growth of these places after the construction of the Shenandoah Valley railroad—Present number and character of the inhabitants of the twin cities—The Front Royal and Riverton Improvement Company—H. H. Downing—Manufacturing and commercial interests of the towns—The development companies—Churches, schools, and social state—One of the coming cities of Shenandoah Valley.

CHAPTER VII—WAYNESBORO.......................... 246

Augusta county—Once a part of Orange county—Cut off in 1738—This county once included all the country between the Blue Ridge mountains and Mississippi river—Its settlement and rapid growth—Population of same—Agricultural and mineral resources—Waynesboro—When laid off and origin of its name—Its original owners and celebrated tavern—Growth of the place, and the Civil war—Advent of the Shenandoah Valley railroad—Development of Waynesboro commenced by Basic City in 1889—The Waynesboro Company—The Waynesboro and Basic City Land Company—Improvements—Manufacturing and commercial interests of the place—Churches, schools, and people of Waynesboro—This town obliged to become a part of Basic City.

CHAPTER VIII—BASIC CITY............................ 253

Basic City—Location—On May 9th the junction of the Chesapeake and Ohio railroad and the Shenandoah Valley—Rapid growth—The cause—Centre of the basic steel section in the South—The Basic City Mining and Manufacturing Company—Policy of the company—Sam. Furrow—J. M. Quarles—Manufacturing and commercial interests of the place—Basic City and Waynesboro—Some general remarks upon the towns in Shenandoah Valley as to their present status and future progress.

DEDICATION.

NOT on account of its merit, but the sincere gratitude and affection of the author, is this work inscribed and dedicated to one, who, though a moving power behind the throne, is none the less entitled to the credit of having swayed the potent influence that led to the conception of the undertaking in the beginning, as, by her love, fidelity, and encouragement, she assisted materially in the execution of it.

THE AUTHOR.

PREFACE.

WHATEVER is wonderful in animate or inanimate nature excites our admiration, and conceives within us an intense desire to inquire into it—to seek out as far as possible the causes which have produced the startling effects.

The rapid development of Southwest Virginia and Shenandoah Valley is almost phenomenal. The beholder, North, South, East, and West, is casting his glance towards these favored sections of the New South in her new era, and astonishment at its rapid strides rests upon his face. In fact, so wonderful is the progression of these sections that the chronicler of dates and events occurring within their borders can scarcely keep apace with them. Everything connected with them is fraught with unusual interest, and the older inhabitants of these communities cannot gauge the rapid pulse, nor comprehend at all the throbbing beats of the arteries of this material progression which is transforming a country ruined by a civil war twenty years ago into a land literally "flowing with milk and honey."

The author here desires to express his earnest thanks to the people of these sections who, by attention, courtesy, and kindness, contributed so materially to the lightening of his labors and his search after knowledge in the way of material and data. He is fully aware of the arduous undertaking now before him, and enters upon the same with many misgivings as to his ability to perform it well, trusting more to the indulgence of the kind reader rather than to any power of his in the execution of so great a task.

As this is purely an historical work, and the author desiring it to rest solely upon its intrinsic merit, it is stripped of all accessories in the way of sketches, views, and cuts, which constitute more or less a charm about a book that has a great deal to do with forming the opinion of a large portion of the public in regard to writings of the present day.

THE AUTHOR.

INTRODUCTION.

SOUTHWEST Virginia and Shenandoah Valley comprise the fairest dominion of any section of country lying within the limits of the Southern States.

The wonderful development of these two sections which has marked the progress of events in the past ten years in the Southern States will be treated in this work rather in accordance with the landmark of time than that of territory. The great Southwest, neither more beautiful nor richer in agricultural and mineral resources than Shenandoah Valley, will be taken first, because, in point of time, it was the first to adorn the robe of material progress and growth.

It will be readily seen that this work is rather an inquiry into the astonishing growth of these sections, than any past, succinct history of them; and, after each as a whole has been treated, historical sketches of the new towns which have grown as if by magic along the lines of the Norfolk and Western railroad, with those on the Shenandoah Valley, will be given in their proper places.

It is not difficult to assign the causes for the rapid development of these sections. First, the location of the countries themselves, with their scenery, salubrious climate, agricultural and mineral resources bestowed upon them in a prodigal manner by the God of nature. Second, the abolition of slavery. Third, the conception, formation, and construction of the New River railroad into the rich coal fields of Southwest Virginia, and Mercer and McDowell counties, West Virginia. Fourth, the developing policy of the Norfolk and Western Railroad Company, in conjunction with the construction of the Shenandoah Valley railroad to Roanoke, intersecting the former. Fifth, the formation of the joint-stock land companies, and their untiring energy and enterprise in locating, encouraging, and constructing vast industrial enterprises, which invariably take their part in a country's material progress.

The inquiry into and history of these causes shall be impartially written, and full credit given to each and every one; while all objectionable features, if there be any, will be fairly discussed.

For reasons already assigned, we will take Southwest Virginia as the first part of our work, and then sketches of the cities and towns most instrumental in aiding in the rapid development and growth of this section.

SOUTHWEST VIRGINIA

AND

SHENANDOAH VALLEY.

CHAPTER I.

Country west of the Blue Ridge, and the first settlers of Southwest Virginia—Their trouble with the Indians—Frontier warfare—Gradual formation of the various counties until 1861—Primitive life of the early settlers: their laws, morals, etc.

THE Blue Ridge mountains, as a landmark, have played an important part in Virginia's history. Long before the fertile valleys and mineral hills west of these mountains were discovered, or the gaze of the white man rested upon New river, the eastern portion of the State had some 80,000 people, and Shenandoah Valley three or four hundred souls. The forefathers of the latter came into this valley by way of Harper's Ferry from Pennsylvania, of whom we shall have more to say in the second part of this work.

The threading of the labyrinth of Rosamond's bower could scarcely have been more difficult than the tracing of the footsteps of these earlier settlers, in any chronological order, who first came into that country now known as Southwest Virginia. The want of all records, which the early settlers failed to preserve, reduces the chronicler of events to groping in the dark, and learning from uncertain sounds the paths trod by our forefathers. Several reasons may be assigned for this unfortunate state of affairs. The primitive, struggling life of those earlier pioneers was not conducive to the recordation of events, and the constant destruction of their settlements by the Indians was often a clean sweep, where the inhabitants could not even escape with their lives, to say nothing of records, if any were preserved. Tradition, therefore, plays an important part in this earlier history, for out of chaos it is difficult to extract facts with any degree of certainty, or bring chronologically down events which have only the palest light to disclose the landmarks as we descend the corridors of time.

In the year 1734 the county of Orange was formed. It then embraced not only its present area east of the Blue Ridge, but all the undefined claims of the Colony of Virginia west of the Blue Ridge mountains to the Pacific ocean. The western portion of this territory at that time was the home of the Indian and wild beasts, who in a great measure preyed upon each other.

In the year 1738 Orange county was diminished in territory by the formation of Augusta and Frederick counties, which comprised all the territorial limits west of the Blue Ridge mountains. With the exception of the small area of country in the lower part of Shenandoah county, called Frederick, Augusta comprised all the territory west of the Blue Ridge. In 1763, by the treaty with France, its western boundaries were limited by the Mississippi river, and it contained all that section of country west of the Blue Ridge, and the States of West Virginia, Kentucky, Ohio, Indiana, Illinois, Michigan, and Wisconsin.

The first white persons who ever trod the wilds of western Virginia were not Governor Spotswood and his knights of the "Golden Horseshoe," as many would have us believe. Although he was knighted and immortalized for having discovered what he then described as "God's country," yet others before him had penetrated those wilds, of which he only took a cursory view. A careful examination, by aid of the best light we have upon the subject, clearly indicates that Colonel Wood was in Southwest Virginia sixty-two years before Governor Spotswood.

In 1654, Colonel Abraham Wood, being of an adventurous and roving disposition, obtained permission of the Governor of

Virginia to explore the country west and open a trade with the Indians. He was a resident of Appomattox, dwelling somewhere near the present sight of the city of Petersburg. There is neither a record of the number he took with him on this expedition, nor as to the particular route chosen by him; but from the fact that "Wood's Gap" lies in the Blue Ridge between Smith's branch of Dan river and the Little river branch of New river, in Floyd county, we may reasonably suppose that he first struck the river now known as New river not far from the Blue Ridge, near the line of Virginia and North Carolina. There can be but little doubt as to this gap being named after him, and if so, this must have been his tread through what was then a howling wilderness. Following Little river he must have first discovered New river at the mouth of the former, and finding a stream undiscovered before, doubtless called it then and there "New River," which name it bears to this day.

As to the result of Colonel Wood's trip, or the fate of his party of humble hunters whom he carried with him, but little if anything is known. That it was not a successful one, so far as any treaty with the Indians went, we are satisfied, because they were extremely unfriendly to the next expedition which went out, the guides refusing to conduct Captain Henry Batte's followers into a certain section of the Southwest, inasmuch as the Indians there were unfriendly to the whites. As Colonel Wood's crowd of traders, with himself, were the only whites who had crossed the Blue Ridge, then it was to this very party the Indian guide was referring. So we naturally conclude that Colonel Wood's efforts to establish anything like friendly relations were fruitless.

In 1666, Sir William Berkeley dispatched a Captain Batte, with fourteen Virginians and fourteen Indians, to make an exploration—all of whom started from Appomattox. What route they pursued is not exactly known; but, as we have stated, when they reached a certain point they refused to go farther, under advice from their Indian guides. In his account of this expedition mention is made by Captain Henry Batte of a river flowing westward, which he pursued downward until he came to some salt springs. Mr. John P. Hale, in his work, "Trans-Alleghany Pioneers," supposes this to have been in the Kanawha Valley, and the salt made at Campbell's Creek Salt Spring. Nothing authentic has been obtained to support this except extrinsic facts which Mr. Hale has so sensibly based his supposition upon. At all events, it is known that Henry Batte and his followers returned to the eastern portion of the colony, for he made a report to Governor Berkeley of such a flattering nature that the latter announced his determination of investigating the country himself, which would have been of infinite service to the future descendants of these people, all of whom have groped in darkness concerning the early history of this country.

Governor Spotswood and his knights of the "Golden Horseshoe" penetrated this section, or at least the valley, at a point known as Swift Run Gap, in 1716. In 1732, Joist Hite, John Lewis, Bowman, Green, Chrisman, McKay, Stephens, Duff, and others came in by way of Harper's Ferry; and in 1734 Morgan, Allen, Moore, Shephard, Harper, and others settled in that portion of the valley known as Shenandoah. From 1735 to 1738, Beverley, Christian, Patton, Preston, Burden, and others settled west of the Blue Ridge. This Patton was the Colonel Patton who in 1736 obtained a grant of 120,000 acres of land west of the Blue Ridge, in the Valley of Virginia. He and his son-in-law, Colonel John Buchanan, located these lands on James river, in what is known as Botetourt now, and the villages, Buchanan and Pattonsburg, which sprang up on the opposite sides of the river, were respectively named after them. A great many of their descendants now reside throughout this section of Southwest Virginia.

About 1744 one Thomas Ingles and his son William, then a young man, made an exploration west of the Blue Ridge, and while on this trip became acquainted with George Draper and his family, who were residing at Pattonsburg, Virginia, on James river. Some time afterwards, George Draper went on a hunting expedition, and as he never returned, his family thought that he was killed by the Indians. The after lives, history, and fate of the Drapers and Ingleses were so intimately mingled and blended that anything touching them is of interest.

The next expedition of which we have any chronological evidence was that of Dr. Thomas Walker, Colonel James Patton, Colonel Buchanan, and others, in the year 1748, when they travelled into Kentucky through Southwest Virginia. It was during this trip that a pass was discovered by Colonel Walker, who named it Cumberland Gap, in honor of the Duke of Cumberland. The creek which flows into New river near Major Cecil's, in Giles county, beyond Pembroke station, on the New River railroad, was discovered during this expedition, and to this day bears the name of "Walker's creek." The parallel ranges of mountains near by were also called in honor of Colonel Walker. This party travelled across the Flat Top mountain, which has since become celebrated for the quantity and quality of its semi-bituminous coal. The object of this expedition was to gain some insight into the country with reference to obtaining a grant; for on their return "The Loyal Land Company" was organized, based on a grant of 800,000 acres north of the line of the Carolinas and west of the mountains, and the company was incorporated June, 1749.

Heretofore these explorers went west of the Blue Ridge merely for the purpose of discovery, and then returned east. None of them crossed into the trackless wilderness for a permanent residence, until some of the most daring and adventurous ones determined at last to make a settlement in this beautiful but wild country.

In 1748, after the return of the Patton party, Thomas Ingles and his three sons, Mrs. Draper and her son and daughter, Adam Harman, Henry Lenard, and James Burke moved westward, with the determination to cast their fortunes farther west and make a permanent settlement. They chose one of the loveliest spots imaginable for their home—that beautiful and level plateau of fertile land on which the site of Blacksburg, in Montgomery county, is now located. This point was called west of the Alleghanies, but it was west of the divide, or floor of the valley raised, just as Massanutton mountain divides Shenandoah Valley in two parts. Here these pioneers settled and erected their crude residences of rough hewn logs, naming the place "Draper's Meadows." Things went prosperously along with them, and by their enconiums upon the fertility of the country, splendid scenery and balmy climate, other settlers were induced to come, among whom may be mentioned William Harbison, George Hoopaugh, James Cull, and the Lybrooks, who settled on Sinking creek, a short distance below the New River White Sulphur Springs. All the settlers were steadily at work engaged in clearing their lands and making themselves as prosperous and happy as the state of their circumstances would admit. They were on the friendliest terms with the Indians who occasionally passed and repassed the settlement, without any hostile signs whatever. In fact, except for one or two small depredations made against Harman and Hoopaugh, there was perfect unanimity between the two races.

But this pleasant state of affairs was not to continue. On July 8, 1755, the day before the English army was so ignominiously defeated under General Braddock, the red-skins made a raid upon this peaceful settlement, killing and wounding or capturing every living soul. Colonel Patton, Casper Barries, Mrs. George Draper, and a child of John Draper were killed, while Mrs. John Draper and Mrs. Cull were severely wounded. Mrs. William Ingles (*née* Mary Draper), Mrs. John Draper, and Henry Lenard were captured prisoners. James Burke would doubtless have shared the fate of these people, but in 1754 he removed to that portion of the country now known as Tazewell, and made a settlement in the fertile valley, hemmed in by mountains, known as "Burke's Garden," and justly celebrated as one of the loveliest and most charming places in Southwest Virginia.

In connection with this raid there is recorded an incident concerning Mrs. William Ingles which is sad and touching to the last degree. This lady, one of the whites captured in the Draper's Meadows raid, was the daughter of George Draper, and married William Ingles, the son of Thomas Ingles. She, with her children and another lady, were conveyed by the Indians down New river, thence by the Kanawha on into Ohio to the camp of the Indians. During this trip Mrs. Ingles, by her useful knowledge, adroit acts, and pleasant address, won the esteem and respect of the Indians, who hoped also to obtain a handsome ransom for herself and children. During this journey into Ohio Mrs. Ingles gave birth to another child, and yet continued her march with the rest, exhibiting a nerve and fortitude rarely seen in a woman. Being of an observant nature, she watched the streams closely as she was marching out, and so placed them in her mind as to remember them distinctly. Her final destination, Big Bone Lick, was at last reached, and her sons having been previously taken from her, she reached this place in company with only one white woman and her infant babe at her breast. Here at this place she again made herself very useful in making salt, and shirts for the Indians out of the checked cloth purchased from the French traders. While residing here, some seven hundred miles from Draper's Meadows settlement, by the circuitous route which they had to come by the rivers, she meditated and planned an escape. She communicated her plans to the other woman, who, although opposed at first on account of the dangers they would have to encounter, finally consented. The parting from her infant, which on the first blush might seem to savor of a want of motherly feeling, was to save herself from a more degrading and worse fate had she remained. With only a blanket apiece and one suit of clothes on their backs, these females plunged into the trackless forest and turned their faces homeward, to walk seven hundred miles. To detail their various adventures and sufferings, their wanderings up and down the streams, their subsistence on berries, wild fruits, and the productions of the forest, their sore feet and intense physical suffering and mental anguish, would transgress our space. For forty days Mrs. Ingles travelled, until worn out and exhausted, she passed around the Anvil Cliffs at New River White Sulphur Springs and came to Adam Harmon's place, who, hearing her cries in his corn-patch, recognized her, and took the tenderest care of her until she could be reunited to her family. Her travelling companion, who during their journey had threatened to kill Mrs. Ingles, was afterwards found by Harmon and safely conducted to the white settlement. This Adam Harmon's place was located on the plateau where the hotel and buildings of the New River White Sulphur Springs are situated at present.

During the year 1755 Vass Fort was raided by the Indians and some of the whites murdered. This stronghold was located about ten miles from Christiansburg, on the head waters of Roanoke river, in Montgomery county. It was near this place that Colonel Washington, Major Andrew Lewis, and Captain William Preston escaped from being attacked, in a wonderful manner, by a mistake of orders given a band of Indians by their chief, who had been stationed to attack Colonel Washington and party. In return for this raid and other depredations committed by the Indians, in March, 1756, General Lewis, with several gentlemen and Captain Montgomery's volunteer company, made what is known as the Big Sandy expedition. They all met at Camp Frederick, and starting out, proceeded by way of Clinch river, Bear Garden, Burke's Garden, over Tug mountain, and down the Tug fork of Big Sandy, now in West Virginia. For some reason this expedition accomplished nothing, being unsuccessful, or perhaps ordered back. Certain it is, these Ohio Shawney Indians were never visited with the punishment they deserved for their unwarranted attacks upon the peaceful white settlers.

About this time the Ingleses, with their families, moved up on New river, and constructed a fort at a place called Ingles' Ferry, which point is about one mile from the present site of

Radford, up the river. The place is still in the possession of Captain Ingles, a descendant of the family. During those earlier days this point and Draper's Meadows settlement were the places of departure for those seeking homes farther west. In 1770 the county of Botetourt was formed from Augusta, taking its name in honor of Lord Botetourt. Mr. William Preston, who, in 1761, married Susanna Smith, of Hanover county, was made surveyor of the county, which in those days was a most lucrative post. He first resided at his farm known as "Greenfield," near Amsterdam, but subsequently removed near the Draper's Meadows settlement to an estate which he acquired in 1774, and in honor of his wife changed the name of the place to Smithfield, which name it bore to the third and fourth generations of the Preston family. The descendants and connections of this family threw out its branches in all directions from Smithfield, and settled much of the country around, among whom may be mentioned the Pattons, Prestons, Buchanans, Thompsons, Madisons, Breckenridges, Peytons, McDowells, Floyds, Bowyers, Harts, Crittendens, Bentons, Hamptons, Johnsons, and many other noted people, who assisted in building up their country and became worthy representatives of Roanoke, Botetourt, Montgomery, Washington, and Smyth counties, as well as other States.

Near Greenfield, in Botetourt county, a widow by the name of Cloyd resided, with one son. She was killed by the Indians prior to 1773, and when William Preston, with his family, moved to Draper's Meadows settlement young Joseph Cloyd accompanied them. He afterwards settled on Back creek, west of New river, in that section of country which lies in the county made in 1839, known as Pulaski. He was the father of General Gordon Cloyd, David and Thomas Cloyd, and grandfather of Colonel Joseph Cloyd, who, with his family, owned the fine estates on Back creek, at the mountain known as Cloyd's mountain, near which was fought the battle of Cloyd's mountain, in 1864. These Cloyds were among the first of settlers in Pulaski, and from that family, by intermarriage, connection, and descent, have sprung the Cloyds, Bells, Kents, McGavocks, and Cowans—all now settled in Pulaski county, and are representative people of Southwest Virginia.

Prior to 1758, one Colonel John Chiswell, who had killed a man in a personal encounter, and who died in jail awaiting his trial, discovered near New river, in that section of country now known as Wythe county, some lead mines. These mines (now known better by the name of Austinville) were the cause of a fort being constructed in 1758 by the State, under the supervision of Colonel William Boyd, who named it in honor of Colonel Chiswell, his friend. In 1772 all of this section of country was formed into a new county, known as Fincastle—named in honor of Lord Botetourt's country home in England—*Fin-castle.* This county was only in existence four years, for in 1776 it was abolished, and the territory divided into new counties, called Montgomery, Washington, and Kentucky. The latter afterwards became the State known by that name.

It appears from the scanty records we have that some time about the year 1763 the Indians were instigated by the French who dwelt east of the Mississippi river to resist as much as possible the settlement of the whites upon their western territory. The French, being now out of all reach of the settlements, could give such advice with impunity. Their red allies, into whose ears the poison of revenge had been poured, bitterly resisted the white men in their onward march westward, and, although the tide continued to pour steadily in that direction, each trail was marked with the blood of some pioneer, drawn by the arrow or tomahawk of the Indian. As time rolled on the disposition of the Indians grew more determined to resist each new footstep made upon their happy hunting-grounds by the pale-faces coming west. From first defending their land, the Indians, finding the superiority they possessed numerically, and the knowledge they had of the country, became aggressive and committed every imaginable kind of depredation upon their white neighbors. In order to check these, an expedition under Colonel Bouquette was sent out, which resulted in staying their atrocities for the while and the recovery of three or four hundred white prisoners who had been captured. In the following year (1765) a treaty of peace was concluded with them, made under the auspices of Sir William Johnson, which for some time caused a cessation of hostilities between the two races. This treaty gave an impetus to western emigration, and by 1772–'74 settlements of the country were made all along this western region by the whites as far as the Ohio river at several points, and the main tributary streams and their smaller branches.

The levying of taxes by England at this juncture to support the expenses of the French and Indian wars occasioned an outcry from the colonists, who deemed such measures not only unjust, but onerous to the last degree. They protested strongly against such legislation, and charged the English with instigating the Indians to resist, in order that a sufficient excuse might appear for their withdrawal of the forces of the colony from the east, where it is said the English desired to carry their oppressive measures through. Although such may have been the *bona fide* belief of the colonists, there is no evidence of any such action by the English. Such a policy would have been self-destructive on their part at that time.

At all events, bad feeling rose again between the races, and several murders were committed. A white man was killed by the Indians while he was in a trading boat above Wheeling creek, and within a few days afterwards Captain Michael Cresap and party killed two Indians. This same captain and followers surprised an Indian camp lower down, and killed nearly all, at the mouth of Captina. Some week or two afterwards, in April, Daniel Greathouse with a party of whites attacked an encampment of Indians near the mouth of Yellow creek, and, after dosing them with whiskey, killed nearly all. Some of the Indians slayed at each of these places were members of Logan's family, and it was he who charged Captain Cresap with the death of his kin. And about this time, to add fuel to the flame, Bald Eagle, an old and friendly Delaware chief, was unjustifiably murdered by some whites straggling around, and set up in his canoe with a pipe in his mouth, and the barge sent drifting down the Monongahela river. The Indians became furious at these murders, and it was evident that they meant to revenge them. In the spring of 1874 they combined for aggressive action.

When the Indians seemed bent on hostile measures, messages were first transmitted the governor, Lord Dunmore, who dispatched Colonel August McDonald with four hundred men to make an expedition of a hostile nature into the Indian territory to occupy them at home and prevent their raids upon the border settlements of the whites. But as this move failed to accomplish its intended object, messengers were again sent to Governor Dunmore, who afterwards summoned General Andrew Lewis, of Botetourt county, with whom to advise concerning a campaign against the Indians. The result was an army of two divisions was organized at once, one of which was to be commanded by General Lewis, the other by Lord Dunmore himself.

Organizing his forces in Augusta, Botetourt, and Fincastle counties, General Lewis and his brother, Colonel Charles Lewis, took command of the army and *rendezvoused* at Camp Union about September 1, 1774, and were to march from there to the mouth of the Kanawha. Governor Dunmore was to collect his army in Frederick and Dunmore (now Shenandoah) counties and those adjacent thereto, go the northwest trail over Braddock's route, by way of Fort Pitt, and thence down the Ohio river, and meet General Andrew Lewis at the mouth of the Kanawha.

On the 2d day of October General Lewis reached the Kanawha river and waited anxiously for Lord Dunmore, who was to have joined him at that time. Hearing nothing further from the Governor, he sent some messengers up the Ohio river to learn his whereabouts. Before these returned several scouts arrived at his camp, on October 9th, with orders from Lord Dunmore to cross the river and meet him in the Indian territory in Ohio. For reasons substantially good Lewis disregarded these messages, and at an early hour on the morning of the 10th gave orders for a general break-up of his camp, intending to proceed at once across the river into the villages of the Indians. But the red-skins saved him that irksome journey. When ready to start he was confronted by an army of a thousand braves commanded by their leaders, Logan, Red Hawk, Blue Jacket, Eliinipsico, and several others. Here took place the largest battle ever waged in this section of the country between the whites and Indians—the memorable battle of Point Pleasant—in which General Lewis won additional laurels and came out victorious. In this fight Colonel Charles Lewis, Colonel Field, and several other prominent gentlemen were killed, and the wounded numerous, among whom were Colonel William Fleming, John Field, Captains Murray and McChannahan, Samuel Wilson, and others. Fifty-three were killed and eighty-seven wounded in the white army. The losses by death and wounds were greater among the Indians.

The result of this battle was the bugle sound for the retreat of the Indians before the whites. A substantial fort was established at this point, and a kind of military school for the training of the white settlers under Colonel Lewis introduced. The Indians receded farther west, and the whites continued to pour in. We hear of no further trouble in this section, except occasional depredations of each race upon the other on the frontier lines of civilization.

The man and general who so ably espoused and conducted the cause of his race in those troublesome times deserves more than passing notice. He was a man of stalwart frame and stern manner and appearance. At the treaty of Fort Stanwix, the Governor of New York said of him: "He looks like the genius of the forest, and the very ground seems to tremble under him." His military career was a memorable one. It began with General Washington at Great Meadows and Fort Necessity, ending with his death just before the surrender of Yorkton, from a fever. He started for his home in Botetourt—now Roanoke—but falling ill stopped at Colonel Buford's, east of the Blue Ridge, where he breathed his last in the midst of kind friends. He was brought home and interred on his estate, "Dropmore," just outside of what is now the corporate limits of Salem. No stone marks his resting-place nor points to the stranger where he lies, and the weeds and grass around his grave have a gentle sigh, as if rebuking Virginia and Roanoke for failing to mark the resting-place of one who died for his country. His acts have lived, and many worthy descendants now residing in Roanoke and other counties revere his memory and his deeds of greatness.

One of the descendants of General Andrew Lewis married a Miss Tosh, of Roanoke county, formerly a part of Botetourt, from which it was taken in 1838. Between the years 1747 and 1767 George the III, King of England, granted to one Thomas Tosh all that boundary of land from near Tinker creek across to Roanoke river, on which is now situated the city of Roanoke, containing some 1650 acres. This family was among the earliest settlers in this section, and Miss Jane Tosh, the mother of Major Andrew Lewis and Thomas Lewis, his brother, married a lineal descendant of General Andrew Lewis of Revolutionary fame. Among the landed possessions of this Tosh family was a grant from Thomas Jefferson, the President. Many branches of this family are throughout the country and assisted in settling it.

Among the depredations made by the Indians after the battle of Point Pleasant was the raid on Burke's Garden, situated in Tazewell county, which was taken from western Augusta in the year 1799. James Burke, the original settler of this lovely spot, had been killed; and subsequently, under license of the "Loyal Land Company," William Ingles had taken up the land. His son, Thomas Ingles, who was given an education notwithstanding his roving disposition, married Miss Eleanor Grills, of Albemarle, and then located in Burke's Garden. He lived apparently contented and happy here until the year 1782, when a raid was made on his home by some Indians commanded by "Black Wolf." Thomas Ingles was away when their attack was made, and they carried off his wife and children and two negro slaves, after firing his buildings, which were soon reduced to ashes. Going to the nearest settlement, which was in the "Rich Valley," on the north fork of the Holston river, he gathered together some sixteen men, and, returning, met Joseph Hix with a squad. Both forces were placed under command of Captain Maxwell, and hot pursuit began after the red-skins. Five days passed before the Indians were overtaken, when they were attacked. Two of Thomas Ingles' children were killed, and his wife, with her infant, barely escaped. Captain Maxwell was shot, and died shortly afterwards. The slaves escaped uninjured. The little girl died on their way home from her injuries, and but for a surgeon who met them at Clinch settlement, in company with William Ingles, father of Thomas, from New river, Mrs. Thomas Ingles would have probably died. The supposition is that several Indians were killed in this engagement.

This blood-thirsty Black Wolf did his part faithfully in the annals of raiding, by attacking and capturing white settlers, who were powerless to resist him. The lovely spot known as Abb's Valley, in the northern part of Tazewell county, and which derived its name from Absalom Looney, who came from Pattonsburg, in Botetourt county, was the scene of Black Wolf's invasions on two occasions. In 1784 he captured James Moore, a son of James Moore, Sr., a resident of the valley, and conveying him to their territory in Ohio among the Shawanee towns, kept him awhile, and then sold him to a white family near Detroit, Michigan. Two years later a party of Shawanee Indians, led by Black Wolf, made a second expedition into Abb's Valley and shot James Moore, Sr., who was salting his stock, and rushing to his home, killed William and Rebecca Moore, his children, and Mr. John Simpson, a hired man. Two hired men fled and made their escape, but Mrs. Moore and her four remaining children, with Miss Martha Evans, from Augusta, were captured and carried off. In their rapid retreat, the boy John, being feeble and unable to proceed with ease, they killed him in his mother's presence, and the baby was brained against a tree a few days afterwards. On arriving at an Indian town on the Scioto river, they learned that several of their braves had been killed in an engagement with the whites, and in a spirit of brutal retaliation, Mrs. Moore and her eldest daughter were tied to a stake, to be tortured to death by cremation. An old Indian squaw, taking pity upon Mrs. Moore's sufferings, killed her with a tomahawk, while the daughter was burned to death. Mary Moore, Miss Evans, and James Moore, Jr., who was captured in 1784, were subsequently ransomed in 1789, and restored to their Virginia home.

In 1779 the third raid was made upon Abb's Valley by the Indians, and Mrs. Andrew Davidson and three children, with two hired youths, were captured and carried off. During their journey westward Mrs. Davidson gave birth to a little girl, who, being somewhat troublesome, was tossed into Tug river by one of the Indians. When they reached the Indian towns her little girls were tied to a tree, and, for sport to the Indians, shot until death came to their relief. An Indian squaw taking possession of her remaining little boy started down the river with him, when the canoe was overturned and he was drowned. For several years Mrs. Davidson remained with a white gentleman as a servant in his family, and finally her own husband, who was in search of her, came to the house. She recognized him, and being reunited they returned to Virginia.

Regarding the Point Pleasant battle and the subsequent raids of the Indians, many writers have expressed the opinion that they were justified in their attacks. Without going so far as to re-echo this opinion in full, justice compels the statement that the Indian chieftain, Logan, had much to exasperate and anger him. Always friendly to the white race; ever ready to aid and assist them, even though his countrymen taunted him; furnishing them with meat and clothes when requested; giving them at all times the hospitality of his cabin and town, we do not wonder that his blood boiled when the members of that very race he so signally defended killed his family at Captina and Yellow Creek, apparently without cause. That the Indian chieftain smarted severely under it there can be no doubt; for though afterwards he assented to the treaty of peace, his celebrated speech is only too indicative of his harrowed state of mind. As a piece of oratory this speech will bear repetition. He said:

"I appeal to any white man to say if he ever entered Logan's cabin hungry, and he gave him not meat; if ever he came cold and naked, and he clothed him not. During the course of the last long and bloody war Logan remained idle in the cabin, an advocate of peace. Such was my love for the whites that my countrymen pointed as they passed, and said : 'Logan is the friend of the white man.' I have even thought to have lived with you, but for the injuries of one man. Colonel Cresap, the last spring, in cold blood and unprovoked, murdered all the relations of Logan, not even sparing my women and children. There runs not a drop of my blood in the veins of any living creature. This called on me for revenge. I have sought it ; I have killed many ; I have fully glutted my vengeance. For my country I fully rejoice at the beams of peace. But do not harbor a thought that mine is the joy of fear. Logan never felt fear. He will not turn on his heel to save his life. Who is there to mourn for Logan? Not one."

Dr. Doddridge's account of Dunmore's war clearly exculpates the Indians from any blame whatever, saying that the killing by Cresap and Greathouse was cold-blooded murder. The reason assigned by the Doctor (and denied by him as true) for the whites attacking the Indians, was the Indians were reported to have stolen some horses from land-jobbers on the Ohio and Kanawha rivers. He says:

"In the month of April, 1774, a rumor was circulated that the Indians had stolen several horses from some land-jobbers on the Ohio and Kanawha rivers. No evidences of the fact having been adduced, led to the conclusion that the report was false. This report, however, induced a pretty general belief that the Indians were about to make war upon the frontier settlements ; but for this apprehension there does not appear to have been the slightest foundation."

The Doctor, however, does not prove, in his account of the war, that a white man was not killed by the Indians in a canoe two days before Captain Cresap attacked the Indians at Captina. The weight of evidence is very strong in favor of the fact that the slaying of the white settler in the canoe was the moving cause of Captain Cresap's attack. Nothing, however, can justify Greathouse in his mode of proceedure when he made the Indians drunk at Baker's and murdered them.

After the raids made by the Indians in Abb's Valley, which we have adverted to, peace seemed to have been restored in a measure throughout this section, and the tide of emigration steadily moved westward. The Indians are like the rattlesnake in two particulars. They are extremely treacherous, and always mysteriously disappear before settlements made by the Caucasian race—not, however, though (like the rattlesnake), before they have given many a poisonous sting. Gradually all that section of Augusta county now composing several counties, was settled up and various names given them. In 1786, Russell county was formed, which lies in the heart of the Blue Grass country. In 1790, Wythe county was inaugurated; in 1793, Grayson; in 1806, Giles; in 1814, Scott; in 1831, Floyd; in 1831, Smyth; in 1842, Carroll; in 1858, Buchanan; in 1861, Bland; in 1880, Dickenson. These latter counties, with the ones already discussed, compose Southwest Virginia, as we will see later on. All of these counties were settled by the same class of hardy, honest, worthy people pouring in from the East to take up lands and establish a permanent abiding place for themselves and families.

In the earlier days, before civilization fled westward and carried in its train the comforts and luxuries of life, these people were crude and primitive in the extreme. Necessarily, having no courts of justice, they were in a measure a law unto themselves. Did any member commit a crime, or injure a neighbor, he was treated with such contempt by the rest of the settlers that he either amended his ways or left the community to avoid the open contempt exhibited towards him. Every man was expected to uphold law and order, and the small number of people living in this section in those earlier days made each and every one a conspicuous character in the eyes of his neighbor. It was impossible for him to commit a civil or moral wrong without his being seen and known by all near that settlement. Debts, which in our day create such an uproar of excitement, bothered the earlier settlers but little, for having no legal tender except an exchange of labor, products, and rude manufactures, a man was only required to fill his bargain. Contracts were held by public sentiment inviolate, and an implied agreement was well settled between each and every one that all should band together in defending themselves from the Indian, whom they held as their common foe.

In matters of morals these earlier settlers were in many things staunch and true. Honor was regarded as a purchasing commodity, and so treated—that is, binding on each and every one. Female chastity was protected by a most stringent code—the shedding of the blood of the betrayer or seducer by the relatives of the girl ruined, with impunity. Sabbaths were observed by the assembling together of the settlers in some particular house, where prayers were said and sermons heard. For lying, any dishonesty, idleness, or ill-fame, the punishment was what we might term "hating the offender out," as the earlier settlers expressed it. This savors somewhat of the old-time custom of the Greeks.

The first settlers, so far as we have any light upon the subject, mortally detested anything in the nature of theft, and said peremptorily: "A thief must be whipped." They carried out their ultimatum in this respect and inflicted this summary punishment upon the offender, as Moses directed, by giving him forty lashes less one. This punishment was followed by exile of the guilty party. When magistrates came into power in the west, they kept up this punishment always for petty thieving until the barbarism was duly abolished by law.

Ladies who were given to evil speaking, lying, and slandering were accorded the same right they have to this day—to speak as much as they desired, and the punishment was the same as now—nobody believed one word they said.

These people were freely given to hospitality in those rude days to all entering their houses, be he ever so much a stranger. Their homes, bread, raiment, and property were ungrudgingly given, and every shield of protection thrown around the guest. In their settlements and forts they lived, worked, feasted, fasted, prayed, and cursed in one cordial harmony, never betraying or injuring one another wantonly in name, reputation, and fame, until the small envies and jealousies of refined civilization came—the latter always having its evils with the good.

The means of subsistence of these earlier pioneers were scanty in the extreme when compared with the luxuries of the present day. Hunting was more an occupation of necessity then than of pleasure, and after summer seasons, when all had been extracted from the ground that was possible in the way of breadstuffs, the men became impatient at home and formed hunting parties, encamping out for weeks, and preyed upon the plentiful supply of game in the forests in those early days. Often they were without bread and had to go out in the morning to find their breakfast. As the country became more populated and civilization advanced, game, with the Indians, gradually receded, and the cultivation of the soil and raising hogs, poultry, and cattle took the place of hunting, and much more than supplied the want caused by insufficiency of game.

The mechanical arts, too, were seen and carried on in their infancy. The dwellings were constructed of logs, in their forest nativity, after being cut; and who is it that does not remember the many tales of "house-raisings" which have been told, describing how these old people all about the settlement would congregate and assist in the "house-raising"? The clapboards covering the dwelling, and flooring of the same, were rude and uncouth, while the very furniture itself was constructed on the same principles. Knots of trees and timbers were curiously wrought into bowls of all sizes and shapes; wooden spoons and platters were the order of the day; and all other vessels used in a domestic way were manufactured from the products of the forest. Labor, produce raised, and wild game were given in exchange for these manufactured goods, and the only currency which these people used in trading with the East were furs and peltry. They were primitive in the extreme, yet on the whole hale, happy, and hearty, when not actually engaged in Indian warfare. All farming utensils were made of wood—the plows, harrows, cooper ware, and sledges. The stripe of red and white cedar wood was regarded as beautiful and deemed a kind of luxury. The looms which made the cloth were constructed by the inhabitants of wood, and from them the simple material was made which covered their nakedness; and the shoes worn were made by themselves, from the thread they spun from the cotton and flax to the hides tanned in their own vats. The medicines used in cases of sickness were extracted from various kinds of herbs and roots, the medicinal properties of which were always familiar to some member of each community.

In the latter part of the eighteenth and earlier part of the nineteenth century the onward march of emigrants in Southwest Virginia, with the gradual departure of the Indians farther west, opened up a new era for this country. These forefathers of the present people, who displayed rare powers of endurance and patience under extreme suffering, who battled every inch of ground they tilled with a savage race, proved themselves in time of peace industrious, energetic, and worthy citizens. They gradually improved and cultivated their lands so dearly earned until peace and plenty crowned them with success and they possessed a surplus of the productions of the soil, which they exchanged with their eastern neighbors for many of the comforts and luxuries of life. The means to gratify suggested wants to the descendants which never occurred to the forefathers. The dwelling houses were constructed on a larger and better scale; the furniture was more comfortable and luxurious; their dress, as well as manners, continued to improve, until the year 1860 found the people of this section in a comfortable, improved condition every way—blessed with a soil of plenty, and numerous advantages unknown to themselves or unheard of as yet. Municipal law had come in to protect the weak and punish the wrong; schools were opening up in which the minds as well as morals of the youths were trained; and houses of religious worship sprang up on all sides, disseminating the seed of Christianity in every direction, which has ever been the one purifying element in this world. Slavery, a badge of intense wrong, was the only blighting wind which retarded the growth of the country, and soon that was to be swept away amidst carnage and smoke, the disappearance of which left the horizon clearer than ever.

CHAPTER II.

The great valley—Southwest Virginia a part of it—Territorial limits of Southwest Virginia—Its geological formation—Its scenery, climate, agricultural and mineral resources—Its advantages as a manufacturing centre.

THERE is a large section of country extending for hundreds of miles, from the Hudson river, at Newburg, to the Tennessee river, beyond Chattanooga. This is called the Great Limestone Valley, and is the main thoroughfare north and south, through which many different systems of railway extend, opening up almost every part of it. This valley has various names in the different States through which it passes, and marks the portion it traverses as the most highly favored. It is called in New York State the Walkill Valley, in eastern Pennsylvania the Kittatinny Valley, in middle Pennsylvania the Lebanon or Cumberland Valley, in Virginia the Shenandoah Valley and the valley of Southwest Virginia. There has been some discussion among writers as to what section of Virginia really comprises the Southwest. The tide-water, Piedmont, and south side of the State are well defined, but not so with this great section about which we are writing, and which has created the utmost wonder and surprise among the whole people by its almost magic growth and development. By some it is contended that all the territory southwest of Lynchburg is the section of which we are speaking; by others, that the Southwest is only that section of country comprising all the counties southwest from Roanoke county, beginning on the top of the table-lands in Montgomery county and including all the watershed of New river and the Holston, embracing the great blue grass section of the State.

Not entering into any controversy as to the geographical positions taken above, there can be but little doubt of the facts that the word Southwest is a key to the situation, and that Southwest Virginia, from the natural position of the country itself, is composed of all those counties lying south of James river and west of the Blue Ridge mountains. It is bounded on the north by James river, south by Tennessee and North Carolina, east by the Blue Ridge mountains, and west by the States of West Virginia and Kentucky. The counties composing it are: a part of Botetourt, Roanoke, Craig, Montgomery, Floyd, Pulaski, Giles, Bland, Wythe, Carroll, Grayson, Smyth, Tazewell, Buchanan, Dickenson, Russell, Washington, Scott, and Wise.

These counties contain an area of some 5,973 square miles, and has territory and extent enough to contain and support a population many times as large as it is at present. In the extreme Southwest, where the counties of Dickenson, Scott, and Wise lie, there are but few people, comparing the number with its immense space, and almost unbounded resources yet to become developed. In this section of Southwest Virginia there are 5,771,454 acres of land on which taxes are paid.

Geographically, this country is most happily situated. Almost the centre of it is pierced by a part of that line which sooner or later will be the great direct thoroughfare from east to west, running from the seacoast at Norfolk, through Lynchburg, Radford, Louisville, St. Louis, Kansas City, and on west. This route by correct estimate is seventy miles nearer from Norfolk to California than New York to California, and one hundred and thirty miles closer than any line could be run from Boston to San Francisco. In this progressive age and generation time has become a commodity of such value that every few miles in a projected railway of unnecessary distance presents an obstacle to be seriously considered. The completion of the Roanoke and Southern railroad (the Elkhorn extension of the Norfolk and Western, both of which are now under construction) will give this section a complete northwestern and southwestern outlet, while the Shenandoah Valley and Cripple Creek extension of the Norfolk and Western give it direct northern and southern connections.

In giving the geological formation of the country, we shall trust to others whose professional life in that line enables them to speak with judgment and confidence. The various stratas underneath the surface of the earth on which the inhabitants tread are full of those valuable ingredients which create ores, such as lead, iron, zinc, coal, manganese, and many other varieties, while the surface itself is capable of the highest yield in the fruits of the earth when properly tilled.

This country is but a division of the Great Limestone Valley of which we have spoken, and everywhere throughout its course presents outcrops of the lower palezoic formations. These formations rest upon the primary rocks of the mountains, which in this region flank the valley on the south and constitute the rocks of Grayson, Carroll, Pulaski, Wythe, and other counties. Many names have been given the members of the upper series, as well as numbers in the States through which they pass; but this is the most easily understood scale of their classification which we have ever seen. It is numbered from below upwards:

XIII. Coal measures proper		
XII. Conglomerate		Carboniferous.
XI. Umbral red shale		
X. Vespertine gray sandstone		
IX. Ponent red sandstone		
VIII. Vergent shale, &c.		Devonian.
VII. Meridial sandstone		
VI. Pre-meridal limestone		
V. Scalent red shale and fossil ore		Upper Silurian.
IV. Levant sandstone		
III. Material slates		
II. Material limestone		Lower Silurian.
I. Primal slates and sandstone		
Primary rocks*		Azoic (archæn).

The principal members of the foregoing series with which any mineralogist or geologist has to deal in examination of minerals in this section are comprised in the three lowest formations—Nos. I, II, III—the Potsdam sandstone, Cambro-

---

* The New-River Cripple Creek Mineral Region. (Page 5.)

Silurian limestone, and the Hudson-river slates, all of which, as is readily seen, are embraced in the division called "Lower Silurian."

This country, taking its whole surface, is not surpassed by any other under the sun for natural beauty of scenery, soil, lumber, or mineral resources. Whether we speed along the succulent valley between Roanoke and Carnegie City, walled in by mountains north and south; whether we cross the floor of this great valley between Shawsville and Christiansburg, amidst the mountain ravines and precipitous passes; whether we go up to the New river plateau, in Floyd, Grayson, and Carroll, or along weird, winding New river into Pulaski, Giles, and Tazewell, we have every delightful prospect of beauty and natural wealth which the eye can desire or the taste suggest. The elevated Blue Ridge division, separated from the valley by the westerly bifurcation of the Blue Ridge, under the names of Pilot Mountain, Poplar Camp, and Iron Mountains, presents every imaginable delightful feature of the greatest interest to either the most scientific geologist or practical miner. The perfect system of drainage, the ledges and bands of rock strata, the heavy deposits of ores and minerals, seem to have been created on the grandest scale, and the intervention of rich, succulent farming and grazing lands make the whole a country which is fast gaining the attention of investors, and a charming place in which to reside.

There is scarcely anything in nature which appeals so strongly to the sense of sight as varied and beautiful scenery. The Southwest is peculiarly fortunate in this respect. In traversing the line of the Norfolk and Western railroad a panorama of different scenes greet the eye almost every moment as the train whirls along westward from Roanoke. The lovely valley, dotted here and there with its comfortable farm-houses and rich fields of corn and green pastures; the blue hills on either side stretching in a rugged manner in every direction; the towns resting in the valley—once quiet, but now active and busy; the mountain ravines and precipitous gorges, overhanging vales which sweep away in graceful folds of hillock and dale; the towering heights of cragged peaks, often capped with snow, all together make up a scene which must be viewed with the naked eye in order to be appreciated. After leaving Radford, upon the New River division of the Norfolk and Western railroad, which runs through Pulaski, Giles, and Tazewell in order to tap the coal region of the Southwest and West Virginia, the scenery becomes grander and more weird, until it culminates in gorges and cliffs, like Cæsar's Arch and Pompey's Pillar, and steep rocks two hundred and ninety-eight feet high, with a base one hundred and fifty feet deep in the river, opposite the New River White Sulphur Springs.

The Peaks of Otter, in Bedford; Angel's Rest, in Giles, and Ball Knob, with the celebrated Mountain Lake near, are places which if once seen are never forgotten on account of their lovely views and the charming scenery surrounding them. Surely, in the choice of a resting-place in this world where one would like to pass his days, it is a matter of great interest and gratification to know that one dwells in a country which is so situated in varied and unique scenery as always to charm the eye and never weary the gaze. The idea that the inhabitants of this section become so accustomed to all this grandeur as to be unimpressed by it is totally erroneous. Take them away from their native heath, and the first void created will be the absence of all these lovely views and the everlasting hills.

This section of country of which we are writing lies between 0° and 8° west longitude from Philadelphia and 36° 30′ and 40° 30′ north latitude. From its position longitudinally and latitudinally the climate must necessarily be salubrious and healthy. This portion of Virginia which lies in the regions of the middle latitudes possesses a climate of means between the extremes of heat and cold incident to the other States south and north of it. The idea prevalent to many strangers that this part of Virginia is very warm during the summer is entirely unjust, for a healthier, more salubrious, and pleasant climate does not exist than the summer seasons of this portion of the

Old Dominion. The days are fresh from the heavy mountain dews which fall at night, and it is always pleasant in the months of July and August to sleep under covering of some kind at night.

But certain it is, whatever may be the carping criticisms as to the summer's heat in Southwest Virginia, people disbelieve them; for during that very season thousands and thousands of persons from north, south, east, and west emigrate to the Roanoke Red Sulphur Springs, Lake Spring, the Montgomery White Sulphur Springs, the Alleghany, the Yellow Sulphur, the New River White Sulphur, Mountain Lake, Wytheville, Glade Springs and Abingdon—all of which places are in this section. These pleasure-seekers all say that the healthy and salubrious climate, the cool nights and delightful days, are the main objects which draw them here, and as they are impartial we rest perfectly satisfied with their verdict. But in order that everyone may know the temperature of this country, a table is here submitted, carefully compiled, giving the average state of the climate:

January	25°	July	73°
February	37	August	71
March	43	September	63
April	52	October	54
May	61	November	42
June	68	December	35

The average for the seasons is:

Spring	52°	Autumn	53°
Summer	70.6	Winter	32.3

Average for the year, 53°.

This climate compares most favorably with the famous health resorts of Europe, such as Geneva, Turin, Vienna, Milan, Weisbaden. The mean temperature of Geneva and Vienna is:

	Spring.	Summer.	Autumn.	Winter.
Geneva	52.2°	70.03°	54.2°	34.0°
Vienna	56.2	71.8	54.6	38.7

Mean for the year: Geneva, 52.07°; Vienna, 55.3°.

This favorable comparison is demonstrative proof that the climate of Southwest Virginia is not only a healthy, equable temperature, but an absolutely pleasant one to the human sense. All doubting Thomases will please examine the foregoing tables and be silent.

There are two other features connected with this climate which it is just to mention. Owing to the mountains the inhabitants are entirely free from all malarial fever, chills, ague, and that debility which exists in the lower countries around and saps the vital energies of the human race. Again, such destructive agencies as tornadoes, cyclones, and terrific storms are unknown here, for the grand old mountains which furnish varying scenery for the eye act as a wall to break and retard the force of these sweeping destroyers which have infested our western sister States, often leaving woe and desolation in their train.

There is another phase connected with the climate of Southwest Virginia which is different from that of other countries.

Generally speaking, when we proceed westerly on the same parallel of latitude the climate becomes colder, as it does if we advance northwardly. But not so is this climate. It is the case to a very slight degree until the summit of the Alleghanies is reached, but advancing westwardly from that point the temperature becomes milder and milder, until it is even warmer in winter than on the sea-coast. This is proven from the fact that catalpas grow spontaneously as far as latitude 37°, reeds as far as 38°, while paroquets grow in winter on the Scioto, in the 39th degree of latitude. A greater portion of Southwest Virginia is west of the Alleghany range, and becomes warmer as we proceed west. This accounts for the fact that the temperature at Wytheville is even milder in a slight degree than that of Radford or Dublin, both of which are east of the former place.

The northeast and northwest winds have more effect upon a climate than is generally supposed, regarding the health and delightfulness of it. The northeast is often loaded and charged with vapor, has a chilling, unhappy, and depressing effect upon the human system, while the northwest is dry, elastic, bouyant, and animating, causing the spirits of human beings to be almost always in the ascendency. In the mountains of the Southwest the northwest wind prevails, which in a measure accounts for the hale, hearty, and bluff appearance of the stalwart mountaineers.

Although the months of July and August are the hottest in the year, they are generally the healthiest, because the weather is dry and less liable to change than in the other months.

The fluctuations between heat and cold, so destructive generally to fruit in the early spring season, prevail much less in Virginia than in Pennsylvania and other States; and the rivers overflow in this period in Virginia a great deal less than in the New England States, because the snows in the former do not lie so long and accumulate so largely as they do in the latter, to be dissolved all at once in the spring, causing frequent, and often disastrous, inundations and floods. The snows in this section are rarely deep—never lasting longer than a few days—often disappearing under the mild rays of the winter's sun in twenty-four hours.

The extremes of heat and cold, after a careful investigation, show the temperature at 93° above, and 6° below zero, in Fahrenheit's thermometer.

Droughts are rarely experienced in this charming country on account of the heavy mountain dews and frequent gentle rainfalls. Timothy, orchard grass, and other forages for hay, which require a given amount of moisture, grow luxuriantly here. In Eastern Virginia, owing to the dry seasons in summer, these grasses suffer, but never here. The rainfall is frequent in summer, consisting principally of mountain showers, which, owing to the natural drainage of the country, seldom occasions any inconvenience, as the surplus water runs off quickly, leaving the grass and herbage fresh and luxuriant. The following statistics will give some idea of the average rainfall during the year.

Spring.	Summer.	Autumn.	Winter.	Year.
10.7	11.9	9.6	9.7	41.9

Owing to the salubriousness of the climate and the health of the inhabitants of this country, a gentleman who has examined this portion of Virginia minutely, and written much upon the subject, says:

"We would call attention to the fact that the Blue Ridge region of Virginia is, as can be proven by the testimony of consumptives fully restored to health, the best *sanitarium* in the United States east of the Mississippi."*

While we are not prepared to assert that this climate is a cure for consumptives, we most unhesitatingly state that we know of none superior in the South, or any other country. The climate plays no small part in the restoration to health of those persons who every year visit Virginia and her watering places, seeking relief from the ravages of disease and various bodily ailments. Its animating and invigorating effect; its freedom from northeast winds, which chill and depress; the entire absence of all malaria from it, renders it a charming temperature in which to reside, or in which to earn the daily bread of life.

The soil in this section of country is somewhat varied as to its productions, but universally productive. In Roanoke, Botetourt, Montgomery, and Floyd the growing of cereals, vegetables, hay, and fruit predominates over "grazing" or cattle-raising, although the latter class of farming is extensively carried on; but in the counties of Pulaski, Tazewell, Giles, Wythe, Carroll, Russell, Wise, Washington, Scott, and Buchanan—the natural home of indigenous blue grass—the business of stock-raising is the chief mode of farming or tilling the land. These latter counties send from their borders every year to market numerous herds of fine cattle, flocks of sheep, and some horses, which find their way into the Baltimore, Philadelphia, and New York markets. Some of the largest cattle men, like Mr. A. H. Stuart and Henry C., his son, of Russell, Charles W. Palmer, of Saltville, and James W. Byars, of Washington county, ship cargoes of live stock to Europe.

---

* Jed Hotchkiss, in *The Virginias*, June, 1884.

In the counties of Roanoke and Botetourt, Craig and Montgomery, the soil is a rich, loamy, chocolate clay, generally speaking, and is admirably adapted to the production of wheat, Indian corn, oats, barley, rye, buckwheat, hay, and vegetables of every description. Fruits of almost all varieties flourish in these counties, and the result is that in Roanoke and Botetourt, especially, the industries of canning fruit and vegetables have become not only extensive ones, but extremely remunerative to the persons engaged in them. Some of the brands of these canning establishments have gained a national reputation almost, and are sold all over the country. Not only does this business consume large quantities of fruit and vegetables, but gives employment to a large number of operatives necessary to carry on the factories. In addition to the fruit consumed by these, large quantities are shipped annually for foreign consumption.

Going westward from the counties we have just been discussing the soil will be found somewhat different. In Floyd, Carroll, Wythe, Grayson, Washington, and Pulaski it is a freestone, with here and there a character of limestone. It results from a decomposition *in situ* of large bands of granitoid rock, gneiss, hornblende, aluminous slates, shales, feldspars—in fact, it possesses all the wide range of silicates of alumina, potash, lime, soda, and iron. Tazewell county is but little different, possessing a richer loam, which is better for grazing purposes. In all of these counties large crops of fruit are grown, and some exported. Wythe, Smyth, and Washington counties are famous for their broad areas of cabbage, which is grown in large quantities and shipped to foreign markets.

But when we speak of agricultural resources we allude more to the capacity of a country for production than to what is being actually produced. No region, in the matters of location soil, climate, and natural advantage, is superior to this for agricultural purposes. In this wonderful development now going on the production of agricultural products will advance with the demand. In the valleys and along the mountains the soil is capable of the highest productive capacity, and the day is not far distant when all this land lying, comparatively speaking, in waste now will be thoroughly utilized and cultivated to an advantage and profit.

There are two industries beginning to dawn in this section which bids fair to become extremely large and productive. We allude to dairy-farming and the planting of vineyards. No country can be more suitable to the production of milk, butter, and cheese than this far-famed blue grass section, in which cattle thrive so fast and yield such an abundance of milk from the peculiar fattening properties of this grazing. From a surplus of milk to the manufacture of cheese is but a step, which we have reason to believe will soon be bridged over. The southern slopes of the mountains are in many instances being utilized as vineyards, an industry which can be rendered extremely profitable, not only from the sale of the grapes, but the manufacture of wines.

The abundant opportunities to farmers with small capital in this country cannot be overlooked much longer, and those who are in possession of these lands have now an opportunity of realizing as much from the slopes of the mountains as their more fortunate neighbors have from the valleys. We know of no soil so capable of producing large crops of cabbage and the Irish potato as this mountain land in Southwest Virginia, to say nothing of it as a fruit-growing region.

Not only are the lands of this section well adapted for the production of all the necessaries of life in ample abundance, but the location of a greater portion of the agricultural country will satisfy the most fastidious taste of those having an eye for the beautiful. The James River Valley, situated in Botetourt; the valley westward of Roanoke; the plateau of country lying around Blacksburg, in Montgomery county; the level lands of Pulaski about Dublin and Pulaski City, where the celebrated Blue Ridge country begins; the beautiful meadows in Wythe, and the justly celebrated Burke's Garden, in Tazewell county, all present agriculturally a picture of scenic beauty, and splendid appearance of fertility equally as true. As stock-breeding and raising is one of the staple industries of this section, we can form some idea of its agricultural resources in this respect by adding a table giving the exact number of each kind in the live-stock department. Then by computing the number of horses we get an estimate of the extent of the tillage of the section. Southwest Virginia has 50,963 horses, 154,931 cattle, 107,565 sheep, 116,546 hogs. The blue-grass counties have by far a larger portion of this live stock, the county of Russell alone having 15,093 cattle.

There is one industry which, though rapidly gaining ground, has still the opportunity and means of becoming one of the largest of its kind in the Southwest—that is, sheep-raising, and in connection therewith, wool-growing. All along the slopes, and even upon the plateaus on top of the mountains, there is the finest character of grazing for sheep. Wherever the trees are cut, and the sun allowed to penetrate with its rays, an indigenous, rich, succulent grass comes, and the whole surface after a while becomes sodded. Sheep of the better grade, for both mutton and wool, thrive well, and experience shows that there is a handsome profit in raising them. In the near future this must necessarily become one of the largest sources of revenue which the agriculturist will have to draw upon.

The rapid growth of towns and cities like Roanoke, Salem, Christiansburg, Radford, Pulaski City, Wytheville, Max Meadows, and others throughout this section, has given an impetus to an industry agriculturally hitherto almost unknown—the trucking business, or market gardening. Wherever there is a demand, the supply for it inevitably follows; and the requirement of vegetables and small fruits by the inhabitants of the foregoing cities can be fully supplied from the country around, because the seasons and soil produce almost every kind that is known, and in sufficient profusion to supply the wants of all.

It is conceded by all who have a knowledge upon the subject that Southwest Virginia is one of the richest countries in mineral resources in the United States. Not only are minerals of almost every variety found in the mountains here, but they are sufficient in quantity and vastly superior in quality. In General Imboden's "Mineral Wealth of Virginia" he says:

"Between the Atlantic coast and the western boundaries of the State the whole 'geological column' is represented, from the foundation granite to the capstones of the upper carboniferous. And in these successive strata are found rocks and minerals peculiar to each all over the world, and usually in greater abundance and of greater excellence than anywhere else in the same area."

McCreath and D'Invilliers, in their report upon "The Mineral Wealth of Cripple Creek and New River," have this to say concerning the country as a mineral territory:

"The New river-Cripple creek mineral region may be assumed to contain three hundred square miles, probably one-half of which may be considered as ore-bearing territory. While it would be injudicious, from the very nature of the occurrence of the brown hematite ore-deposits everywhere, to estimate the tonnage that any single square mile of this territory would yield, yet it must be manifest from the details given in this report that the total amount of iron ore to be mined in the region will be very great. The quality, uniformity, and richness of the ore is unsurpassed by any other developed brown hematite iron-ore district. The accessibility of the ore deposits to the Cripple Creek extension, and their proximity in a large part of the field to unusually good washing facilities, as well as the small cost of mining the ore itself, should result in the production of a cheap and well-prepared ore for furnace use. The occurrence here of a first-class and cheaply-mined ore; the proximity of a magnificent coking field, with limestones for fluxing purposes everywhere throughout the region; with a constant supply of pure water; surrounded by a fertile agricultural and grazing district capable of supporting a large population, and with numerous eligible sites for manufacturing purposes, this New river-Cripple creek region certainly offers unusual advantages for the investment of capital."

This region so rich in ores is situated in Wythe, Pulaski, Carroll, and Grayson. Floyd, too, an adjoining county, is rich in ores.

In this New river-Cripple creek mineral region an iron ore of peculiar quality has been found, termed *Gossan ore*. It gives, when mixed with other iron ores a peculiarly good character to the iron, while by itself it produces an admirable iron. It is one of the most important discoveries found in the South, in the way of iron ore, and it is admitted to be the only "red short ore" that has been found south of Mason and Dixon's line. Mixed with the brown ores, it gives a first-class iron for foundry or mill purposes, and permits the use of thousands of tons of high phosphorus and manganese ores that could never be utilized successfully by themselves. By means of the Reed Island extension, completed about June, and the Cape Fear and Yadkin Valley extension, finished this last summer, this ore is available for most of the furnaces situated around. By the means of this they will be in a position to make, as they wish, either a red, cold short, or neutral iron—stimulating to a very high degree the establishment of industries requiring as raw material cheap as well as varied classes of pig-irons, and by so doing build up wonderful adjuncts to the furnaces established. The analysis of the iron ores compare most favorably with that of any other ore we know of mined anywhere. McCreath and D'Invilliers, in their report mentioned above, give the analyses of various openings made throughout this favored section. We give several, as an average sample, showing the quality of the ore.

From samples taken from a ton lying at Cedar creek opening it yielded:

Metallic iron 57.300
Phosphorus 045
Siliceous matter 4.620
Phosphorus in 100 parts of iron 078

In the Buddlefield tract samples clipped from all along the ore surface yielded:

Metallic iron 57.700
Phosphorus 058
Siliceous matter 4.280
Phosphorus in 100 parts of iron 100

On the Widow Stephens' tract, from a sample of lump ore taken from three different pits, the following analysis was obtained:

Metallic iron 54.075
Phosphorus 073
Siliceous matter 7.950
Phosphorus in 100 parts iron 135

In the same work, the general average character of the ore is well represented by the following analysis of a sample (176 pieces) taken from nine different openings:

Bisulphide of iron	None.
Protoxide of iron	None.
Sesquioxide of iron	76.214
Sesquioxide of manganese	.051
Oxides of nickel and cobalt	.040
Oxide of zinc	None.
Oxide of lead	None.
Oxide of copper	None.
Alumina	2.365
Baryta	None.
Lime	.820
Magnesia	.486
Sulphuric acid	.157
Phosphoric acid	.171
Water	12.072
Siliceous matter	7.480
	99.856

Metallic iron	53.850
Metallic manganese	.036
Sulphur	.063
Phosphorus	.075
Phosphorus in 100 parts of iron	.140

There can be no doubt but that this is a magnificent ore-bearing section in the way of iron. Every facility for manufacturing iron in this country on the very cheapest basis is apparently good, and already its reputation in that respect has caused several large furnaces to be erected.

But it is not in this section of the Southwest alone that we have an abundance of ore. In Roanoke and Botetourt counties both the Houston and Rorer iron mines have been successfully worked for a number of years. The former supplies much of the raw material for the Crozer iron and steel furnace, while ores from the latter are shipped in all directions. The ores from this section of Virginia are good, too, and, upon an analysis from McCreath's "Mineral Wealth of Virginia," yield from the Houston mines, in Botetourt county, the following:

Metallic iron	52.200
Metallic manganese	1.419
Sulphur	.016
Phosphorus	.194
Phosphorus in 100 parts of iron	.371

The opening near Cloverdale, in Roanoke county, also worked by the Houston company, known as the Murray Bank, analyzes well. From twenty-five pieces selected by Mr. Warne, superintendent of the mines, Mr. McCreath gives the following analysis:

Metallic iron	53.050
Phosphorus	1.266
Siliceous matter	6.630
Phosphorus in 100 parts iron	2.386

Near Salem, Virginia, there are large deposits of ore, from which the furnaces at that point will draw their raw material in the way of ores. The Bott property is particularly good as to quantity and quality, for Mr. Edmund C. Pechin, general manager for the "Virginia Development Company," in his report to the stockholders in April, 1890, says:

"After considerable negotiations, the furnace has secured the lease of the Bott property, about seven miles from Salem. A late inspection of this property shows, as the result of extensive developments, what promises to be one of the very best ore properties in Virginia. Not only is the amount of the ore apparently very large and of good quality, but it lies in the foot-hills and on the mountain side in such a shape as to allow easy opening up and cheap mining." * * * * * * * * * * *

In this very particular of "cheap mining" most of the ore-bearing country throughout the Southwest is alike. On all sides it is conceded that ores can be mined cheaper in this part of Virginia than in any other country known. In various parts of the section, from experience and careful, prudent estimates, it has been repeatedly shown that iron ore can be mined and placed at the furnace for an average price of $2.30 per ton of ore. In Pennsylvania it costs on an average of $4.25 per ton to place it at the furnace—almost twice what it costs in our own country. This difference must necessarily gradually drive the iron manufacturer south, and substantiate Chauncey M. Depew's advice when he said: "Go South, young man!"

Many counties in this vast mineral section contain mines of iron ore in sufficient quantities to furnish material for large amounts of capital to be used in their development, and to give employment to thousands of mechanics and laboring men for years to come. Magnetites, limonites, and specular ores are found in different regions and localities. The magnetites abound in the James River Valley; on the plateau; in counties drained by New river and its tributaries; in Floyd, Carroll, Pulaski, and Grayson. In Smyth and Washington counties, as well as others, a semi-magnetic ore has been discovered, and pronounced excellent on account of being low in phosphorus, and therefore adapted to the manufacture of Bessemer steel, which is rapidly succeeding iron in all structural work. The hematites, both red and brown, are distributed all through the Southwest—on the western slopes of the mountains, and in the hills and valleys. This section is truly an iron-ore bearing field, and the fact that the railroads direct from coking fields near at hand run through it proves that Virginia, at no great future day, will be one of the foremost States in the Union for the manufacture of iron and the adjuncts thereto.

Other minerals as useful and necessary to humanity have been discovered in Southwest Virginia, and many of them are successfully worked at this day.

Lead has been extensively mined for over one hundred years in Wythe county, and at this time the largest lead works in the South are carried on there, with an apparently exhaustless quantity. In this same section other mines of the same mineral have been found and developments set on foot to have their products utilized. These will, beyond doubt, prove a success, and give employment to many people in manufacturing a most valuable commodity in every respect. The analysis made of a sample of lead ore, second separation, taken from the property of the Wythe Lead and Zinc Company, yields:

```
Metallic lead . . . . . . . . . . . . . . . . . . . . . . . 65.836
    "    zinc . . . . . . . . . . . . . . . . . . . . . . .  5.408
```

In the Cripple creek–New river mining region have been found the best samples of zinc ore ever discovered in the South; and the "Bertha Zinc Works," situated at Pulaski City (of which we will have more to say when we reach that place), are not ônly the largest, but manufactures the purest spelter in the United States. Up to the year 1887 this company had manufactured or smelted 12,775 tons of ore, which they derived from their mines not far off. An analysis of this zinc shows:

> Metallic zinc 37.836
> " lead . . . . None.

In many other localities in this section this mineral has been found, and will undoubtedly be successfully operated.

The allotment of space in this work forbids an analysis and description of each class of minerals already discovered in Southwest Virginia, and we refer the reader to various geological and mineralogical works on this subject. But we have conclusive evidence that, besides the minerals already mentioned and classified, this section has copper, tin, manganese, mica, and plumbago, kaolin and fireclays, lime and cement, plaster (gypsum), salt, marl, and building stones of every variety from the grey to the brown sandstone—all of which can be seen by any one interested in the mineral resources of Southwest Virginia.

We have not omitted the great coal sections thoughtlessly, but will recur to them at the proper place, in connection with a history of the New River railroad, which was constructed into that section to haul out the vast quantities of this mineral.

With these mineral resources in the midst of an agricultural country like this, it is but safe to prophesy that Virginia will ere long occupy her natural position in the foremost rank of manufacturing States. Even now there are within her borders many furnaces being erected, and some in blast. The Crozer Furnace, the West-End Furnace, at Roanoke; the one at Salem; the Crane Furnace, at Radford; the Pulaski Iron Company's furnace; the furnace of G. T. Mills, at Pulaski City; the Ivanhoe Furnace on Cripple Creek extension; the furnace at Speedwell; the furnace of the Max Meadows Company; the Graham Furnace, all indicate and point to the fact that the Southwest bids fair to become a great manufacturing centre.

Another powerful lever which Virginia has to substantiate her position as a manufacturing centre in the way of iron in this section is the cheapness with which the article can be made. Having the iron ore, limestone, and coke all within her borders, no country can manufacture it cheaper than it can be made here. Actual costs of making a ton of pig-iron are here given. The cost at Roanoke, as furnished by the Crozer Company, is:

Ore, 2¼ tons, at $2.26	$ 4 81
Coke, 1¼ tons, at $2.95	3 69
Limestone	75
Labor	2 10
Incidentals	1 25
Total	$12 60

The cost at Pulaski City, as given by the Pulaski Iron Company, is:

Ore, 2 tons, at $1.35	$ 2 70
Freight, at 35c.	70
1¾ tons coke, at $1.75	2 40
Freight, at 90c.	1 24
Limestone and labor	2 15
Incidentals and repairs	1 00
Total cost per ton	$10 19

This cost of $10.19 at Pulaski is the average expense of making iron in the New river-Cripple creek regions. Comparing these estimates of actual cost with those of Pennsylvania, we readily see the advantageous position which Virginia holds as an iron-producing State.

In middle Pennsylvania the cost is:

	1882. Actual Cost.	1884. Estimated.
Ore	$ 9 37	$ 7 75
Fuel—coal and coke	5 02	4 62
Limestone	1 00	1 00
Incidentals, labor	2 35 48	3 25
Total	$18 22	$16 62

In the lower Susquehanna district the cost is $18.16 per ton, and in the Lehigh Valley district $20.38 actual cost, and $17.02

estimated cost for one ton in 1884. This difference in cost in that State between the years 1882 and 1884 arose from the fact that in the latter year the cost of both ore and fuel was much less.

These facts are invulnerable, and, so far as the manufacture of iron is concerned, place Southwest Virginia in a most enviable position.

If steam as a manufacturing power does not totally supersede water, this section has an ample quantity for manufacturing purposes. James river in Botetourt; Roanoke river running through Montgomery and Roanoke; New river through Giles, Pulaski, Floyd, and Carroll; the Bluestone through Tazewell, and other streams, place this section on a sound basis as to water-power. But we have by careful observation come to the conclusion that the old cry, "there can be no city without water-power," is *effete*, and that money and energy will rear any structures under the sun except culture and refinement—they go a long way towards assisting those.

The immense and valuable bodies of timber throughout Southwest Virginia has caused manufacturing in lumber to become a distinct and remunerative business. Not only right at home is there any quantity of it, but the demand for it is there, too, and an ever-increasing one. All the varieties are found—walnut, ash, cherry, pine, poplar, oak, spruce, cedar, hemlock pine, hickory, chestnut, locust, birch, and tulip poplar—and the supply is almost exhaustless, for so quickly do the forests replenish themselves that a continuous supply is the result. Huge saw-mills, planing-mills, and wood-working factories, such as sash, door, and house-furnishing wood-work, are springing up on every side; while manufacturing establishments for fancy wood-carving are beginning to be erected at one or two places.

When we think of a country's possessing all these advantages bestowed upon it by the God of nature—its gorgeous and beautiful scenery, its salubrious and healthy climate, its agricultural and mineral resources, its certainty of possession of all those adjuncts which make a country a manufacturing center—should we wonder at energy and capital pouring in to develop it? And having taken a cursory view of the original grand cause, let us look now at the auxiliary causes which have played no small part in the history of its progress.

CHAPTER III.

Slavery : Its effect upon the country, upon the people owning them, and upon the slaves themselves—Abolition of slavery one of the causes of the progress of Southwest Virginia.

UP to the year 1865 slavery was an institution in the Southern States, and in the particular section of country of which we are now writing. It was not only a stigma to the country in a moral sense, but a stumbling-block in the way of its material advancement and progress. History but repeats itself that slavery, in every form and shape, is an insuperable obstacle to the development of the general interests of a people at large, though it may render the slaveholders opulent and extremely rich as a class. Taking the people of any country as a whole, the tendency of the institution is to retard their growth, development, and welfare, and the interest of any people as an unit should always be considered before that of any particular class.

The fact that slavery exists in some form or shape the world over does not justify the kind of which we are writing. There may be such things as political, moral, mental, social, and pecuniary slavery, yet it is a badge adopted by the slave himself to serve some particular cause or end, and one for which he is to blame. But the governing, directing, and training of minds and bodies by one class of men without the consent of the other necessarily entails ideas, views, and thoughts of life contrary to divine as well as true human wisdom.

The effect of this institution upon the proprietor of the slaves was in many respects very bad, although in others it advanced him. The owner of hundreds of human beings accustomed to obey his slightest wish, never questioning the right or wrong of the command, could scarcely brook opposition or contradiction from any quarter whatever. In his behavior to any whom he deemed his inferiors there was that hauteur of class superiority, almost unconsciously on his part, which made the life of the inferior degraded and contemptuous, often causing the latter to be convinced that he possessed the right of living and nothing more. The poorer class, or "overseering" population, was almost as degraded as people could well be, and even the slaves had an unbounded contempt for them. This unfortunate state has been amply proven by subsequent events to have proceeded from the institution itself, because, after the abolition of slavery and those galling chains were removed in a social way, that very class improved and bettered themselves until they have become broad, representative citizens. On the other hand, the effect of slavery, from various causes, gave the slave-owning people and their families the means of improving themselves morally, mentally, and physically until they inaugurated a *régime* which for culture, elegance, and refinement has never been excelled, nor ever will be; for as the general condition of the people has improved, that has retrograded, we are sorry to say, although recognizing both the force and necessity for it. Furthermore, slavery unfitted a large class of people from any self-reliance whatever, and inoculated a reign of luxurious ease which of itself gave the possessors an erroneous idea and view of life, and, when the slaves were freed, nothing but the pluck, virtue, and moral excellence of the Southern people themselves prevented them from drifting into absolute destruction.

The results of this institution upon the slaves in bondage necessarily depends upon the people themselves in a great measure. To some races (for instance, the Caucasian) it would mean a total elimination of the race itself, for they would never stand it; but the negro people as a race have no objection to it. Even when placed in their native country now they relapse into barbarism, and people who cannot govern themselves properly are necessarily slaves to those who can. To them slavery was an honor rather than otherwise, and it was as much their joy and pleasure to look up to and serve their masters and mistresses as it was to breathe the air around them.

As a class, happier beings never existed, and they had a most unbounded contempt for a free negro—"Cuffee," as they called him—and shunned him as they would a leper, and even to this day that prejudice still exists in the mind of the negro who can recall the days of slavery. A crowning proof, however, that the colored race was not dissatisfied with its existence was this: When the civil war was raging in all its fury, and the negro knew that the bone of contention was his freedom, he remained not only perfectly quiet, but aided and assisted his owner in every way possible, and had a death-like enmity towards the North. Of course there were exceptions to the rule in this as in all other cases. It is contended by some that the negro had no such feelings of loyalty, but this quiet demeanor arose from superior virtue on the part of his race. No one can divine the motives and desires of the human heart of the negro any more than any one else, and they are capable of deceit at times; but their uttered thoughts and acts supported the position taken by us above.

They were treated kindly as a whole, and were well cared for in every way, having their prerogatives and rights guaranteed them by an unwritten law as binding and well defined as our laws from which we draw many of our strongest customs. The many accounts written about cruel treatment of them were untrue, although there were some owners who were harsh. Particularly have some dwelt upon the lash as a means of torture and barbarism, but they appear not to have given both sides an impartial examination. Punishment in some form must be administered to prevent vice, and if a negro committed theft or any other crime, his owner, being in a measure amenable, administered punishment instead of the law. Shall it be said to be cruelty that a negro's liberty is snatched from him because he violates the law? Try him to-day, and see which would be his choice—thirty-and-nine, or the penitentiary for one year—for the commission of grand larceny.

Of all the means for advancing the material interest of a

country, manufacturing is the most successful. It gives a demand for both the raw material and the labor with which to work it up. Whatever has a tendency to advance the manufacturing interest of a country promotes its general welfare, while anything which retards it necessarily obstructs its material development. The necessary results of the institution of slavery invariably have this latter result. Slavery first has a tendency to encourage and foster agricultural pursuits, and discourage those of the manufacturing business; therefore the owner of the slaves must exchange his surplus agricultural products for the manufactured machinery and products of some others. Except for the needs of the plantation and slaves themselves, mechanical arts were not encouraged and education vetoed among them. It would not have been policy to have taught them the art of mechanics, or given them learning any farther than was necessary for their absolute maintenance and support and the purposes of the master, which were to give him the necessaries, comforts, and luxuries of life. The owner cared not for manufacturing when his slaves could make his meat, his clothes, his farming implements, and do his blacksmith work. The capitalist who desired to institute such an enterprise as an establishment for manufactured goods, except in a few instances, was discouraged. When class distinctions ran high, and the ensign of a gentleman was to have no virtual occupation except one of pleasure, to be engaged in trade was rather a stigma than otherwise; so the capital of the country was not invested in such pursuits. Mining and iron-manufacturing were not resorted to, but if a man became possessed of any capital the first impulse was to invest in a plantation and negroes.

The labor of any country has much to do with its manufacturing interests. Manufacturers require generally a class of skilled labor, which is not necessary in agricultural pursuits. In the South, where slavery existed, the skilled white mechanic rebelled against working with the slave, which he deemed degrading to himself, and thus the emigration of this class of labor into the South was extremely small indeed. Not until after the abolition of slavery did they come here and seek employment in developing our vast resources.

Whatever virtues the negro may possess, experience shows that they are only capable of the lowest class of manual labor as a race, although instances have been, and are known, which vary the rule. Skilled work—mechanical art—is far beyond their powers, nor are they placed in any such position. The friends themselves of the colored race, who advocate their having equal rights and being pushed forward in every way, are a living contradiction to such views, when the negro applies for an engineer's place to run a locomotive, or to fire one, or to take the place of a skilled laborer in any other of the numerous departments of the gigantic enterprises now set on foot. This is but right and correct, because the negro is incapable of reaching that state of intelligence necessary to fill these important posts as the Caucasian can do. Again, in addition to the necessary skill and knowledge which is requisite to fill these positions, there is more or less responsibility attached to them which requires more or less truth and honesty to fill them properly. A negro might be trusted implicitly to plow your field, but there would be some objection to his having a passenger train crowded with human freight under his care, although he might be cognizant of the *modus operandi* of a locomotive engine.

When slavery was abolished and the whole phase of life in Virginia changed in this respect, the agricultural interest began to develop on a new basis, while capital slowly crept in until the wonderful resources of the country were made public, and then it began to pour in. The old large estates were cut up into smaller ones, and the true agricultural policy adopted—that of cultivating the most on the least possible ground. This new *régime* in farming caused many people to turn their efforts and energies in other directions. The opening up of the great western granaries, with through railroad facilities, caused agriculture here to have a hard time, and people turned their attention towards the vast wealth imbedded within their mountains.

But the native population had no means with which to develop these large hidden treasures. Their property consisted of slaves, which had been swept away, and they turned their attention to foreign capitalists, who, on viewing the wonderful resources of the country, came in with their money, energy, and varied business experience. The result was that the Virginia young men gradually disrobed themselves of all false pride and became by apprenticeship the skilled labor of the southwest of Virginia in a great measure. To-day ninety per cent. of the fifteen hundred mechanics working at "The Roanoke Machine Works" are skilled laborers and from the surrounding country in Virginia.

This false pride to which we have just alluded is one of the logical results of the institution of slavery. Where all the labor in any country is performed by slaves or an inferior race, to become a laborer is to brand yourself with a stamp of counterfeit disgrace from which it is hard to recover; and during slavery the white man who earned his bread by the sweat of his brow in a social way was but little better than a slave, except he possessed personal liberty and the right of property. When the cruel war was over the abolition of slavery did not eradicate all his preconceived views concerning labor all at once. He still thought that to labor with his own hands was a shame, and it was not until necessity and the changed condition of things were apparent that he threw off this device of pride and went manfully to work. He then, with his superior mental and moral parts, soon took his natural position as a skilled mechanic, while the negro continues to perform the lowest manual and menial service, and will continue so to do to the end of the chapter.

The burden of slavery to the owner was more retarding to the material growth of a country than any one would imagine from a cursory view. Upon every estate there were so many superannuated negroes, as well as young ones, who were a constant drain upon the working ones without yielding any return themselves. They had to be supported and cared for like the rest, who worked. If there was a failure in crops, why there was no shutting down and saving of expense as in other branches and states of business. The expense still went on. So if a man during slavery desired to invest in manufacturing pursuits he found it difficult so to do, because his capital was generally all invested in land, negroes, and a sufficient bank account to meet any exigencies which might arise from any unforeseen accident. In this respect he was completely unfettered by the abolition of slavery.

So far as manufacturing industries were concerned, the want of knowledge concerning them was a serious hindrance to their either embarking in them as proprietors or employees. They first had to learn—*i. e.*, begin at the bottom and master the rudiment of their occupations, as well as conquer their pride. Years were necessarily spent in becoming acquainted with those minor details which any ordinary mechanic's son would know at sixteen or seventeen years of age, and which they would have known had they lived in a country where labor was regarded as honorable and virtue brought out through dire necessity. This very want of knowledge on the part of the native men at first—which is attributable to the institution of slavery—was one of the causes of the pouring into our borders throngs of new people. If a furnace, a machine-shop, a rolling-mill, an iron mine, or a coal mine was started, the necessary operatives had to be imported to do the labor, which meant, of course, the influx of families, too, and the necessary grocerymen and clothiers to supply their wants. There are no better illustrations of this salient fact than Roanoke, Salem, Radford, Pulaski City, and Bluefield. In these cases the opening of shops, furnaces, and other industries required skilled laborers at once, and the natives, from their want of knowledge, could not take hold at first, so the importation of the necessary clerks, skilled laborers, and mechanics who understood the business caused them all to grow as if by magic. When the young men found that the heads of these great establishments had worked as mechanics; that there was no disgrace in it;

that good, remunerative wages were paid, they took hold, and in every case nearly made the best class of workmen, and numbers can now be pointed out who own their homes and smoke the pipe of peace by their own hearthstones.

Taking the people of this country as a whole, and the general welfare of the section itself, a greater boon could not have been bestowed upon them than the abolition of slavery. Before that time they manufactured but little, and purchased everything except the plainer necessaries of life made by the slaves at home. Now it is the wish, desire, and will of these people to draw upon the wealth embodied in their mountains, and, in preparing it for the immediate use of the people, to give employment to thousands of their brethren, so that each and every ramification of society may perceive its benefits, which they cannot fail to do. The day when manufactured goods have to be brought from the North is over. From the raw material which composes the locomotive engine to the skilled labor which construct it we are full-handed, and everything made in the way of iron, from a shovel to a bridge, will soon be manufactured here—not only to supply our wants, but those of other people, because we can make them cheaper.

That the abolition of slavery, which is one of the chief causes of the rapid development of this country, was attended with some evil results is undeniably true. No great upheaval or revolution can occur in any country without some disaster, it matters not how much good its results may finally accomplish. The ideas, views, mode of life, and habits of a people can never be changed without trouble and great misery at first. Those who were reared to gratify every wish, to enjoy and possess the best of everything, suffered intensely when the means of gratifying their desires were swept away suddenly; but the fiery ordeal in crushing the few benefited the many, and made the New South in her new era a greater and really wealthier country than she ever was before. And this view is becoming indoctrinated everywhere in the United States, for the old cry of "Go West" has been revised and changed, and now it is, "Go

South." We cannot better illustrate this fact than by quoting the words of the Honorable Chauncey M. Depew, in an address to the Alumni Association of Yale University. He said, just after a tour through the Southern States:

"The net results of this visit to the South, to my mind, is just this: that *the South is the bonanza of the future.* We have developed all the great and sudden opportunities for wealth—or most of them—in the Northwestern States and on the Pacific slope, but here is a vast country *with the best climate in the world;* with conditions of health which are absolutely unparalleled; with vast forests untouched; with enormous veins of coal and iron which yet have not known anything beyond their original conditions; with soil that, under proper cultivation, for little capital, can support a tremendous population; with conditions in the atmosphere for comfortable living winter and summer which exist nowhere else in the country; and that is to be the attraction for the young men who go out from the farms to seek settlement, and not by immigration from abroad, for I do not think they will go that way, but by the internal immigration from our own country it is to become in time as prosperous as any other section of the country, and as *prosperous by a purely American development.*"

The continual emigration of people into this section since the war is proof that Mr. Depew's utterances are truthful and prudent. Many of the people of the very State in which he delivered that address are locating in this section, and are pleased with it. And he is not alone. Many persons in all directions of the compass are pointing towards this country with the same sage and salient advice: "Go South, young man!"

CHAPTER IV.

The New River branch of the Norfolk and Western Railroad Company—Part played by the New River railroad in the development of Southwest Virginia—Its inception and beginning—The original charter—General G. C. Wharton—Dr. John B. Radford—First organization—Meeting at Eggleston's Springs—Resolutions of incorporators—Richard B. Roane—Thomas Graham, J. D. Sergeant. and Walter Wood—Governor Gilbert C. Walker—Options and coal lands, and the manner in which the road was captured from its original incorporators—Country which was opened up by this railroad—Pocahontas and the Flat Top coal regions.

OF all the auxiliary causes which have played their parts in the development of Southwest Virginia, the New River branch of the Norfolk and Western Railroad Company stands pre-eminently in the front. This road runs from Radford, in Montgomery county, through Pulaski and Giles counties, Virginia, and Mercer county, West Virginia; thence on through Tazewell county, Virginia, touching the West Virginia line at Bluestone Junction, and goes to Pocahontas, Virginia. The branch running from Bluestone Junction goes into the Flap Top coal region, and on to Elk Horn from Mill Creek Junction, which latter branch is being extended to Ironton, Ohio, through West Virginia.

Such a marked effect did the formation and construction of this route have upon the section of country of which we are writing, that every person who acted a part on the theatre of its earlier history deserves special notice, and if there should be some stage by-plays among the *personæ dramatis*, all deserve either the praise or blame of posterity as well as its thanks.

In the fall of 1862, General G. C. Wharton, of Radford, was marching through West Virginia with his brigade, on his way to Fayette by the Raleigh turnpike. When beyond Princeton, after crossing Bluestone river, the troops stopped to rest for a few moments in ascending the mountains. Two of his officers, Captain Pole French and Captain Pack, were lying under a train wagon. Whilst conversing with these gentlemen he remarked:

"There is coal in this vicinity."

"Certainly," replied Captain Pack; "there is plenty of it. Right below here you will see where they have been getting it out."

So far as we can gather from history this was the first discovery of this coal region which led to any beneficial results. This point was on the head-waters of Camp creek, in Mercer county, West Virginia.

Later on during the war, General G. C. Wharton married a daughter of the late Dr. John B. Radford, after whose family the city of Radford is named. Settling there on New river, on some land given his wife by Dr. John B. Radford, General Wharton, who was well acquainted with the iron ore regions of Floyd, Carroll, and Pulaski, conceived the idea that if the coal regions he had traversed during the war could be opened up and coke made, the point where he was living might become in some time an iron-manufacturing centre. Nor were his ideas on that subject at all chimerical at the time.

New river, which borders his land, rises in North Carolina, and flowing northwest, cuts directly through the range of mountains between Radford and West Virginia, giving an outlet. General Wharton, being satisfied that the charcoal furnaces could not continue long in blast for want of fuel, thought of penetrating this coal region for coke. With this idea framed in his mind, he determined to set the plan in operation at the earliest possible moment. In 1871 he was elected to the Legislature, and while there, on March 7th, 1872, obtained a charter incorporating what was then known as "The New River Railroad, Mining, and Manufacturing Company," with John B. Radford, John T. Cowan, Joseph Cloyd, James A. Walker, William T. Yancey, William Mahone, Charles W. Statham, Joseph H. Chumbley, A. H. Flannagan, Philip W. Strother, John C. Snidow, Joseph H. Hoge, William Eggleston, G. C. Wharton, William Adair, James A. Harvey, A. A. Chapman,

Robert W. Hughes, A. N. Johnston, Elbert Fowler, David E. Johnson, John A. Douglas, W. H. French, R. B. McNutt, James M. Bailey, and A. Gooch as incorporators.

The charter obtained by General Wharton gave the company power upon its organization "to construct, maintain, and operate a railroad from New River depot, a point on the line of the Virginia and Tennessee division of the Atlantic, Mississippi and Ohio Railroad Company, in the county of Pulaski and State of Virginia, to such a point as may be agreed upon at or near the head-waters of Camp creek, in the county of Mercer and State of West Virginia; and the said New River Railroad, Mining, and Manufacturing Company shall have the privilege of constructing, maintaining, and operating such branch roads as may be necessary to bring out coal, iron, and other ores from the counties of Mercer, Somers, and Monroe, of West Virginia, and the counties of Giles, Bland, Pulaski, and Montgomery, of the State of Virginia. And the said New River Railroad, Mining, and Manufacturing Company shall be further empowered to acquire ownership of land for mining and manufacturing purposes, and shall be entitled to enjoy all the rights and privileges respectively conferred by the laws of the States of Virginia and West Virginia upon railroad corporations and mining and manufacturing companies, and shall be subject to the restrictions imposed by such laws upon like corporations.

2. " The capital stock of the said New River Railroad, Mining, and Manufacturing Company shall not exceed two millions of dollars, to be divided into shares of one hundred dollars each, each share subscribed to be entitled to one vote in all meetings of said company; and one hundred thousand dollars shall be taken as the minimum subscription on which said company may be organized."

While the General was applying for this charter, his friends ridiculed the idea of a railroad being run through the mountain gorges and clifts bordering on the wild banks of New river. But he, nothing daunted, continued his course. When the bill came up to be passed, his brother law-makers said: "There's nothing in it, but we will vote for it because Wharton wants it."

Finally, as we have said, the bill became a law in March, 1872, and General Wharton, with the power conferred under this charter, proceeded to put his plans in operation.

On the 17th day of June, 1872, a meeting of the incorporators of this road was held at Pearisburg, in Giles county, Virginia. From the Pearisburg *Gazette* of date June 22, 1872, we find that the following business was transacted:

The roll was called, and a quorum being present the meeting proceeded to business. Dr. John B. Radford was elected president, and Elbert Fowler secretary. Dr. Radford had given much of his time and attention to the construction of this company, and was a worthy gentleman in every way to place at the head of the scheme in its infancy.

On motion of General G. C. Wharton, numerous committees were appointed to receive subscriptions at Norfolk, Richmond, Lynchburg, Philadelphia, and all points along the line of the projected railroad. Two other resolutions were passed at this meeting, as follows:

"*Resolved*, That Richard B. Roane be authorized and requested to visit the coal-fields in Tazewell and Mercer and secure such grants and subscriptions in land, material, money, and, as far as possible, the right of way on the line.

"*Resolved*, That this meeting adjourn to meet at Eggleston's Springs on Tuesday the 23d day of July."

Richard B. Roane came from Eastern Virginia, a descendant of one of the best and most influential families in that country. He came to Southwest Virginia in 1871, to follow his profession of engineering, and in connection with that became well acquainted with the topography and mineral resources of the land. To him was entrusted the onerous duty of securing options, grants, material, right of way, and mineral properties for the New River Railroad, Mining, and Manufacturing Company. He proceeded at once to the counties named, and during this trip laid the foundation for securing grants of the celebrated coal lands on Flat Top and around there which have since proven to be worth millions. He saw and negotiated with the following parties, as appears from the following memorandum, which is unquestionably true:

"The following parties seen, and negotiations entered into with them for their coal, in the interest of the New River Railroad, Mining, and Manufacturing Company: A. A. Spotts, G. W. Spotts, Jonathan Smith, John Smith, India and Sarah Taylor, Amos Read, W. L. Moore, Jacob Buckland, W. H. Whitten, George Reid, Thomas Franklin, I. Q. Moore, Lewis K. Harvey, John J. Jeffress, the tract on centre of Laurel; Osborne tract, near the same, 500 acres (Laurel); Daniel Bolling, D. H. Dean, Daniel K. Perdue, J. Parker, Mosby Davis, George Tabor, Arch Thompson, C. H. Gleaner, 500 acres."

These parties were willing to make certain donations and grants, provided the road was constructed in five years. Most of these lands were in the very heart of the Flat Top region; and the New River Railroad, Mining, and Manufacturing Company, with the options upon such property as this, would have been one of the richest corporations in the South, and made the originators of the scheme rich, had justice played a role on the stage of this railroad theatre.

On July 23, 1872, the meeting appointed to take place at Eggleston's Springs was held, and from a subsequent copy of the Pearisburg *Gazette* of date July 27, 1872, we find the following proceedings concerning the New River Railroad, Mining, and Manufacturing Company:

"A quorum for business being present, on motion, Richard Wood was appointed chairman, and A. L. Fry and George W. Easley secretaries.

"The committees appointed at a former meeting to canvass for subscriptions to capital stock, not being ready to report, were severally continued.

"Richard B. Roane, who was appointed to visit the coal-fields in the counties of Tazewell and Mercer to secure grants and subscriptions, and as far as practicable the right of way, returned an interesting and flattering report, which was read and accepted."

A resolution was then passed by the company with reference to subscriptions, and the meeting adjourned after appointing Gen. G. C. Wharton, Hon. P. W. Strother, John T. Cowan, and George W. Easley as a committee to solicit aid from the

Atlantic, Mississippi and Ohio and the Chesapeake and Ohio railroads. Although the *Gazette* does not mention the fact, yet there is evidence that at this meeting John T. Cowan was elected president, with Wood, Strother, Radford, Fowler, and Wharton directors.

In the session of 1872–'73, the charter was amended in several respects to meet the wishes of parties desiring to become connected with the company.

Early in the spring of 1874, Richard B. Roane visited Richmond, Va., and while at the Exchange Hotel was introduced to one Thomas Graham, from Philadelphia, by Governor Gilbert C. Walker, at that time occupying the highest post of honor in Virginia. Roane exhibited some samples of ores and minerals to Graham which pleased him very much, and he made minute inquiries regarding the country, resources, minerals, and all, to which Roane politely gave him all the information possible, desiring to interest every one he could in the New River Railroad, Mining, and Manufacturing Company. Finally he asked Roane if he would meet him and take him over the line of the country—through Tazewell and Mercer—where the coal was situated. Roane agreed to meet him at Dublin, in Pulaski county, and did so, taking him for a trip through the counties above named, and then he returned to Philadelphia, carrying with him a box of specimens to be analyzed.

Hitherto, in detailing the history of this little company, which was struggling to place itself upon its feet, we have done so with great pleasure; but from this on a canopy of darkness comes over the transactions concerning it which we would gladly leave drawn, but truth in chronicling these events requires that it be unfolded.

What passed between R. B. Roane and Thomas Graham during this trip through the country we are unable to say, nor can we explain why Walter W. Wood should have appeared on the scene in Philadelphia about this time, but we find that in this same spring he wrote the following letter:

PHILADELPHIA, PA., *April 10, 1874.*

DEAR ROANE,—I have had a further interview with the parties to-day. Graham's box of specimens has arrived, and he is proceeding immediately to analyze them. The parties are in dead earnest, and nothing will disconcert them unless the ores turn out bad on analysis—a contingency that they do not contemplate. Whether you deem it advisable to see Colonel Harman or not, you come to Richmond to see me, as the parties want the railroad *captured* right away. I repeat, they mean business.

Very truly yours, W. W. WOOD.

Who the parties were that wanted the railroad *captured* right away we cannot say from Wood's letter, nor have we any idea what plans had been formed for capturing the same. But three days later the following letter was written, which in a measure gives us some idea who the capturing parties were:

THOMAS GRAHAM, *President.* T. B. ENGLISH, *Sec'y-Treas'r.*
OFFICE NORTH CAROLINA CENTRE IRON AND MANUFACTURING CO.,
PHILADELPHIA, *April 13, 1874.*

MR. R. B. ROANE, ESQ., *Dublin, Pulaski County, Va.:*

DEAR SIR,--In conversation with our friends on the subject of the New River railroad and matters connected therewith, they join me in the opinion that it will be expedient to see you here, in order to have more definite information. I therefore invite you to come to this city, and meet us, with Governor Walker, in order that you may personally explain and confer with us. Should this meet your wishes, will you please advise Governor Walker, to whom I have written to-day, and also inform me, appointing the time? I would suggest that you bring with you all necessary papers of information, with maps. Inclosed I hand you Girard National Bank check on New York for one hundred dollars, which please acknowledge.

Very truly yours, THOMAS GRAHAM.

The friends of whom Thomas Graham writes in the above letter were, in all probability, J. Dickinson Sergeant, Richard Wood, Harvey Beckwith, and Lewis Rodman, including Governor Walker, of course. From the best light we have upon the subject, these were the parties then attempting to capture the New River Railroad, Mining, and Manufacturing Company. In his letter of April 13, 1874, Thomas Graham advises R. B. Roane to put himself in communication with Governor Walker. But it appears that Roane had already communicated with Governor Walker, for two days after Thomas Graham wrote Roane, this letter followed:

RICHMOND, VA., *April 15, 1874.*

MY DEAR SIR,—Your valued favor of the 7th instant reached here during my absence.

After my return I had a conference with General G. C. Wharton, who promised to write you, and I presume has done so last evening. I received a note from Mr. Graham, stating that he had written you suggesting a conference between us and others in Philadelphia. I am compelled to be in that city next week on other business, and I have so written him. If you can go on, I think it would be well to do so; and if you will name the day most convenient to you, I will try and arrange to go on at same time. *Much caution* and good management will be required in all these matters, which of course you fully appreciate. Hoping to hear from you by return mail,

I am very truly yours, G. C. WALKER.

R. B. ROANE, ESQ.

In a short while from the receipt of those letters Roane went to Philadelphia. By some people it was thought that as Thomas Graham was not in any way connected with the road, Roane should not have carried the papers, maps, and information which he had gathered as a duly appointed agent of the New River Railroad, Mining, and Manufacturing Company to him and his Philadelphia friends; but upon reflection, we are inclined to think that in this instance Roane should not have been censured, because he wished to show Northern parties the many advantages which his company possessed in the way of minerals and ores. In fact, others knew that Roane was going on, because General Wharton met Roane in company with Thomas Graham; thought that the latter was a Philadelphia capitalist, as he represented himself as such, and from his statements believed that he and his Northern friends could construct and equip the road. But General G. C. Wharton at that time had not the ghost of an idea that Thomas Graham and his friends were in concert to capture the coal lands, strip them from the New River Company, and let the latter shift for itself. Nor had such a plan ever entered the mind of John T. Cowan, then president of the company, because, as we shall see directly, he and Hotchkiss were working in the interest of the New River Railroad, Mining, and Manufacturing Company, endeavoring to obtain options and grants for land. Prior to this time we find, by a memorandum endorsed, that in 1872 and 1873 all negotiations, bargains, and purchases were being secured by Roane in the name of the New River Railroad, Mining, and Manufacturing Company. On the back of the list of men seen in Abb's Valley, in reference to their lands, we find this written memorandum:

"Abb's Valley coal men seen and negotiated with by Roane in 1872 and 1873."

And within we find written:

"In the interest of the N. R. R. R., M. & M. Co."

So we may reasonably conclude that in the capturing minds of Thomas Graham and friends, of Philadelphia, alone rested the idea of gobbling up these mineral lands, at this time, without respect to the wishes or rights of the New River Railroad, Mining, and Manufacturing Company.

What passed at the conference in Philadelphia which Roane attended we cannot say farther than what was subsequently stated by R. B. Roane—that "a plan of action was determined upon."

We are not left, though, in the dark as to what that plan was, for Mr. Roane, upon being asked, frankly stated that Thomas Graham desired to become a stockholder in the company, with some friends of his. At all events, Roane called a meeting of the directors, which took place in April, 1874—about the 24th—at the Norvell-Arlington Hotel, in the city of Lynchburg. He requested that Thomas Graham and others be allowed to subscribe, but for reasons unknown the directors refused to allow it, doubtless feeling then that things were not going on as they ought. But the stockholders having carelessly omitted hitherto to pay the two per cent. on the fifty thousand subscribed, Thomas Bocock, an astute attorney, at the suggestion of Roane, gave it as his opinion that the whole thing was invalid on that account, and that the books should be re-opened in order to collect the two per cent. Three of the directors consented; the books of subscription were re-opened, and checks were given by the subscribers for the two per cent., and other subscriptions made. At this meeting it seems that Roane made a subscription of five thousand dollars, conditioned upon the fact that he should be satisfied with the organization to be made at the Montgomery White Sulphur Springs, in June, 1874. We further infer from facts which we will give directly that at this meeting Richard B. Roane was in some manner passed over and ignored in a way which he thought was but a poor return for the services he had given this company. From now on we find that he gave the Philadelphia parties every assistance possible, until they broke faith with him, and by their own actions, as we shall see, treated him abominably.

Shortly after the adjournment of this meeting Thomas Graham wrote a letter, which we copy *verbatim*. It was as follows:

THOMAS GRAHAM, *President.*   T. B. ENGLISH, *Sec'y-Treas'r.*
NORTH CAROLINA CENTRE IRON AND MANUFACTURING CO.,
PHILADELPHIA, *April 28, 1874.*

MR. RICHARD B. ROANE, ESQ., *Dublin, Va.:*

MY DEAR SIR,—Mr. Richard Wood returned, and called on me yesterday. He related what had occurred at the meeting at Lynchburg. His explanation of the results is not made clear to me up to this time. I also have your letter of the 26th, which is very clear, and I coincide with the opinions therein expressed. Until I see you I will reserve any further comments. I fully appreciate your surprise and disappointment. I think it just to warn you that you are likely to be ignored. I do not know yet what steps myself and friends will take—surely some, however—of which I will inform you ; but I would advise you to strengthen yourself by laying hold of red hematite and magnetic ore, marble, and lithographic stone ; also, fossil ores near and tributary to the line. Advise us of properties you can secure, with description, terms, &c., and we will inform you what we will do. Get leases and options. Tell us what you wish us to do for you. If it meets with our views we will do as we agree. It will be wise for you to confine yourself for the present to properties close to the line of the railroad, and where you know good bodies of mineral exist—the best of such properties—without encumbering yourself with heavy bodies of property. It will be proper to furnish you with funds for your expenses whilst engaged in this work, and the further compensation or interest that may be determined on secured to you by contract. Should you entertain these suggestions, we would prefer that leases, options, or any direct important purchases of mineral property, or strategical points of importance, if approved by us, should be made in the name of or conveyed to J. *Dickinson Sergeant*, attorney at law, Philadelphia, Pa., subject to the contract of interest or compensation agreed upon with you. I call your attention at once to the magnetic property (No. 3) north of Snidow's Ferry; to Charles Parker's red hematite, No. 2; to No. 5 brown hematite, Laurel creek; to the magnetic ore near A. M. & O. R. R.; to the marbles and litho stone. Mr. Wood considers that Mr. Cowan and Mr. Hotchkiss are in positions to enable them to accumulate property for the New River railroad. Probably they are. In writing you this letter, however, it is simply business between us. I shall be glad to hear from you, and I will advise you. Please write me on the matter contained in this letter, and believe me to be sincerely your friend,

THOMAS GRAHAM, 233 St. (over).

P. S.—You will pardon me if I further advise you to make *no* confidants. When you write, will you inform me more particularly as to the occurrences of the meeting at Lynchburg, and whether General Wharton agreed *entirely* with Mr. Wood in the course he pursued? I wish to remark that Mr. Wood was authorized, and agreed to make the requisite subscription, and my telegram inferred further aid, if necessary. T. G

This remarkable letter was written on the 28th day of April, 1874, almost three months before Thomas Graham or J. Dickinson Sergeant became officers in that company. Notwithstanding the fact that Sergeant had no connection whatever with the company, Graham writes the authorized agent of the New River Railroad, Mining, and Manufacturing Company to have "all leases, options, or any direct important purchase of mineral land, or strategical points of importance," conveyed to J. Dickinson Sergeant. Graham had some object in view in wanting the New River Railroad, Mining, and Manufacturing Company completely separated from the options, leases, and purchases of the mineral lands, and that object could be but one. Had the leases, purchases, and options of this great coal section been obtained in the name of the New River Railroad, Mining, and Manufacturing Company no disposition could have been made of them without the consent, sanction, and authority of the directors of that company, and the general stockholders—not Graham, Sergeant, Wood, Beckwith, and Rodman—would have been entitled to a participation in the profits. The fact stares us directly in the face, that the very property which the company knew was most valuable and upon which it based its calculations was being snatched away and forever sundered from her chartered rights, without any knowledge of the president or board of directors, who were the legal guardians of its property, rights, and franchises. By virtue of the authority vested in R. B. Roane to secure grants, options, leases, and contracts of mineral land, the New River Railroad and Mining Company was entitled to them, and Graham and Sergeant well knew that their steps were in violation of that express authority to have them gotten in the name of a total stranger to that company.

It was now absolutely necessary that such a change should be made in the governing body of the company as would enable Graham and Sergeant to continue their concerted plan of operations without question from any president, vice-president, secretary, treasurer, or director. So, at the meeting held in June, 1874, at the Montgomery White Sulphur Springs, Thomas Graham appeared for the purpose of becoming a subscriber in the sum of $50,000, to make up the necessary one hundred thousand dollars required by the charter.

At this meeting the stockholders again objected to the books being re-opened or Graham being allowed to subscribe. There seemed to be some insuperable difficulty to his coming in, for at the former meeting in Lynchburg the directors and stockholders had objected. But Roane again came to his rescue, and withdrawing his subscription of $5,000, and his check for 2 per cent. cash, the books were re-opened, and Thomas Graham subscribed $50,000, and at last became a stockholder in the company with which he had been hitherto connected *"sub rosa."* At this meeting a new organization was effected, and J. Dickinson Sergeant was made president, Thomas Graham vice-president, T. B. English secretary and treasurer, and R. B. Roane land agent and mining engineer.

The surprise which Thomas Graham expressed in his last letter to R. B. Roane, at the proceedings in Lynchburg, can be easily understood now. This last reorganization he expected in Lynchburg early in the spring. His taunting Roane with being ignored was but a card played to prejudice him as much as possible against the Virginia board of directors. Doubtless that very objection which they had to Graham's subscribing was apprehensiveness less the road passed from their hands.

After this last meeting there was no longer any concealment on Graham's part, so far as Roane was concerned. He distinctly asserts that the land grants, contracts, and options are their private land interests. The following correspondence forever sets this matter at rest, and shows that the options gotten under, by virtue of, and through the authority of the New River Railroad, Mining, and Manufacturing Company were appropriated *in toto* by Sergeant and his capturing friends:

PHILADELPHIA, *July 22, 1874.*

MR. RICHARD B. ROANE, *Dublin, Va.:*

MY DEAR SIR,—Mr. Sergeant wishes you to come here and bring with you all papers and memoranda you have in connection with our *private* land *interests.*

We are deliberating on our plans on this and railroad matters, and your presence with papers and information is necessary.

Mr. English writes you to-day.

Very truly yours,   THOMAS GRAHAM.

With this letter from Thomas Graham one came from T. B. English, which reads as follows:

NO. 233 SOUTH 3D ST., PHILADELPHIA, *July 22, 1890.*

MR. RICHARD B. ROANE, *Land Agent and Mining Engineer, New River Railroad, Mining, and Manufacturing Company, Dublin, Va.:*

MY DEAR SIR,—I am instructed by the president to request you to come to this city, and to bring with you all papers, contracts, deeds, maps, &c., appertaining to the business of this company in your possession, for examination, &c.

Please draw on me at sight for one month's salary and travelling expenses, and advise of the probable time of your arrival here, in order that Mr. Sergeant may arrange to meet you.

Very respectfully,   T. B. ENGLISH,
Secretary and Treasurer N. R. R. R., M. & M. Co.

Is it not passing strange that Thomas Graham should have to write such a letter, underscoring "private interests," at the same time that the secretary of the company writes to Roane to come in his official capacity? There is but one reasonable solution: these land options had been gotten apart from the railroad company, which was justly entitled to them, and Thomas Graham, fearing that Mr. Roane would not consider these as a part of the railroad papers, deemed it more expedient to speak plainly as to the meaning of the request in Secretary English's letter. That Richard B. Roane did not consider them as in any way connected with the New River Railroad, Mining, and Manufacturing Company is conclusively shown later on.

What took place at Philadelphia when Roane went on is not positively known except between the parties themselves. But from evidence before us the options, leases, grants, contracts, and so forth, were deposited with J. Dickinson Sergeant. There has been some little question as to what properties those options, leases, and contracts included. Some have contended that they were simply leases and options of iron mines in and about Giles and Tazewell, but the following letter, coupled with the memorandum already given, shows that they were options on those valuable coal lands around about Laurel creek, in Tazewell, where the mining town of Pocahontas now stands, and some of the Bluestone coal lands:

Abb's Valley, Tazewell County, Va., August 22, 1872.

Richard B. Roane:

Dear Sir,—I hasten to reply to your letter received a few days since. Sqr. Moore says there is no doubt but that you can get the Osburn land, as he is now holding correspondence with said Osburn to make the purchase, and expects to let you have it. I saw Nelson, and he promised that you should have the refusal, and will sell to no one else before giving you the first chance. I saw my son and many others, all of whom seem to be willing now to give one-half to come up to your terms—myself with the balance. It is difficult for me to ascertain the exact amount of acres, but I know one thing: that is, the company can secure one-half of all, or nearly all, of the mineral lands on Laurel, and that is all they want. There is only two persons but what is willing to come into the arrangement, so I hope that this will satisfy the company. Dr. Johnson is doing well. He, Mr. Moore, and myself are the working men for the company. Write me without delay, and if there is anything that I can do, let me know, and it shall be attended to.

Respectfully, A. A. SPOTTS.

This property which Mr. Spotts speaks of, on Laurel creek, is among the best of the coal mines in that section now, and worth probably many millions of dollars. Mr. Spotts was under the impression that the negotiations were in favor of the New River Railroad, Mining, and Manufacturing Company. The memorandum which we have quoted from shows that his impression was correct.

By some means or other Governor Walker failed to participate in the new arrangement and reorganization for some time afterwards. W. W. Wood appears upon the scene again by writing the following letter:

515 OLIVE STREET, ST. LOUIS, MO.

DEAR ROANE,—What's become of the railroad and the mineral property? I saw Graham in Philadelphia, and he gave me an account of the proceedings at the reorganization of the New River railroad, with the name of the president-elect, &c. He told me that the president would immediately organize things and proceed actively to work in building the road. He told me that Governor Walker was not in it, but that he intended to protect you fully. Write me all about it, and anything of interest besides that you can think of. I am here at above address—have stuck out my shingle as attorney at law. My prospects are good, and I believe I will do well. Write me all about the iron. Very truly yours, W. W. WOOD.

In 1875, the line was surveyed, commencing at New river. It was to run to Hinton, with power to build any branch roads that might be necessary to bring out minerals. Of course this branch line had indirect reference to the counties of Wise, Giles, Bland, Buchanan, and others, but pointed more directly to the rich coal-fields near Abb's Valley, in Tazewell, and the county of Mercer, West Virginia. There was but little known regarding this company until 1878, when the State convicts were placed upon the line and grading begun for a narrow-gauge railroad, and the plan conceived by General Wharton in 1871, which was deemed almost impossible by every one, became a living reality. These convicts were secured through

General Wharton, who not only succeeded in getting an act passed to that effect, but personally went security upon Thomas Graham's bond, which had to be given to the State before the Governor would allow them to go.

In the meanwhile, between the years 1875 and 1878, R. B. Roane was still seeking leases, grants, and options upon the mineral properties adjacent and tributary to the proposed line. Several of these original options are still extant, with the name of owner of land, the county in which it was situated, amount specified, and terms of lease. All were obtained in the name of J. Dickinson Sergeant, of Philadelphia. Most of these contracts which did not go into Sergeant's possession were obtained in the counties of Bland and Giles, Virginia, and Mercer county, West Virginia. They appear to have been gotten on or about the 17th or 18th of May, 1877. Why these failed to reach their destination is accounted for from the fact that in the year 1878 there was a difficulty between Roane and Sergeant in reference to the part Roane should have for services rendered. We give below copy of a contract drawn by Sergeant, which will show that he acknowledges indebtedness for Roane's services. There seemed to have arisen some misunderstanding, because a letter of Roane's, which we will give later on, clearly shows that. This agreement is signed by J. Dickinson Sergeant, and was evidently forwarded by him to R. B. Roane for signature, who refused to append his name to it on the ground of its being defective. The contract is as follows:

Agreement made this —— day of October, A. D. 1878, between J. Dickinson Sergeant, of the city of Philadelphia, president of the New River Company, and trustee holding certain lands and leases on and near New river, in Virginia and West Virginia, for himself, Richard Wood, Harvey Beckwith, and Lewis Rodman, of the one part, and Richard B. Roane, of the other. Whereas the said Roane has rendered services, time, and labor to, for, and about the business of the New River Railroad Company, and about the obtaining and negotiating for the *lands and leases* now held by the said Sergeant, as trustee aforesaid, upon the stipulation that he should have the privilege of taking at the cost thereof, with interest and expenses added, one sixteenth part of the stock of the said company, and a similar proportion in the said lands and leases : Now this agreement witnesseth, that the said Sergeant, in consideration of the services of the said Roane as aforesaid, and of one dollar unto him in hand paid by the said Roane, the receipt whereof is hereby acknowledged, doth declare and agree that the said New River Railroad Company shall and will issue to the said Roane, on payment by him of one-sixteenth part of the cost thereof, with interest and expenses added, one-sixteenth part of the stock of said company; and that he, the said Sergeant, shall and will, on payment by the said Roane of one-sixteenth part of the cost thereof, with interest and expenses added, grant and assure to the said Roane, his heirs, executors, administrators, and assigns, one-sixteenth part of the lands and leases on and near New river held by the said Sergeant as aforesaid, and that upon any sale of the stock, leases, and lands before the said Roane shall have obtained said transfer, the said Roane shall be entitled to receive one-sixteenth part of the profits of said sale, to be ascertained by deducting from the sum realized the cost of acquisition of the same, with interest and expenses thereof.

Provided, however, that nothing herein contained shall be deemed to vest in the said Roane (prior to the payment by him of the one-sixteenth part of the cost, interest, and expenses aforesaid) any further or other right or title than the right to participate in the profits from sales of the stock, lands, and leases aforesaid, should there be a sale of the same by the parties holding title thereto. And the said Roane hereby agrees to accept the interest hereby intended to be secured to him in full payment and satisfaction for his services to the said New River Railroad Company, and to the said Sergeant and those for whom he is acting as trustee. In witness whereof, the said parties have hereunto set their hands and seals the date aforesaid.

(Signed) J. D. SERGEANT. [L. S.]
Witness present:
(Signed) SEPTIMUS E. NORRIS.
A true copy: PARK PHIPPS (Witness).

In this agreement the evidence is conclusive that Sergeant did not hold these grants, leases, and options for the benefit of the New River Railroad, Mining, and Manufacturing Company, but for the personal benefit of himself and three others. Where had gone the stockholders' interest in these valuable options and leases originally negotiated for in the name of the company? Echo answers, "Where?"

Mr. Roane misunderstood the contract in two particulars. He thought that the interest he should have in the option and leases should be entirely distinct from his participation in the stock of the New River railroad. He regarded the two as totally distinct transactions, just as Sergeant really held when he termed one interest for himself as trustee for others. Moreover, Roane evidently understood that he was to have the interest for services rendered without any payment of cost and expense. That this was the original agreement there can be no doubt, for the correspondence, as well as extrinsic facts, prove it. But J. Dickinson Sergeant, having possession of these leases and options, chose to take a different position. Mr. Roane's letter written concerning the contract gives his views thoroughly upon the subject. It is as follows:

J. D. SERGEANT, ESQ.: NEWBERN, VA., *March 17, 1879.*

DEAR SIR,—I return one of the contracts unsigned. I have examined it carefully for the first time. It is very much mixed, and susceptible of too many constructions—that is, the railroad company and the land company is mixed up together in such a way that one cannot be distinguished from the other; in fact, they are made to appear in the contract as one and the same, while, as I understand it, they are separate and distinct. If this understanding be correct, they should be separated and made distinct in the contract, or there should be separate contracts. The wording of the contract is such that it brings the railroad and land company together in such a way that they cannot be separated. I am sure this was not your intention. Again, the wording of the contract is such that it makes the interest intended to be secured contingent only in the event of a sale, or upon my paying such a portion of prime costs; and even this is foreshadowed with some doubt from the phraseology. And under the programme, as I understand it, there will be no sale; hence I am excluded from the contract unless I can by some chance raise the money necessary to be paid from some outside source, which is simply impossible, as I am dependent on my daily labor for sustenance. I am therefore forever excluded under the contract, unless some one will take it off my hands at whatever they may choose to give, although the enterprise may pay for itself in one year, and its net earnings may thereafter be large. Yet I can never participate under the contract unless there is an actual and absolute sale of the stock, lands, leases, rights, franchises, &c., or by my paying the certain proportion, in some source independent of the enterprise, whatever its net earnings may be. Thus, suppose the parties now in interest continue, the road built, the mines and lands utilized, worked, and ore shipped and manufactured—in one year the thing has paid for itself, and the next there is a net profit. Under the contract I am excluded from participation because I am unable to pay my proportion independent of the earnings of the enterprise. If there is no sale, there is no contract unless I can get the money from some outside source to pay the proportion as mentioned, which I am not able to do, and doubtless never will be, unless

the earnings of such operations are to be applied in this way, which the contract does not provide for. While this may be implied, we may die at any time, and this implication disregarded. The contract is imperfect and worded wrong. My first impulse was to sign it without comment, but knowing that you meant and intended differently from what the contract expresses, I thought it best to return the contract and call your attention to its defects. There is not a court in the land but what would construe this contract as I have.   Yours very truly,
                              RICHARD B. ROANE.

In regard to his having gotten these options in J. D. Sergeant's name, Mr. Roane's explanation is this:

"When I went into Tazewell and Mercer I was under the impression that the organization of the New River Railroad and Manufacturing Company was illegal, so I obtained them in limited grants, in an independent capacity."

Messrs. Graham and Sergeant failed signally to liquidate Roane's claim, as just as it was, so far as they were concerned, and he was on the eve of bringing suit to recover his rights when the New River Railroad, Mining, and Manufacturing Company was said to have passed into the hands of *innocent purchasers*—the Norfolk and Western Railroad Company. The exact time at which the New River Railroad, Mining, and Manufacturing Company passed into the possession of the Norfolk and Western railroad, or Clarence H. Clark and *his associates*, is not exactly known, but we gather from the first annual report for the year ending December 31, 1881, of the Norfolk and Western Railroad Company, that the negotiations for the New River Railroad, Mining, and Manufacturing Company, and all its branches, properties, and rights, were completed at the time that Clarence H. Clarke and *his associates* were purchasing the Norfolk and Western railroad, which at that time was the Atlantic, Mississippi and Ohio railroad. The purchase of the latter was made under sale by decree of court on February 10, 1881. Their first annual report shows this fact on page 6. It reads:

"In the proceedings on the bill the said court, on the 9th day of May, 1879, pronounced a decree of foreclosure and sale; and on the 10th day of February, 1881, the road, property, franchises, and rights were sold to Clarence H.

Clark and his associates for the sum of $8,605,000, subject to liens and encumbrances amounting to $4,898,159.14, including the interest calculated to the first day of January, 1881."

In this same first annual report there is something said concerning the New River Railroad, Mining, and Manufacturing Company, on page 15 :

"The Norfolk and Western Railroad Company has acquired the control of the various roads in the States of Virginia and West Virginia, which, aggregated, constitute what is known as the New River Railroad Company. This line commences at the junction with the Norfolk and Western Railroad Company at New river bridge, and running down the New river and its tributaries, as at present projected, will be about seventy miles in length, with authority under its charters to extend up New river to the North Carolina border, and in various directions upon tributaries to the river. At its proposed terminus it strikes a superb body of Kanawha coal in what is known as the Flat Top region. The surveys were completed and work commenced August 3, 1881."

When we come to the beginning and inception of the Norfolk and Western Railroad Company, in the chapter containing its history, this subject will be reverted to again.

The Pocahontas and Flat Top coal regions, opened up by this company's railroad, is one of the best coal countries in the United States. These lands lie in a part of Tazewell county, Virginia, and Mercer, McDowell, Wyoming, and Raleigh counties, West Virginia. The coal is not only of first-rate quality, but apparently of almost inexhaustible quantities. Throughout a large portion of Flat Top Mountain the coal is above water level, and lies most conveniently for cheap and expeditious mining. The mineral is deposited in layers throughout the mountain, and mined by an entrance cut into the solid bank of coal, on the side of the hill. Tipples are erected near this entrance, and through them the coal goes into a railrod car—after being screened and the fine coal separated.

These coals, geologically, are the lowest members of the coal measures, and are the equivalent of the Quinimont group of the Kanawha region and the Pottsville conglomerate of Pennsylvania. They are low in sulphur and ash, and unusually high in fixed carbon. The coal-bed everywhere presents, so far as discovered, a working thickness of 11'3'' around Pocahontas, and holds its working dimensions until it reaches Flipping creek, six or seven miles off, where it divides into two beds, each some 4½ and 5½ feet thick. Westward of Pocahontas, along Laurel creek, the bed carries its thickness fairly well for a distance of eight miles, and shows pretty well the same section for quite a distance north of the dividing ridge, on the waters of the Elkhorn and the Tug Fork of Sandy. A large area of country is underlaid with this coal, and it has been estimated that it should yield 10,000 tons per acre, while the upper beds should add probably 6,000 tons more. The quality of it has been tested both in the laboratory and by actual practice, and for steaming and coking it has been found very superior. As a domestic coal, it is generally used, and pronounced good. But a safer and better idea of its quality can be gained from McCreath and D'Invillier's analysis. In their report on "the New river-Cripple creek region," they give the following analysis in connection with its quality from an average of fifteen samples:

Water.	Volatile Matter.	Fixed Carbon.	Sulphur.	Ash.
1.011	18.812	74.256	.730	5.191

By analysis, this coal is superior to the Cumberland, Clearfield, Broad Top, Connellsville coking, Westmoreland and Cardiff (Wales) coals.

Its analysis as a coking coal is superior in every respect. The same valuable report already quoted gives the analysis of the coke taken from these companies' ovens in that region:

Water	.182	.196	.664
Volatile matter	.719	.494	1.059
Fixed carbon	92.248	92.585	92.816
Sulphur	.565	.677	.548
Ash	6.286	6.048	4.913
	100.000	100.000	100.000

Since the discovery of this valuable field many coal operations have begun. At present the following works are in active operation in Tazewell county, Virginia, and Mercer and McDowell counties, West Virginia:

In Tazewell, the Southwest Virginia Improvement Company.

In Mercer county, West Virginia, in what is known as the Bluestone region (because the Bluestone river flows through the country), are John Cooper & Co., the Caswell Creek Coal and Coke Company, the Buckeye Coal and Coke Company, the Booth-Bowen Coal and Coke Company, the Good-will Coal and Coke Company, the Louisville Coal and Coke Company.

In McDowell county, on the Elkhorn extension of the Norfolk and Western Railroad Company, we have the Coaldale Coal and Coke Company, the Elkhorn Coal and Coke Company, the Shamokin Coal and Coke Company, the Norfolk Coal and Coke Company, the Lick Colliery, the Turkey Gap Coal and Coke Company, the Crozier Coal and Coke Company, the Houston Coal and Coke Company, the Powhatan Coal and Coke Company, the Lynchburg Coal and Coke Company.

These are all actively engaged in shipping. Many others are obtaining leases, and as the railroad extends on through McDowell towards Ironton will begin shipping. To give an idea of the immense amount of coal and coke shipped from these regions we subjoin a table of the shipments since 1883:

	Coal.	Coke.
1883	54,552 tons.	23,762 tons.
1884	153,229 "	56,360 "
1885	499,138 "	48,571 "
1886	739,018 "	59,021 "
1887	992,260 "	151,171 "
1888	1,343,312 "	202,808 "
1889	1,543,900 "	310,504 "

These figures do not include the coal mined altogether, because the miners and their families burn an unlimited supply for their own consumption.

As we may easily understand, the opening up of these works was the cause of the growth of towns and the country as if by magic. Pocahontas in two years grew into a city number-

SOUTHWEST VIRGINIA AND SHENANDOAH VALLEY. 75

ing its inhabitants among the thousands, while Bramwell, Graham, Simmons, and Mill Creek soon followed. From a howling wilderness of mountains the whole community in those sections became, as if by an electric shock, a rushing, thriving business place; and now in that mining section embracing a corner in each of the three counties of Tazewell, Virginia, and Mercer and McDowell counties, West Virginia, the population is hardly less than twenty thousand people. The wages of the miners are good, and as they are a class of people who do not believe in denying themselves, there has been a steady business rush all the time. A great deal of money has been made in speculating and dealing in coal lands, and the formation of joint stock companies of various kinds have, more than anything else, tended to develop each and every resource of the country. Certainly, just from this section alone, the New river division of the Norfolk and Western Railroad Company has almost inexhaustible supplies from which to draw. But, in addition to this great coal section, over this line of road will come the mineral products of the Clinch Valley country, which more properly belong to the history of the Clinch Valley extension of the great Norfolk and Western system.

CHAPTER V.

The Norfolk and Western Railroad Company: Its inception and beginning—The Norfolk and Petersburg Railroad Company—The Southside Railroad—The Virginia and Tennessee Railroad—The Virginia and Kentucky Railroad—The New River branch—Creation of the extension mortgage—The Cripple Creek extension—The Norfolk Terminal Company—The Bluestone extensions—The Clinch Valley extension—The Elk Horn extension to Ironton, Ohio—The Scioto Valley Railroad—The Southeastern extension into North Carolina—The Shenandoah Valley division—Increase in mileage of the Norfolk and Western Railroad for the past ten years—Increase in passenger and freight traffic—Increase of its rolling stock—Its financial advance.

THE Norfolk and Western Railroad Company has played such an important part in the development of Southwest Virginia that it deserves a full account of its various operations from its inception to the present time; and the rapidity with which it has advanced in every way for the past nine years makes everything connected with it of more than ordinary interest. There is scarcely another railroad in the Southern States which has done so much for the development of the country through which it runs, or enriched its owners more. So phenomenal has been the success of the company in the section of country of which we are writing that its name has a kind of talismanic effect there and its objectionable features cheerfully borne on account of its developing policy.

In 1851 the Norfolk and Petersburg railroad was chartered, and opened for traffic in 1852. This road ran between Norfolk and Petersburg, a distance of some eighty-one miles. It passes through what is known as the Great Dismal Swamp, which at that time was a scene of horror, but is now being gradually reclaimed and cultivated; thence on through Nansemond county, by Suffolk; next the road runs through Isle of Wight county by Windsor, Zuni, and through Southhampton, Sussex, Prince George, and Dinwiddie counties, until Petersburg is reached—a city of some thirty thousand people. As may well be imagined, this railroad did a small business until others connected with it were put in operation.

As far back as 1846 the Southside Railroad Company was chartered, but was not constructed and placed in operation until the year 1857, when it was opened for traffic between Petersburg and Lynchburg. This road runs from the former place through Dinwiddie, Nottoway, Prince Edward, Appomattox, and Campbell counties to Lynchburg, in the latter county, one hundred and twenty-three miles from Petersburg. The country through which it passes presents an uninviting aspect to the eye, but is really a good one. The railroad, in order to select the best grade possible, runs as much along the ridge as practicable, excluding from sight many fertile spots and good farms. Leaving Farmville, in travelling westward, the plateau begins, which is really a fine section from there on to Lynchburg. Many towns have sprung up along this route since its earlier history, among which may be mentioned Blackstone, Crewe, Burkeville, Farmville, Prospect, and Pamplin. The live, business capacity of some of these places argue with force that the possibilities of this section of the country are great.

The Virginia and Tennessee railroad, chartered in March, 1849, and opened in 1857, runs westward from Lynchburg through Bedford, Botetourt, Roanoke, Montgomery, Pulaski, Wythe, Smyth, and Washington counties to Bristol, Tennessee—a distance of two hundred and four miles from Lynchburg. This line traverses a part of the great Southwest of which we are particularly writing, and the towns, cities, and counties contiguous to this branch of the road will not be especially mentioned now.

Another road was chartered, and partially constructed, in connection with the three we have mentioned, which was known as the Virginia and Kentucky railroad. This route was to extend from Bristol to Cumberland Gap. The road was, however, placed in other hands, as we shall see later on.

On June 17, 1870, the Legislature of Virginia passed an act entitled, "An act to authorize the formation of the Atlantic, Mississippi and Ohio railroad," which was for the purpose of merging, absorbing, and consolidating the Norfolk and Petersburg Railroad Company, the Southside Railroad Company, the Virginia and Tennessee Railroad Company, and the Virginia and Kentucky Railroad Company, all four of which were in a separate existence at that time. This consolidation was not effected without a great deal of trouble, and even at this day queer lobbying tales are told of how champagne flowed and Havana cigars were handed around among the law-makers on the evening of the day previous to that of the passage of the act. People along the lines of the companies were opposed, on the ground that it would not be to their interest—why, it was impossible to divine. That the consolidation was a good measure for the country at large is beyond all doubt, for by that means a traffic was established which redounded to Virginia's benefit. This new company was placed under the management of General William Mahone, who has since rendered himself famous in Virginia politics; who, though censured by some for the manner in which he conducted the affairs of the company, undoubtedly improved and added to the condition of the road. It was during the year 1874, in April, that by an act of the Virginia Legislature the stock of the Virginia and Kentucky railroad owned by the Atlantic, Mississippi and Ohio Company passed from its control. The road apparently was prospering under General Mahone's rule, for the traffic increased, while new stock, iron, and station-houses were all placed along the line of the road. This road controlled the branch from Petersburg to City Point, and the extension from Glade Springs, in Washington county, to the salt works, about nine miles distant. On October 1st, 1874, the Atlantic, Mississippi and Ohio Railroad Company failed to pay the semi-annual interest due upon the mortgaged debt it had created. This was a surprise indeed, and still more did consternation stare all in the face when on April 1, 1875, the semi-annual interest was in default again. This second failure caused the trustees, under deed of September 9, 1870, to file their bill in the circuit court of the United States for the Eastern District of Virginia, praying that a receiver be appointed to take an account of all liens and incumbrances, and a sale of the property, rights, and franchises of the road. On the 9th day of May, 1879, the court decreed a sale of the property, and who should purchase the Atlantic, Mississippi and Ohio railroad became an absorbing topic in railroad circles.

At this time this company owned and operated four hundred and twenty-eight miles of railroad, running through a good portion of Eastern Virginia and the very heart of the great Southwest. At Bristol it connected with the East Tennessee, Virginia and Georgia, while at Norfolk it possessed harbor facilities unexcelled on the Atlantic coast. A rich, succulent, agricultural country enclosed it on both sides, and it had more than a modicum of advantages usually possessed by railroads in the Southern States. The mineral resources along its lines were superb.

It was to these that the Northern capitalists were turning their attention—the coal and iron in Southwest Virginia—and on the tenth day of February, 1881, the Atlantic, Mississippi and Ohio railroad, with its road, property, and franchises, was purchased by Clarence H. Clark and his associates for the sum of $8,605,000, subject to liens and incumbrances amounting to $4,898,159.14, including interest calculated to the first day of January, 1881. This sale was duly confirmed by the court on the fourth day of April, 1881, and then the purchasers were designated as the "Norfolk and Western Railroad Company," under which the reorganization was perfected. The purchase money was paid on the third day of May, 1881, and the road, with its property, franchises, rights, and privileges, was deeded to the Norfolk and Western Railroad Company by M. F. Pleasants, who was the commissioner appointed by the court, which deed was duly recorded in the clerk's office of the hustings court of the city of Norfolk. On the same day the Atlantic,

Mississippi and Ohio Railroad Company deeded to the Norfolk and Western Railroad Company all the shares of the capital stock of the Norfolk and Petersburg, the Southside, and the Virginia and Tennessee railroad companies; the Virginia and Kentucky railroad stock having been already disposed of by the Legislature of Virginia in 1874.

Then burst upon the financial horizon one of the most remarkable pecuniary reorganizations that ever startled the sober business sense of any man. The Atlantic, Mississippi and Ohio Railroad Company, which was sold for $8,605,000, with divisional liens and incumbrances amounting to $4,898,159.14, including interest calculated to January 1, 1881, was reorganized under the name of the Norfolk and Western railroad, with an authorized capital stock of $25,000,000 and a general mortgage indebtedness of $11,000,000.

The organization stood thus:

To amount authorized capital stock		$25,000,000 00
To 150,000 shares preferred stock issued Clarence H. Clark	$15,000,000 00	
Common unassessable stock, subject to preferred stock, and general mortgage bonds, issued Clarence H. Clark	3,000,000 00	
Unissued capital stock	7,000,000 00	
Total amount issued	$25,000,000 00	
General mortgage bonds		$11,000,000 00
Amount issued to retire divisional liens	$5,137,000 00	
For use of the treasury of the company	500,000 00	
Issued to Clarence H. Clark	5,363,000 00	
	$11,000,000 00	

A railroad which sold for about $13,503,159 was reorganized for $36,000,000. People wondered at this financial operation, and many predicted that the company would not pay interest upon the bonds, and that it would soon go into the hands of a receiver. Not knowing at that time anything about the New River Railroad, Mining, and Manufacturing Company, which was the moving power behind the throne, one would have supposed that Shakespeare was totally wrong when he said there was nothing in a name.

In the first annual report of the Norfolk and Western Railroad Company, on page 7, we find the reorganization stated to be a compact between Clarence H. Clark and his associates. Who the latter were is a matter which is not disclosed, but from the reading of the language of the report itself they paid Clarence H. Clark a very good sum to purchase this property, if they believed in its being of any value. The report reads:

"By the terms of the agreement between Clarence H. Clark and his associates, it was provided that in consideration of Clarence H. Clark's furnishing and paying the purchase money ($8,605,000) in cash, the Norfolk and Western Railroad Company should deliver to Clarence H. Clark its general mortgage bonds amounting to $5,363,000, one hundred and fifty thousand shares of its full-paid and unassessable preferred six per cent. capital stock, and also thirty thousand shares of its full-paid and unassessable common capital stock; and it was further agreed that general mortgage bonds amounting to $5,137,000 should be reserved to retire existing divisional liens, and that general mortgage bonds amounting to $500,000 should be reserved for the treasury of the company."

If the $5,363,000 of mortgage bonds were worth par, and the stock was worth par, which was given C. H. Clark for purchasing this company, then for paying some $8,605,000 for the road he received the sum of $23,363,000—a very substantial rate of interest. That the $15,000,000 of preferred stock came out all right we cannot doubt, since in the annual report of the Norfolk and Western Railroad Company for 1883, on page 18, we find the following:

"Your directors, believing that so long as it was considered advisable to use the surplus earnings of the company for the purpose of bettering its property or increasing its facilities for doing business, the preferred shareholders are entitled to scrip dividends representing the amount which has been so applied, and which would otherwise be applicable to cash dividends, at a meeting held December 26th, declared a scrip dividend of 3½ per cent., payable January 15, 1884, on the $15,000,000 of preferred shares then outstanding. The scrip, when presented to the company in sums of $500, is exchangeable into convertible debenture bonds, payable in 1894, bearing six per cent. interest, payable semi-annually."

The interest is paid upon these bonds, as well as the others received by Clarence H. Clark, making the sum of $20,363,000 interest-bearing and good. What did Mr. Clark's associates get? Whatever may have been the public opinion as to this reorganization, Clarence H. Clark and his associates well knew that the increased rate of freight and passenger traffic over the lines of the Norfolk and Western Railroad Company would justify the issue of the increased amount of stock and bonds. They had possession of premises and facts concerning which the general public was totally ignorant. Those were in connection with the New River Railroad, Mining, and Manufacturing Company, from which the coal options had been so ruthlessly torn. Subsequent to the year 1878, after Sergeant and Roane had arrived at a misunderstanding, as seen heretofore, there must have been a reorganization of the New River Railroad, Mining, and Manufacturing Company, because afterwards it comes out under the new title of the New River Railroad Company. In all probability the stock originally owned by the shareholders of the New River Railroad, Mining, and Manufacturing Company had been purchased by Mr. Sergeant and his friends, and afterwards the company reorganized under the latter name, *with J. D. Sergeant's options, contracts,* and *mineral leases attached,* transforming virtually a poor corporation into one worth millions. At all events, the first and second annual reports of the Norfolk and Western railroad expressly dwell upon the fact that the expected traffic from the opening of the coal mines would greatly increase the earnings of the Norfolk and Western Railroad Company, and that the latter owned the New River Railroad Company. But those reports are not explicit as to how the Norfolk and Western Railroad Company came into the control and ownership of the New River Railroad Company. Yet we are not without some evidence on that score, for in Poor's Railway Manual for 1883–84, on page 361, we find the following in connection with the report on the Norfolk and Western Railroad Company:

"On the 9th of May, 1882, the New River Railroad Company of Virginia, the New River Railroad Company of West Virginia, and the East River Railroad of West Virginia, which were chartered to build extensions of this road hereinafter named, were consolidated into this company [the Norfolk and Western Railroad Company]. By the terms of the consolidation the preferred stock of the Norfolk and Western Railroad Company was exchanged share for share for the preferred stock of the New River Railroad Company, (of Virginia) and the common stock for the common stock share for share of the same company and for the ordinary stock of the other companies. Under this plan the company issued 30,000 shares of its preferred stock during the year in exchange for a like amount of the New River preferred. The stocks of these companies having been wholly owned by the Norfolk and Western Railroad Company, the preferred stock so issued is held in that company's treasury for future use.''

This merger and consolidation especially state that the Norfolk and Western Railroad Company owned wholly and entirely this preferred New River railroad stock. So we see that previous to this date (May 9, 1882) the fruits of Graham's and Sergeant's transactions had passed into the Norfolk and Western Railroad Company's hands. The evidence is almost conclusive that upon this New River railroad, already owned, the Norfolk and Western Railroad Company based its organization, and made an issue of stocks and bonds founded upon the traffic of the railroad company, after a consolidation with the New River Railroad Company, whose stock it controlled at the time. Nor were the calculations of Mr. Clarence H. Clark and *his associates* at all wrong as to the increase of traffic that would arise for their road subsequently to a consolidation with the best known coal and coking fields in the South. From that time on the success of this company was almost all that could be desired.

This New River division was opened to the coal-fields May 21, 1883, and the first shipments of coal made in the following month of June, 1883. The beginning of shipping coal from these great mineral fields was marked in letters of red for the Norfolk and Western Railroad Company, and the abundance of coke which would naturally be produced led to the abolishing of the charcoal furnaces in the Cripple creek region and coke furnaces erected in their stead. To form a connection between the coking fields of the Flat Top region and the ore belt about Cripple creek was the next step of the Norfolk and Western Railroad Company—a wise and judicious one.

The first step taken by the company was the creation of an improvement and extension mortgage for $5,000,000, with power under certain restrictions to increase the sum to $8,000,000, for the purpose of double-tracking. Under this mortgage the bonds issued were to bear 6 per cent. interest and the first issue limited to $2,500,000. Proposals having been made for these bonds which were satisfactory, the proceeds were to be used as follows (Third Annual Report, page 21):

"First. The construction of the Cripple Creek extension of the New River division is about fifty (50) miles in length. This work was put under contract December 10, 1883, and the line is expected to be completed and in operation before the close of the year 1884.

"Second. For increased terminal facilities at Norfolk. Contracts for this work were entered into December 28, 1883, the work to be completed prior to August 31, 1884.

"Third. To build short lines to new coal-fields.

"Fourth. For additional sidings, stations, and other improvements on the main line. The remainder of the improvement and extension (mortgage) bonds, $2,500,000, can, under the terms of the mortgage, be sold only when the stockholders so vote, and only for the purpose of providing funds for making improvements upon the main line, for increased terminal facilities, for new rolling stock, and for new branches or extensions. If bonds are sold for the purpose of constructing branches or extensions, the amount of bonds sold for this purpose is limited to $25,000 per mile. In case of an issue of bonds for the purpose of double-tracking the line, said issues are to be made at the rate of $10,000 per mile, and no bonds are to be issued for this purpose until at least fifty (50) miles of double track of standard quality has been constructed."

The building of the Cripple Creek extension, one of the purposes for which this improvement and extension mortgage was created, opened up a mineral region rich beyond conception in iron ore and heavy bearing in lead and zinc. We have already touched upon the mineral deposits in this section, but some better description is deserving as we follow the tortuous windings of the extension through Pulaski, Wythe, and Carroll. When this extension was first proposed, two routes were thought of—one, by way of New river, beginning at New River bridge, near the station by that name, thence up New river into this ore region. For many reasons this route was considered by some as the most practicable, since it would be but a continuation of the New River division already constructed into the Flat-Top coal region. But a route was drawn by Mr. James McGill, of Pulaski county, who lived not far from what was then known as Martin's Tank, but now called Pulaski City. He enclosed a sketch, drawn January 24, 1882, of the present line of the Cripple Creek extension to Mr. George F. Tyler, then president of the Norfolk and Western Railroad Company, and the latter's reply shows that at this time (1882) the route south of 110-mile post had been chosen. The letter is as follows:

PHILADELPHIA, *January 27, 1882.*
MR. JAMES MCGILL, *Martins, Pulaski County, Va.:*

DEAR SIR,—I have received your communication of the 24th instant in respect to the line which you think the most practicable for us to take in the extension which we propose to make of the New River railroad above New River bridge.

We have ourselves come to the conclusion that the line which you have so neatly sketched is no doubt the one for us to take, and I am very much obliged to you for the suggestions on the subject which you make.

Truly yours, GEORGE F. TYLER,
President.

This sketch of Mr. McGill's is very neatly drawn, showing the comparative distances of the two routes, and the territory of the one desired by him. In 1883 the contracts for the construction of the road were let, and this extension became not only an assured fact, but opened up the finest mineral region in the Southwest. This line has ultimately two objects in view, as can be easily seen if we trace its meanderings. It leaves the main line of the Norfolk and Western railroad two miles east of Pulaski City, running first in a course that has a southern direction until it touches New river, when it sweeps away in a western course almost parallel with the main line of the Norfolk and Western railroad, with an intervening space of some twelve miles of country between the two roads. It continues on by Reed Island, Allisonia, Barren Springs, Pierce

Furnace, Foster Falls, Austinville, to Ivanhoe. From this latter point is the extension on to North Carolina, to connect with the Cape Fear and Yadkin Valley railroad, which will be the southern outlet from Ohio after the Ironton extension is finished from Elkhorn, in West Virginia, to Ironton, Ohio.

Another branch of the Cripple Creek extension runs from Ivanhoe westward up Cripple creek to Speedwell, and this route will undoubtedly be continued through the Rye Valley iron district to the waters of the south fork of the Holston, and thence to Abingdon, making a loop line with the main route to Bristol. This extension has branch routes running to furnaces and mines throughout this fine ore-bearing territory, the principal of which are: The Pulaski Iron Company, Boom Furnace, Barren Springs Furnace, Bertha Zinc Mines, Pierce Furnace, Foster Falls, Ivanhoe Furnace, Ravencliff Furnace, Beverley Furnace, and Speedwell Furnace. Many iron, lead, and other mineral mines have been opened tributary to this route, and will furnish much of the ore which will run furnaces eastward in the valley. The scenery along the line is beautiful and picturesque in the extreme, whether we go by winding, romantic New river, with its mountains and cliffs, or by wild, weird Cripple creek, with its cascades and gorges. The quality of this rich ore-bearing territory can best be gathered from the analyses and opinions of experts on the subject. McCreath and D'Invilliers, in their report on the New river-Cripple creek region, has this to say concerning the ore. (Page 155.)

"All of the iron ore at present mined, and to be mined, in the New river-Cripple creek region proper may be conveniently classed under the general heading of *brown hematite* ore, and is found associated in at least four well recognized horizons or belts, extending in a general northeast and southwest direction through the region, with the trend of the rock formations to which they have been referred. The first and lowest, *geologically*, of these is the 'Pottsdam sandstone ore,' occurring in the body of the formation from which it takes its name. These ores are locally known as the 'back vein,' or 'bed,' and are characterized by having a dark brown to pitchy black color, and are generally quite dense and brittle. Their composition is shown by the following average analysis of samples already incorporated in the body of this report:

"Average composition of the Pottsdam sandstone ores :

```
Metallic iron . . . . . . . . . . . . . . . . . . . . . . .  50.200
Phosphorus . . . . . . . . . . . . . . . . . . . . . . . .   1.007
Siliceous matter . . . . . . . . . . . . . . . . . . . . .  10.012
Phosphorus in 100 parts iron . . . . . . . . . . . . . . .   2.006"
```

The next class is the mountain ores, which yield 48.750 of metallic iron. The limestone ores are particularly fine, of which the report speaks as follows, on page 155 :

"The limestone ores, on the other hand, by reason of their greater accessibility, higher percentage of iron, and more ready reduction in the small charcoal furnaces, which have hitherto alone occupied this field, have been sufficiently developed and worked in a large number of places to warrant an opinion as to the richness of the ore material. From the last information we could obtain bearing upon this subject, the general claim is that two tons of ore material will yield one ton of clean wash ore, and this would seem to be confirmed by our own tests made from five different pits and from samples weighing from 14 to 93 pounds, which yielded the following percentages of clean ore : 41 per cent., 53 per cent., 57 per cent., 59 per cent., and 60 per cent."

In addition to this rich ore deposit, the extension runs through what is known as "the Blue Ridge Plateau," and has the reputation of being one of the finest grazing sections in the State. From Pulaski City to Ivanhoe is some thirty-two miles, making about forty-one miles from Pulaski City to Speedwell, beyond Ivanhoe, the present western terminus of this extension. And lastly, this region is the home of the "*Gossan ore*," to which we have already alluded as being peculiarly adapted to the permitting of the use of high phosphorus and manganese ores, which by themselves could never be used, and with this ore a "red, cold short, or neutral iron" can be made.

The improvement of the property of the Norfolk Terminal Company is so intimately blended with the opening of the coal mines that some notice should be given of it, although not situated in Southwest Virginia, because it is one of the improvements of this company which has a significant bearing upon the mineral regions of the section of country of which we are writing. To meet the growing demands made upon the company for increasing terminal facilities, and for the purpose of speculation, the Norfolk and Western Railroad Company, under the name of the Norfolk and Terminal Company, obtained a charter in 1882 from the Virginia Legislature, and under it an organization was effected. The reason for this charter and incorporation is given in the second annual report, on page 15, which says:

"The Legislature, at its last session, granted a charter incorporating the Norfolk Terminal Company. Under it an organization was duly effected. Although it is a separate and distinct organization, yet the control and ownership is in the interest of your company. The charter authorizes the ownership of land, the construction and operation of a line of railroad, the building and operating of wharves, store-houses, cotton-presses, grain elevators, chartering of vessels, &c., and in other ways gives ample power and authority for the conduct of such business as will be necessary at so important and growing a port as Norfolk, and will enable the company to carry into effect the recommendations of the stockholders at the last meeting in regard to improving and increasing the terminal facilities at Norfolk. Power is given the Terminal Company to consolidate with this company, and the board recommend that such consolidation be effected when it is the interest of the company to do so."

By virtue of the charter, the Norfolk Terminal Company purchased several valuable wharf properties below the city, near Lambert's Point, embracing about four hundred and thirty-eight acres of land, and one and a half miles of waterfront, and the necessary right of way to construct a railway line connecting Elizabeth Station with Lambert's Point. Improvements of all kinds were made for the storage and proper handling of grain, cotton, tobacco, and other produce, while piers were erected for coaling vessels and ocean steamers. The company also invested largely in the stock of the Old Dominion steamship line, and purchased barges for the transportation of grain, cotton, and coal. So great and rapid were the improvements on this property that in the year 1884 they had constructed a railroad from Norfolk to Lambert's Point, a distance of 5.3 miles, together with yard room and sidings necessary for the accommodation of the Norfolk and Western's tidewater coal traffic.

A magnificent pier, 894 feet in length and 60 feet wide, with a height above water-mark of 48 feet, had been constructed, which terminates at the United States lighthouse known as "Lambert's Point Light." This superb structure is divided into upper and lower stories, from each of which vessels can be loaded, and is capable of storing 150 tons in each bin, having 45 bins in all. This pier is equipped with every modern appliance for loading, unloading, and handling of cars, and not less than 3,500 tons per diem can be received and discharged, while the depth of the water in the approach to the main channel is twenty-five feet at low tide.

Not only was this undertaking of great advantage to the city of Norfolk, but a credit in many respects to the Norfolk and Western Railroad Company. For the coal regions in Southwest Virginia it was an undoubted benefit in many ways. This semi-bituminous coal is said to be the best steaming fuel known, and the number of steamers which coaled at Lambert's Point gradually increased from the first construction of the pier until the quantity consumed by them was a traffic of no small magnitude in itself, and gave employment to thousands of miners in the coal regions who would doubtless have been idle had the coal trade depended entirely upon the inland traffic. In the year 1885, between March 12th and December 31st, 402 vessels of all kinds were loaded at the pier, among which were forty-five ocean steamers. In 1886, 676 vessels of all kinds were loaded, among which were ninety-five ocean steamers. The increase in this business alone was something enormous, while the storage houses erected for cotton, grain, tobacco, and other produce for foreign shipment did an extensive business. In 1884 the capital stock of this company fully paid in amounted to $322,026, of which $321,900 is owned by the Norfolk and Western Railroad Company, and the operations of the former are completely governed by the latter company. As amounts were furnished the Norfolk and Terminal Company by the Norfolk and Western Railroad Company, the latter took the bonds of the former. In this way every particle of funds derived by the Terminal Company were furnished by the railroad company, until the mortgage of $1,000,000 was created on the properties of the Norfolk and Terminal Company. These terminal facilities reflect unquestionable credit upon the Norfolk and Western Railroad Company, and the latter showed great wisdom in expending the necessary sums for such proper facilities, without which it could not well handle its large traffic. But why should this Terminal Company have purchased more real estate than was necessary for the use of the railroad company?

That the Norfolk and Western railroad furnished this Terminal Company with the necessary means to purchase this real estate is a fact admitted in their annual reports, for out of $322,026 owned by the Terminal Company, the railroad company owned $321,900. (See Fourth Annual Report, page 24.) It is further shown in one of their reports that *lots* were sold. In the seventh annual report, on page 20, the language is this, relating to this Terminal Company:

"The property of the Norfolk Terminal Company is operated by your company, and the revenue derived from such operations is included in your gross earnings. Of the real estate not required for the purposes of the company, there were sold during the year lots to the value of $12,245, which amount has been deposited with the trustee of the mortgage of the company, and will be expended in improvements to the property."

Again, in the eighth annual report, on page 21, the language reads thus, in reference to this same company:

"Of the real estate not required for the purposes of the Terminal Company, there were sold during the year lots to the value of $8,805.02."

The only reason which can be assigned for the company's purchasing more land than is necessary for the use of the railroad is, it desired to sell the lots at a profit. Whilst commending the wonderful developing policy of the Norfolk and Western Railroad Company, we cannot help deploring the fact that, under the name of another company, it should have violated section 1073 of the Code of 1877, of the State of Virginia, which expressly provides that no railroad company in the State shall own more than forty acres in one parcel for its main depots, machine shops, and other necessary purposes connected with the business of said company. This statute was supposed to be passed for the purpose of preventing railroad companies from speculating. By some it is contended that the land was not purchased in the name of the Norfolk and Western Railroad Company, but by another company. Considering that the Norfolk and Western railroad furnished the funds, and the revenues were placed with their gross earnings, such contention imputes to the Norfolk and Western Railroad Company an amount of ignorance that is stupendous, or a subterfuge just as contemptible. Again, some claim the right to be vested in the company by its charter. It would seem passing strange that the Legislature of Virginia should, by a special act of legislation, set aside and nullify a general law passed in the interest of the State.

The first shipments of coal from the Flat Top region, as we have seen, began in 1883, and during the years 1884 and 1885 the extension into the Bluestone country was completed. This line, running from the New River division at Bluestone Junction, to Mill Creek, Bramwell, Simmons, and Duhring, has at last been completed as far as Goodwill, and opens up a coal region of magnificent quantity and quality both. This extension was made with a view to hauling out coal, and is some ten miles in length, with branches to the various mines located on the Bluestone river, and which yield a large output of coal daily. Mill Creek, Bramwell, Simmons, and Goodwill are flourishing places, and their growth appears almost magical when we consider that a few years ago this portion of Mercer county was nothing more than a lot of rugged, impassable mountains, without any vestige of settlements except the huts of mountaineers, who, though poor and lowly, were as brave and loyal men as one could find anywhere.

The penetration of this country by this branch of the Norfolk and Western was a transformation of this part of Virginia and

West Virginia into a rushing, thriving, tax-paying community, which in 1881 was almost a sterile wilderness of mountains. During the year 1887 the extension from Mill Creek was completed as far as the station now known as Elkhorn. The tunnel through the mountain, some two miles from Mill Creek, is a massive structure, and the trestles bridging the mountain gorges wonderful in the extreme, showing the energy, pluck, and determination of the Norfolk and Western Railroad Company to bridge not only these seemingly impassable chasms, but every difficulty presenting itself in the way of their onward progress towards developing the country. This extension opens up the vast coal-fields in McDowell county, where any quantity of it lies buried, and thousands are daily employed to unearth it. We will have more to say of this section when we come to speak of the Ohio line to Ironton. In this coal region up to January, 1888, there were 2,030 coke ovens in course of construction and completed.

Prior to the year 1886 a charter had been obtained for the construction of a railroad called "The Clinch Valley railroad," and at the annual meeting of the stockholders in 1886 a resolution was passed empowering the directors of the Norfolk and Western Railroad Company to make a consolidation of this Clinch Valley extension with their company. By the terms of the charter this company was given authority to locate and construct a road "commencing in Tazewell county, at a point at or near the New River division of the Norfolk and Western Railroad Company, and running thence to such a point on or near the Clinch river, Powell river, or either, or any branch thereof, in Russell, Wise, Scott, or Lee counties, and by such route as might be deemed most suitable to the directors of said company."

On March 8 and May 2, 1887, the Norfolk and Western Railroad Company and the Louisville and Nashville Railroad Company entered into contracts by which both agreed to construct and finish—each one respectively from its lines—this extension to a point in Wise county, Virginia, both connecting there. Work upon this extension by the Norfolk and Western Railroad Company was begun on June 20, 1887, and pushed forward as rapidly as possible. This road has been about completed, and runs from Graham, on the New River division of the Norfolk and Western, to Norton, at which latter point it will connect with the Louisville and Nashville railroad. The section through which it runs is by far one of the finest in Southwest Virginia. It first traverses Tazewell county, running by Tazewell Courthouse, Richlands, and Cedar Bluff; then through Russell county, touching Honakers, Cleveland, Saint Paul, and Minneapolis, and on through Wise, by Guest, to Norton, where it connects with the Louisville and Nashville railroad. On leaving Graham the line goes through the far-famed grass section of Tazewell, noted for its fine stock and agricultural products. As an outlet for these alone the road would have been a boon to the county—a success to its company; but, on leaving Tazewell, it touches upon the very borders of the now celebrated Clinch Valley coal region, which has a coal excellent for gaseous uses as well as domestic purposes. Russell county, too, through which it runs, is celebrated for its grazing capacity as well as fine stock, and has many mineral-bearing properties. When the line reaches Wise county it penetrates the heart of the coal country stretching from this part of the county on towards Big Stone Gap. Numerous towns have sprung up in a few years, such as Richlands, Honakers, Minneapolis, Saint Paul, Norton, and Big Stone Gap, all of which bid fair to become cities at no great future date. Mineral City, near Big Stone Gap, claims to be the centre of a variety of minerals for manufacturing purposes. This route opens up a regular kingdom of lumber and coal, the latter of which has been most complimentally noticed on account of its gas properties; while in live stock and agricultural productions no place in the Southwest is superior and richer. Mines are being opened and branch roads constructed to them, and on all sides can be heard the sound of the axe and the saw culling the best of hard-wood lumber. The traffic from this section alone will be something great, and the Norfolk and Western railroad can hardly fail to reap the profits in passenger and freight traffic to which its energy and spirit in opening up the country entitles it to. The scenery all along the line is beautiful in the extreme, and every variety, from the peaceful, charming valley to the rugged, snow-capped mountains, greets the eye as the train rushes onward through fertile Tazewell and Russell and mineral-laden Wise.

With a view towards perfecting northwestern and southeastern connections, and for other purposes deemed advisable by the Norfolk and Western Railroad Company, on the 29th day of October, 1889, this corporation created what is known as the one-hundred-year mortgage, which is a first lien upon the property when all underlying liens are refunded. This mortgage first provides an issue of $10,000,000 5 per cent. bonds, to be applied as follows:

"$1,000,000 for redeeming Norfolk Terminal Company's first mortgage.

"$975,000, to reimburse the company for expenditures by way of improvements, extensions, sidings, &c.

"$6,000,000 for construction of Ohio extension (Northwest).

"$1,500,000 for the North Carolina extension.

"$525,000 for retiring the convertible debenture loan of the company."— (Ninth Annual Report, page 21.)

The creation of this mortgage enabled the Norfolk and Western Railroad Company to construct the two extensions named above, and since these have added materially to the progress of this company about which we are writing, they deserve mention, although the Northwest (or Ohio) branch does not run through the southwest of Virginia.

The Ohio extension, as located and partly constructed, "follows the waters of Big Sandy river from the present northwestern terminus of your line, at Elkhorn, in McDowell county, West Virginia, for about ninety-five miles; thence about fifteen miles over a low summit to the head-waters of Twelve Pole creek, which it follows for about seventy-one miles, and crosses the Ohio river by a steel bridge, and runs about fourteen miles to Ironton, Ohio, making a total distance of not less than one hundred and ninety-five miles."

The value of this line, not only to the Norfolk and Western Railroad Company, but Southwest Virginia, can readily be appreciated when the results of its construction are calculated. The city of Norfolk, being one of the best harbors on the Atlantic coast, will have a direct route from Ironton, Ohio, and the purchase of the Scioto Valley railroad, with the route under construction from Ashland, Kentucky, to Kenova, on the borders of Kentucky, Ohio, and West Virginia, will place Norfolk, Virginia, in almost instant communication with Columbus, the capital of the State of Ohio. The granaries of the West, with the live stock bred in the same country, will be poured into the East, giving this extension an importance and bearing which is not easily calculated. The coal regions through which it goes are of almost endless quantity and consist of several varieties. In the county of McDowell the Flat Top coking coals of the Pocahontas region are traversed, while farther on the line penetrates the domestic coals of Logan county. Near Warfield, in Martin county, Kentucky, the road bends to the right, and in Wayne county, West Virginia, it divides the cannel and splint coal region, which will give a splendid traffic in these latter varieties.

This route will not only cause Norfolk to increase as a shipping point for foreign exports, but will be the means of connecting the Northwest with the Southeast. The line extending south from Ivanhoe, on the Cripple Creek extension, will push its way forward until a connection is established with the Cape Fear and Yadkin Valley railroad at Mount Airy, in North Carolina, which will place Columbus, Ohio, in immediate connection with the Southern sea-coast at Wilmington, North Carolina. Coal will be shipped there and cotton brought back into the Northwest and on to Norfolk. The connection will give the Norfolk and Western railroad outlets south, southeast, west, and northwest; and the northern connections it possesses by way of the Shenandoah Valley makes its system of great value as a leading trunk line north and south and east and west. With these advantages the company will be in a condition to do a large traffic in every direction.

While we may imagine, it is impossible to ascertain with any degree of certainty the growth of this corporation without an inquiry into the rapid increase of the mileage, traffic, and rolling stock of the company. In the year 1881, when the Atlantic, Mississippi and Ohio railroad was reorganized as the Norfolk and Western Company, there were four hundred and twenty-eight miles of railway. Now, with the Cripple Creek, New River, Flat Top, Clinch Valley, Ironton, Scioto Valley, and the southeastern extensions, and the Shenandoah Valley railroad, there are almost twelve hundred and thirty-four miles of track, not including sidings, switches, and what double track that has been constructed. The construction of these lines has been effected in the best manner possible—the heaviest steel rails, iron bridges, the most approved masonry, and solid stone ballast being used in order to procure comfort and safety in the highest degree possible.

It is not difficult to see that with such a wonderful extension of railway the passenger and freight traffic has grown accordingly. Both departments are taxed to their utmost to accommodate this increase, as the following tables will show.

The passenger traffic was as follows:

In 1881	215,904
1882	263,347
1883	307,927
1884	412,452
1885	388,087
1886	400,269
1887	558,951
1888	771,248
1889	841,986

This route has become a favorite one, and the opening up of all this section has been the means of thousands of passengers travelling over the line. The usual number of passenger coaches to each train is four and five, and they are invariably crowded. The freight statistics also show a marked increase. There were carried over the road—

In 1881	538,102 tons.
1882	609,727 "
1883	797,255 "
1884	892,512 "
1885	1,199,790 "
1886	1,555,867 "
1887	2,208,688 "
1888	2,763,376 "
1889	3,435,797 "

We cannot refer to any common carrier within our knowledge which has increased so rapidly in freight traffic. Of course it is mainly due to the opening up of the vast mineral regions in Southwest Virginia and the large increase in the agricultural resources throughout the country. The minerals began to be shipped about the year 1882, and a comparison of the number of tons carried that year with the number in 1889 will give some idea how rapidly the Southwest has advanced:

	1882.	1889.
Iron ore	1,399 tons.	249,374 tons.
Pig-iron	13,372 "	161,215 "
Coal	4,735 "	1,543,900 "
Coke		310,504 "
Stone	6,181 "	87,965 "
Salt	9,270 "	14,453 "
Plaster	3,405 "	5,580 "
Zinc ore	2,872 "	12,321 "
Zinc spelter	490 "	2,972 "
Manganese	1,648 "	152 "
Miscellaneous	4,939 "	48,321 "

We cannot fail to give our praise to this company when we see the wonderful progress it has made in aiding and assisting in the development of Southwest Virginia, and the untiring energy it has exhibited in giving an impetus to everything. In 1881 the rolling stock of the company consisted of 81 locomotives, 24 passenger coaches, 2 sleeping cars, 4 postal cars, 12 baggage, mail, and express cars, 1 pay car, 556 box cars, 199 stock cars, 315 platform and gondola cars, 65 ditching cars, 42 conductor's cars.

At the close of the year 1889 we find that the rolling stock has increased in proportion to everything else, and that notwithstanding this addition the transportation department is taxed to its utmost capacity to accommodate and move the heavily increased traffic of the road. The number at the end of 1889 was as follows : 195 locomotives, 87 passenger cars, 7,880 freight, caboose, and other cars.

A further comparison of the earnings of the company will show that its financial status has kept apace with its rapid growth in every way. These earnings have been generally appropriated as far as possible to the improvement of the road and adding rolling stock for transportation facilities. The following amounts for 1881 and 1889 gives us an idea of the great pecuniary advance made within that time :

	1881.	1889.
Gross earnings	$2,267,288 62	$5,597,124 58
Net "	1,104,055 87	2,113,772 17

We cannot deny that this company in every way has more than doubled its carrying capacity and intrinsic pecuniary value. When we think of the amount of material necessary for constructing these extensions, the number of mechanics and laborers necessary to perform the work, the emigration brought in by reason of this work, we cannot withhold the credit it is justly entitled to, nor fail to express our admiration at its policy, which has been one of the causes of the rapid development of Southwest Virginia.

CHAPTER VI.

Norfolk and Western Railroad Company continued—Policy of the company—Its equipment, service, and regulations—Its adjuncts (the Roanoke Machine Works, the Virginia Company, and real estate operations of the latter)—Speculations of the Norfolk and Western Railroad Company through the Virginia Company—Statutory regulations regarding railroads holding real estate—Commissioner of Railways of the State of Virginia the proper governing authority in these cases—General remarks on this company as a railroad corporation.

THE general policy of the Norfolk and Western Railroad Company is an aggressive one in every way, which tends to develop the country through which it runs, as well as its own property and holdings. Whether the modes adopted by it to accomplish this end are entirely legitimate do not in the least alter the fact that the prime object of the company is to develop everything coming in contact with it, in order that such a course may eventually redound to an increased rate of traffic for the Norfolk and Western Railroad Company. This corporation uses every means in its power to draw a foreign element into the State, and along its lines has every inducement which can possibly attract, from a good hotel to women in the reception rooms at the stations, to render its passengers as comfortable as possible. No amount of money has been spared to insure the traveller not only a safe but as pleasant a passage as possible over its line. The road itself, with all the wonderful resources of the country through which it runs, are annually set forth and duly advertised by the company, which are the means of many settlers coming in and being attracted here. Their method not only builds up a community, but pays them handsomely for the outlay expended in placing these many advantages before the public.

The equipment, services, and regulations of the company are not only first-class in every respect, but far ahead of those of any other railway system that we know of in the South. The track is not only well ballasted and laid with the best steel rails, but a double track is now in construction along the line wherever it is necessary for the safety of the passengers and the expeditious handling of freight and minerals. The rolling stock, while greatly taxed, is amply sufficient to serve the traffic, and consists of elegant, comfortable, and pleasant passenger coaches, stout, safe freight cars and coal gondolas. The heavy ten-wheel locomotives carry along over the mountains a train of nine and ten coaches on schedule time, and give an ease and steadiness to the whole train which is far superior to the motion of the cars when drawn by lighter engines. The stations along the line are being replaced by much more commodious buildings, some of which are really ornaments to the places where they are built, besides affording passengers every reasonable facility for pleasure and comfort. All of the through trains carry the Pullman vestibule and sleeping cars, the comfort and luxury of which are well known and appreciated by the travelling public in general.

This road is under control of a splendid class of officials, from the president to the brakemen. Seek as diligently as you may and each position will be found occupied by some man who has the necessary acquirements and knowledge to fill it as it should be. The president, vice-president, general manager, as well as engineers, conductors, and guards, have each their prescribed territory, and in these respective departments every one carries out, without fear or favor, his various duties and the rules and regulations of the company. Whoever you may be, unless you are in the employment of the company the guard will promptly march you in from a platform while the train is in motion. The conductors do not lounge in the seats nor smoke cigars with the passengers, but walk their beats along the aisle and see that the travellers have all they want, and carry out the rules of the company. No passenger is ever allowed to ride upon an engine, and every rule is required to be strictly carried out under pain of dismissal, for the safety and comfort of the passenger traffic is the first consideration of the company. In the mining regions around Bluefield, Bramwell, Pocahontas, and Elkhorn, where the population is necessarily rough, a well-disciplined police force is on hand to protect the most unprotected traveller, not only from any possible outbreak of violence, but drunkenness, profanity, and loud talking—the usual concomitants of the inhabitants of a new and almost uncivilized country.

The regulations of the company are made in the broadest and most prudent manner possible. Printed rules are furnished every employee, and he is required to conform to them in every way, and never deviate from them unless special orders to the contrary are given, or circumstances unforeseen arise which on account of safety to the travelling public demand a departure. These rules smack greatly of a kind of military discipline, which is really essential to the good government and well-being of any set of men who have certain orders to carry out in order to attain a given end. In view of the large amount of traffic over the road the regulations which govern the transportation department are not only well planned, but executed with marked ability, for considering the number of trains which go over the road the loss of life by accident is extremely small and the number of wrecks few. Sometimes employees are killed and wounded, but no one has a right to exclaim at that, unless gross negligence is shown, because incident with the employment are the risks which the law says every man must assume who goes into the employment of the company. Taking out the "Thaxton Switch" disaster, occurring in the early part of 1890, we know of no other wreck in which a passenger has been injured, except by the direct cause of Providence, over which this company can exercise no authority whatever. In all its government the Norfolk and Western Railroad Company is run on a mathematical scale which causes every department to be properly filled beyond even a reasonable certainty.

The Norfolk and Western Railroad Company has two adjuncts—the Roanoke Machine Works and the Virginia Company—in both of which the railroad owns a large controlling interest. They have played no unimportant part in the progress of the railroad company.

Prior to the year 1882, a company was formed for the purpose of constructing and erecting engine and car-shops. The capital stock of this company was $365,000, and the Legislature of Virginia, by act approved April 1, 1882, authorized the Norfolk and Western Railroad Company to own as many shares in said company as the directors of the railroad company should deem proper. This authority was most properly conferred, for it was but natural that the company should have a controlling interest in the works which constructed its engines and cars and repaired its rolling stock. These shops were placed in the corporate limits of Roanoke, and the necessary buildings took at least fifteen acres of ground. The buildings consisted towards the end of the year 1883 of—

Smith-shop	350′x72′
Machine-shop	348′x72′
Annex to same	33′x72′
Engine-erecting shop	516′x64′
Foundry	252′x72′
Paint-shop	206′x50′
Planing-mill	252′x72′
Lumber kiln	71′x38′
Store-house	150′x72′
Engine-house	22 stalls.
Passenger and freight car erecting shop (semi-circle)	21 "
Lumber-yards.	

Before the construction of these shops reached completion, in 1883 a mortgage of $500,000 was created and the bonds purchased by the railroad company, which soon owned a controlling share, and at this time they belong virtually to the company. These gigantic works compare favorably with any in the Northern States and surpass anything in the South, and since their erection not only have they done all the repair work for the Norfolk and Western and Shenandoah Valley railroads, but much new equipment work. Many of the engines which pull the heavily-loaded coal trains from the mines to Lambert's

Point were made in these shops, while all the box cars, gondolas, and some baggage and passenger cars, have been constructed here. All the most approved machinery for manufacturing an engine is placed in them, from the heavy planing and slotting machines to the rivets which go in the boilers. The capacity of the shops are some four engines per month and twenty freight cars *per diem*, besides repairing and building passenger cars. At one time these shops filled orders for other railway lines, but owing to the increase of traffic on the Norfolk and Western railroad line of late, its utmost capacity has been taxed to construct new equipments and do the repair work of this latter company. The construction of the works was in a thorough manner—brick buildings and iron truss roofing being used—and the ground and buildings at night are lighted by electricity. The locating and building of this gigantic plant was a wise act on the part of this company, for the very material from which our northern friends manufacture their work comes from a section of country tributary to the lines of the Norfolk and Western railroad; consequently the cost of manufacturing here is so much less that the company was more than justified in this erection. The number of employees are about fifteen hundred men, and the works have played no small part in the development of this section, as will be seen when we come to discuss the city of Roanoke. The organization has not only been a self-supporting one, but paid a handsome dividend on its stock. For the year 1887 it paid $61,305 on the capital stock, while in 1888 it rendered a dividend of $50,088 to the stockholders of the company, and in 1889 $25,044 were declared in dividends.

Another adjunct of the Norfolk and Western Railroad Company, which has become a part of the latter, is the "Virginia Company." This company was originally known as "The Iron-Belt Land, Mining, and Development Company," which was chartered prior to the year 1883. At what particular time the Norfolk and Western Railroad Company began to be an investor in this company is not known exactly to us, but in its third annual report, on page 29, we find the following:

"Your company [the Norfolk and Western railroad] owns a controlling interest in the Iron-Belt Land, Mining, and Development Company, holding three hundred and thirty shares out of a total of five hundred shares. Under the charter of the Iron-Belt Land, Mining, and Development Company, real estate is held at Roanoke, Central, Martins, and at other points. The real estate is either at junction points, or at localities which from the nature of the ground and abundance of water are suitable for manufacturing purposes. The lands were purchased in the interest of your company, so that parties desiring to erect furnaces or other manufacturing establishments could secure proper locations at reasonable cost."

Why these lands were purchased in the interest of the company is not stated in this report, but in their fourth annual report, for the year 1884, on page 24, the reasons for investing in this company are given. It reads:

"For reasons similar to those which led to the organization of the Norfolk Terminal Company, your company acquired control of the Iron-Belt Land, Mining, and Development Company. The cost to your company of its interest in this corporation is $43,955.07, which amount represents the actual cost of the real estate purchased at junctional and other points. It was apparent that additional yard room and sidings would ultimately be required at these points in order to accommodate the growing business of your company, and it was considered expedient to secure the lands before they could be built upon or occupied for other purposes. Such land as may not be required for the uses of your company will be disposed of to parties desiring to locate manufacturing establishments."

It seems from this that the actual cost of real estate to the railroad company through this Iron-Belt Land, Mining, and Development Company was $43,955.07. The object of the company in obtaining this real estate was for additional yard room, sidings, divisional round-houses, and certain necessary accommodations for the rolling stock of the company. This was but right, and a praiseworthy, legitimate undertaking. But why should the railroad company desire to purchase more real estate than was necessary for its own use? Some calculation could have been readily made by which the requisite quantity for shops, sidings, yard room, and round-houses could have been arrived at, and purchased. Their reason for so doing is very clearly stated in the eighth annual report. Prior to 1889, by act of the General Assembly of Virginia, on March 5, 1888, the Iron-Belt Land, Mining, and Development Company was changed to the "Virginia Company," under which name the buying and selling of real estate by the Norfolk and Western Railroad Company is still continued. In the eighth annual report, for the year 1888, we find the following statement concerning this "Virginia Company," on page 22:

"For several years the title to valuable real estate at junctional and other points upon your line has been vested in the Virginia Company. Owing to the redivision of its line during 1888, it became necessary for your company to construct yards, engine-houses, repair shops, store-houses, and other improvements at various points, and it was deemed advisable, when acquiring the real estate actually needed, to purchase such outlying and adjoining land as would be made valuable by the improvements, so that your company might derive the benefit. The land required for the purposes of the railroad was paid for and deeded directly to your company, and the adjoining lands were acquired and paid for by the Virginia Company. The properties so acquired at Crewe and Bluefield were laid off into lots, of which a considerable number were sold during the year; upon other lots dwelling-houses were erected and sold or rented to the employees of your railroad company. * * * * * To provide means for the expenditures required, the capital stock of the Virginia Company was increased to $100,000, all of which was taken by your company, and such further sums as were required were advanced by your company. The balance-sheet attached to this report shows the acreage and cost of real estate and improvements at the several points. The net profits of the Virginia Company during the year (1888) amounted to $44,156.32, out of which a dividend of six per cent. was paid, and the balance, $38,156.32, was carried forward as a surplus. Your investment in this company promises to be very remunerative."

The avowed object of the Norfolk and Western Railroad Company in purchasing more land than was necessary for the actual use of the railroad was for the purpose of speculating in real estate. There is no other reasonable construction when their own report, from which we have just quoted, says:

"and it was deemed advisable, when acquiring the real estate actually needed, to purchase such outlying and adjoining land as would be made valuable by the improvements, so that your company might derive the benefit."

Why did the Norfolk and Western Railroad Company only purchase and pay for just such a quantity as the railroad needed? Why should the balance have been purchased by this Virginia Company, and yet the profits derived go to the Norfolk and Western Railroad Company? That the railroad company invested its money in the Virginia Company for speculative purposes is forever settled by the latter sentence of the statement just quoted, which reads:

"Your investment in this company promises to be very remunerative."

And the financial report, on page 62 of the eighth annual report, reads as to the liabilities of the Virginia Company:

"Norfolk and Western Company, $140,808.71."

If the railroad then advanced this Virginia Company the necessary funds upon which to speculate, and participated in the profits arising therefrom, then it is virtually the railroad company speculating under a *nom de plume*. It is the Norfolk and Western purchasing this land about, with as sure an eye to profit by speculation as to obtaining the requisite amount of ground for its divisional points, shops, round-houses, and yard room. But why should the railroad company only purchase and have deeded in its name a certain portion of the real estate—so much as they may deem necessary for the use of the railroad company? Why not have it all conveyed to the railroad company, instead of a portion to the Virginia Company? To these questions, so far as we can see, the Norfolk and Western Railroad Company answers: because under the statute no railroad company can own and hold over a certain quantity of real estate. If more than that is purchased, then it must be in the name of another company. No other reply can suggest itself to us after reading the statement in their own annual report already quoted. And this solution becomes almost a certainty when we turn to section 1073 of the Code of Virginia, 1877. There it is expressly provided that no railroad company shall own more than forty acres for its principal shops, yard, &c., in any one parcel. It is usually conceded that the statute was passed for the purpose of preventing corporations from speculating in real estate—especially railroad companies. Then, if such is the intention of the law, the use of money by the railroad company under another name for the purpose of profiting by speculation is a clear invasion of the law, besides being a direct evasion of the statute.

Whether or not such operations on the part of the railroad company are intentionally an evasion depends much upon the terms of their charter. If the Legislature gave them the power to own stock in this company for the purpose of purchasing real estate with which to speculate, then they are clearly right to pursue such a course; but it is scarcely reasonable to suppose that an intelligent body of men would confer by special act a power upon one corporation which by a general act is denied all others throughout the State engaged in constructing and operating railway lines. If, on the other hand, power was given the railroad to purchase through this company lands for its use alone, and under this property was bought which was more than the company needed, then that corporation is clearly wrong to proceed, under and by virtue of such power, to speculating in real estate. By their own reports the company shows that at several points large quantities of real estate were purchased and lots laid off and sold, besides houses constructed for renting purposes. In the eighth annual report, page 62, the following real estate is mentioned as belonging to the Virginia Company, which the Norfolk and Western owns through having purchased all of its stock. We name the real estate at those points only which exceeds the statutory allowance:

Real estate at Oakvale—43 acres			$ 3,595 47
"	"	" Norton—1,810 acres	41,922 42
"	"	" Bluefield—242 acres	24,355 31
"	"	" Crewe—334 acres	17,719 97
"	"	" Ivor—64 acres	5 09
Houses at Crewe—46			47,055 63
"	" Bluefield—29		34,883 72

In addition to this, the company owns splendid inns at Radford, Pulaski City, and Roanoke, all of which comprise a part of this Virginia Company. All of these well-known hostelries are admirably kept, and made as luxurious and comfortable as possible, and is another evidence of the energy and progress of this railroad company. The hotels have much to do with the pleasure and attractiveness of the towns in which they are located, adding to the beauty as well as comfort of the same. For such purposes, as well as for the erection of the necessary yard room, sidings, shops, and round-houses, we unhesitatingly think the railroad company had a right to own the requisite real estate, and the statute made provision for such; but the buying and selling of lots and construction of houses apart from the purposes named seems to be an invasion of the law, whether intentional or not, on the part of the company. But at all events, the people of Virginia have a railroad commissioner to govern and to look into such matters, and if he sanctions it without complaint, and makes no objection to the company's indulging in such operations, then the people can scarcely blame the Norfolk and Western Railroad Company, but should look to him to whom full power and authority has been delegated to see that all provisions respecting railways throughout the State are properly carried out. So long as he does not complain, it is fair to presume that the spirit, as well as the letter, of the law is carried out, until the contrary is shown by some means or other.

Throughout the southwest of Virginia the Norfolk and Western Railroad Company wields a potent influence in every way. Everything connected with it commands a respect which it is hard to estimate or describe. Each movement of the company is anxiously watched by the people at the various places along the line, in order to have something done for the town or city which is their residence, fully recognizing that it is within the power of the railroad to give any place either a tremendous impetus forward or a fearful stroke backward. The policy of this corporation is of such a progressive nature that every section of the country hails its advent with delight, feeling sure that if it comes there will certainly be rapid strides made in a material way, and for this reason people bear much from this company cheerfully which ordinarily they would never submit to from other companies. And it is but right that it should be so, for where much good comes from any undertaking to the people at large the objectionable features can easily be submitted to on that account. It is rare, indeed, that the best of human undertakings for mankind have not something connected with them which is subject to adverse criticism, and the Norfolk and Western railroad is not exempt in this respect; yet, so great has been the material development of, Southwest Virginia through its policy and influence that the people of Virginia should accede to any request made by the company that is within reason and not a violation of the laws of the land.

CHAPTER VII.

The joint-stock land improvement companies—Their origin, formation, and mode of government—Their effect upon Southwest Virginia—These companies the means of manufactures and enterprises being brought in—The general results of their efforts—Speculation in connection with them—Its effects—Various opinions concerning the same—Lieutenant-Governor Tyler, James S. Simmons, L. L. Powell, L. S. Calfee, A. M. Bowman, E. S. Stuart, J. Lawrence Radford.

WHATEVER may be the individual opinion of any one on the subject which we now have in hand, a careful investigation of the facts in connection with it, and salient points upon the operations of joint-stock land companies, show that they have been one of the strongest auxiliary causes of the rapid development of Southwest Virginia. So important a part have they played among the causes which we are seeking to investigate, that some information concerning their origin and formation, with a slight history of the first ones in Southwest Virginia, is not amiss.

Generally, any five or more citizens who desire to form one of these companies apply to the circuit court of the county in which they reside, or hustings court of the city, to be incorporated as a body politic, with all the rights, powers, franchises, duties, and obligations of such bodies conferred upon them. In this application the amount of capital stock to be issued by the company, with its minimum and maximum limits in that respect, are set forth, as well as the amount of each share specified. The names of the incorporators, place of business, and officers of the company are given also. When the court approves this application and gives them the powers prayed for, that is termed the charter, which, upon recordation in the office of the Secretary of the Commonwealth, gives them the requisite authority to proceed at once to business.

Upon their first meeting so many shares of stock are issued, and after that is taken there is a meeting of the stockholders, when by-laws are passed, and generally an election of president, vice-president, secretary, and a board of directors—the latter of whom govern the affairs of the company. As the board and stockholders may direct, a certain quantity of real estate is bought, and the necessary assessments made upon the stockholders to pay the cash payment upon this, and to have it surveyed off in lots of proper sizes, which, after being properly improved, are placed upon the markets and sold, either by way of public auction or privately, as the company desires. The proceeds from the sale of these lots are put in the treasury, and after payment of the necessary expenses the profits are divided among the stockholders in proportion to the amount of stock held by each shareholder. This stock, from the time it is issued until it is redeemed, has always a value upon the market generally governed by the confidence the public has in the company and the approximate value of the dividends it is likely to pay. From the formation of the first land company in Southwest Virginia to the present time many fortunes have been made by a participation in the profits of these companies, as well as buying and selling the stock, but not a single man has ever lost one dollar as yet from investing in the stock, that we can find out after a most diligent inquiry.

As an evidential fact of the marvellous success of these organizations we mention the transactions and pecuniary workings of one of the oldest companies, which is still in active operation—the "Home Building and Conveyancing Company," which was formed in the primitive days of land companies, and the parent of many in existence now. The capital stock of this company at the date of its organization was $5,000. The investments and operations of the concern were on the soundest basis, and so successful that the capital stock paid up to-day is $200,000 and net assets at least $500,000. This concern may justly claim to be the mother of almost all the investment companies in and about the city of Roanoke, which have done so much towards building up her material interests. The

West End Land Company, the Belmont and the River View Land and Manufacturing Companies, owe their origin to this Home Building and Conveyancing Company. The Iron-Belt Land, Mining, and Development Company of Virginia (known now as the "Virginia Company") was among the earlier companies in the Southwest, and has been of vast assistance in developing the country at Bluefield, Radford, Pulaski City, Crewe, Norton, and other points. This company is now owned and controlled by the Norfolk and Western Railroad Company, of which we have already spoken in a former chapter. Nor should we omit to mention the Roanoke Land and Improvement Company, one of the oldest, and said to have been the cause of "the Roanoke Machine Works being located in Southwest Virginia," and gave an impetus to business which has never been forgotten to this day, although the organization is virtually wound up. From the earlier days on the land companies have multiplied and increased until their number is very large and the influence they wield immense.

The effect of these organizations on Southwest Virginia is simply marvellous. No one expects any undertaking inaugurated by man to be perfect, and all readily acknowledge that everything good has its accompanying evil, so it is that some objectionable features have necessarily come in; but the results accomplished by them in materially advancing the growth of the country counterbalance and overwhelm any evil ones. In the very first instance, their corporate and joint existence gives them a power to carry out their objects and aims which an individual could never succeed in carrying out from his want of the proper amount of capital and concert of action. By these organizations men become bound together not only in unity of plan and action, but what is much more to the point, unity of pecuniary interest. Each shareholder is deeply involved in the ultimate result of the undertaking, and therefore advances the whole with all his power and ability. He cannot injure his fellow-man's prospects and interest without attacking his own, so the whole is moved forward. The appointment of a board to act, with capable assistants to advise, in the shape of a board of directors, and unlimited capital to draw upon, gives the company the means of seizing any opportunity which presents itself and would be most likely to enhance their pecuniary interests. As every one is more or less bound up, every known lever is brought to bear to increase the value of their joint interest.

As an increased value of the property which they possess in common is the main object of these organizations, every legitimate means is seized to enhance it. Manufacturing enterprises, with their train of merchants, mechanics, artizans, and laborers, are invited, sought out, and induced to come and locate on their property. Free sites, donations of lots, and subscription by the company to these industries are some among the many inducements held out by them in the effort they make to increase the value of their property. Each and every advantage of their particular locality in the way of agricultural and mineral resources, climate, scenery, and population are thoroughly advertised and placed before the people. The result is, foreign capital—manufacturing interests—seek investments within the limits of their possessions and build up a community almost as if by one magic stroke. Roanoke, Salem, Radford, Pulaski City, Max Meadows, Wytheville, all owe their prosperity and material progress to the untiring efforts of these joint-stock concerns, which have brought in enterprises and industries that would never have sought their borders but for the inducements of the land companies.

Let us take an illustration of this fact: Since April, 1890, Salem, Virginia, has doubled her population, and from being a lovely residential seat of learning, has become a rushing, thriving, business place, with manufacturing plants, stores, and hotels all around. The investigation of the cause of this leads to but one conclusion as to why it grew so rapidly: the united efforts and boundless enterprise of the development companies there, headed and managed by men like D. B. Strouse, A. M.

Bowman, Mr. Allemong, Mr. Allen, and several others. If any manufacturing establishment wanted a location in which to pursue its vocation, Salem offered almost irresistible inducements in the way of free donation of sites, and subscribed capital to the undertaking.

The number of enterprises and foreign capital which they have drawn into Southwest Virginia in the last two years is almost incredible. Many Northern, Eastern, and Western capitalists are interested in the stock of these companies, and induce and persuade many of their friends to either build new manufacturing enterprises or remove their old ones here. They, too, tell of Southwest Virginia's resources in minerals, and the many opportunities held out through her wealth for men to better themselves pecuniarily, as well as the temptation to locate in a land with such glorious climate, scenery, soil, and productions. Most of the working capital now in our country is that of people who either dwell out of it, or of those who have emigrated here and cast their fortunes among us. There is scarcely a development company that we know of that does not have a journal, periodical, or publication of some sort, setting forth the many advantages of the country, city, or town in which it is located.

The general result of all these efforts is for the good of the country at large. But for these there are many manufacturing industries that would not be in existence, and many a town never thought of. Individuals could never have accomplished the same and given the whole country such an impetus in a business way as to cause the whole land to seem on a boom, and in many cases a manufacturing place to come into existence as if through the fairy power of some *genii*. Yet here they are living realities and monuments to what the combined force of energy and capital can do.

One of the necessary results of actions of these joint-stock companies in opening up and developing the country is speculation, which is sure to follow. . Speculation is nothing but a fictitious value placed upon properties which are being generally bought and sold; and whether the values of properties come in that class or not depends not upon the rapid advance in price, but whether there are resources and causes of development enough in a country to support more than its present population. If the inhabitants of any community absorb all the profits from the agricultural, commercial, and manufacturing interests that it is capable of supporting, then of course any rapid advance in property at values not truly supported would cause untold pecuniary trouble. But property may advance rapidly in price, and on that account seem to be reaching a purely fictitious basis; yet, if the full commercial, agricultural, and manufacturing resources are not developed, then there is no such thing as a fictitious value of property, although its price may double many times in a week. There have been many predictions in the past six years about the great crash that was sure to come, and some persons were disposed to regard the rapid advancements going on as indicative of a "South Sea Island scheme"; but those people have looked only at the buying and selling of property, without investigating carefully the wonderful resources of Southwest Virginia and its agricultural and manufacturing powers. These latter have kept apace, and in a great measure by these development companies, who, though apparently engaged in selling lots, yet have never lost an opportnnity to locate an enterprise wherein and whenever they could. In this they had but little trouble, especially in iron and wood, because manufacturers who can be convinced that the raw material is in a country in great quantities, and that it can be worked there cheaper than anywhere else, are sure to invest their capital. And until the population of any country is sufficient to consume all those resources fully developed, which we have named, there can be no fictitious value of property; because as long as there is a supply people will come to demand it, and as long as they come and are obliged to have property, then, however much it may advance in price, there can only be real values attached to it.

Any one who is at all familiar with either the agricultural

or mineral resources of Southwest Virginia knows full well that the former is only partly developed, while the latter is but in its infancy, and that the manufacturing industries are at present far ahead of the needs of the present population, to say nothing of those whom the abundance of raw material is sure to draw here. The buying and selling of real estate in Southwest Virginia has been, and is to-day, as safe as dealing in sugar and coffee, and the proof is, not one individual has ever lost a dollar at it yet.

The desire in the greater portion of humanity to grow rich as quickly as possible is as inherent in the people of Southwest Virginia as in any other that we know of. And on this account, while there may be no fictitious value upon the properties, yet there may be too much buying and selling of real estate to the exclusion of other trades and callings. Men ordinarily cannot pursue but one line of business successfully at the same time, and the danger in this country is not any great financial or real estate collapse, but the pecuniary failure of an individual now and then, who, being engaged in other pursuits, draws out his money from that business to engage in speculation, and not be able to meet his business obligations. This is the danger. Not only is too much capital withdrawn from what are known as legitimate pursuits, but the latter are totally deserted, and have to be rebuilt again when entered into. Individuals may be hurt financially after awhile from the cause stated, but there will be many a year yet before property in this section reaches its maximum figures, because the resources have yet to be fully developed. Everything in this life has a great tendency to settle itself in its proper channels, based upon supply and demand, and there can be but little doubt of the fact that this business which people occasionally exclaim at will settle itself upon a proper basis if there are fictitious values placed upon the property.

But regarding this subject no one opinion should be advanced, so we here give the views of some of the most prominent gentlemen in Southwest Virginia on the score of advance in the values of real estate. Lieutenant-Governor J. Hoge Tyler, president of the Radford Development Company, said, when questioned upon this subject:

"I regard Southwest Virginia as one of the most favorable sections in the South. It is the direct line from East to West, and a route from Norfolk to San Francisco can be made via Lynchburg, Radford, Louisville, St. Louis, Kansas City, one hundred and forty miles shorter than by the route running from New York to the western slope. The causes of the rapid development of this section are its superb agricultural and mining resources, combined with the developing policy of the Norfolk and Western Railroad Company. So far from thinking that there are fictitious values upon property in this country, owing to the resources I have just named, I am of the opinion that property will advance for years to come."

Mr. James S. Simmons, who was vice-president of the Home Building and Conveyancing Company, and who has been for a number of years connected with real estate in almost every way—a member of the leading real estate firm in Southwest Virginia—says:

"The development companies have been one of the principal causes of the onward march towards prosperity. Real estate for years has steadily increased in value, and will continue to do so until the many resources of the country are fully opened up. Property is very low in Southwest Virginia, when we consider the amount of wealth which lies around, and it must increase in value as that is brought out."

Mr. L. L. Powell, a son of the accomplished and learned D. Lee Powell, of Richmond, Virginia, and who is the senior member of one of the leading real estate firms in Roanoke, made this statement concerning the matter:

"No one has ever lost one dollar speculating in real estate in this country, because it has had the best opportunities to thrive. Industries have been brought in ahead of the demands of the country, thereby making an increase in the value of property all the time. Speculation is on a solid basis, and, in my judgment, will continue so until the manufacturing interests cease to come in. As these are just in their infancy, we may readily conclude that property has not reached any fictitious value. In times gone by, when industries were not half so many, property was almost as high then as now, and fortunes were made even more readily than at this time. I think the country has a golden future before it."

Mr. L. S. Calfee, of Pulaski City, says:

"The situation of the ores and coking fields almost together gives Southwest Virginia an impetus in the way of manufacturing which must make this section an iron centre. Being in the infancy of this great enterprise, it will be years before property in Southwest Virginia will reach its true value."

A. M. Bowman, president of the Salem Development Company, and a partner of George W. Palmer in their great stock enterprise, gives his views as follows:

"This country has a wonderful future before it. Its vast resources in the way of minerals, and the low rates at which they can be manufactured, are certain to cause it to progress for years to come. When those are fully developed and manufactured up, then we can tell something as to what values the property may go. Being in their infancy now, it must continue to increase and grow."

Mr. E. S. Stuart, of Roanoke, who has grown up with the Southwest, and a gentleman who has done as much as any man in the country for its growth, and the originator and promoter of some of the largest developing concerns, says:

"The wonderful deposits of minerals throughout this section, with the fine lands for agricultural development, gives Southwest Virginia a basis for both agricultural and manufacturing powers. These are but beginning to grow, and as they progress property must necessarily continue to increase in value. I am very sure the values are not fictitious, but on a solid increasing basis."

Mr. J. Lawrence Radford, son of the late Dr. John B. Radford, a gentleman of varied knowledge and observation, in speaking upon the subject, says:

"My grandfather, Mr. John McCandless Taylor, in whose judgment all of us had great confidence, used to speak of the tremendous ore-bearing country in the Southwest, and took much interest in hunting minerals. He purchased a great deal of land around, and had unbounded faith in the future of this country. I think the wonderful development in ores in this section and the natural advantage in the way of climate make the future of it great, and at present, with all the advantages, I am sure property is not only sold at reasonable prices, but that it will continue to advance in value as the resources are developed."

Strange as it may seem, an investigation of this whole section can but lead to the same conclusion which all these gentlemen from whom we quoted have reached. When we gaze upon the farming and trucking facilities, with an increasing home demand for them; the thousands upon thousands of acres of all kinds of minerals in their native stage, and the cheapness with which they can be manufactured, we cannot fail to become convinced that the values upon properties, so far from being fictitious, have nothing like reached their maximum price.

When we think of the energy and untiring efforts of these development companies, their inducements to manufacturing industries, their own capital invested, we cannot withhold our tribute of praise, nor question the fact that they have played their parts well in the development of Southwest Virginia. We will revert to them more minutely in giving an account of the towns and cities along the lines of the Norfolk and Western Railroad Company and its tributaries. In the rapid growth of many of these places they have played an important part, and no history of these cities can be given which is not more or less entwined around them.

In the space allotted to us we have discussed as briefly as possible the causes of the development of Southwest Virginia, and now turn to our historical sketches of the cities and towns along the line of the Norfolk and Western Railroad Company in this section which are the natural results of this wonderful growth, and which have played no small part themselves in the progress of this great section of country of which we have been writing.

CHAPTER VIII.

Lynchburg—Gateway to the Valley of Southwest Virginia—Something of its earlier history—Gradual growth of the town from ante-bellum days until the present—Its commercial and manufacturing interests—Its capital—Its business progress — Its climate — Its religious privileges, educational facilities, and social status—General remarks concerning Lynchburg.

LYNCHBURG is situated in Campbell county, on the border of James river. Although it is not within the borders of Southwest Virginia territorially, yet so great has its influence been in developing the sections of which we are writing that it is but proper to give some account of it. The Virginia and Tennessee railroad, which was the first to penetrate the Southwest, was largely subscribed to and supported by Lynchburg, which was the eastern terminus of the road at one time. Lynchburg was largely interested in the James River and Kanawha canal, which penetrated the Valley of Virginia to Lexington, and made a handsome subscription to the Virginia Midland and Lynchburg and Durham railroads, both of which afford Southwest Virginia northern and southern outlets. To-day, with its geographical situation and railroad facilities, Lynchburg occupies the position as gateway to this fertile valley.

This city, set upon hills, is one of the oldest and most interesting places in Virginia, and has contributed largely to every undertaking which it deemed for the benefit of the State. Like most places over which time has passed its hoary hands, it is conservative in all things, requiring a certain degree of confidence in whatever it grasps. As far back as the year 1786 Lynchburg had her auction and private sale of lots, for in a revised copy of the ordinances published in 1880 of the city we find this sketch:

"The Legislature of Virginia, in the year 1786, vested in certain trustees forty-five acres of the land of John Lynch 'lying contiguous to Lynch's Ferry,' in the county of Campbell. The village thus laid out was named 'Lynchburg,' after the owner of the soil. The trustees sold this land in half-acre lots at public auction at first, and subsequently at private sale, for the benefit of John Lynch. The lots brought an average of £50 in the Virginia currency of that day. The first meeting of this board of trustees was held on May the 8th, 1787, at which John Clarke, Jesse Burton, Joseph Stratton, William Martin, Micajah Moorman, and Achilles Douglas were present. Richard Smith was appointed to lay off the town. According to his map the eastern boundary of the town was Lynch street; the western, Court street; the northern, a line running between Sixth and Seventh streets at right angles to Lynch and Court streets; and the southern, a line running between Eleventh and Twelfth streets parallel to the northern boundary. These trustees met from time to time between the years 1786 and 1817 for the transaction of business. They had no control in the town except over the legal titles of the unsold lots. The money they received for the lots was paid over to John Lynch."

The Lynch name has been handed down to posterity as the founder of a city and "Lynch law." One is as much a credit to it as the other a disgrace to the annals of any civilized and respectable community. The city taking its name after this family grew slowly until the year 1805, when, on the 10th day of January, it was incorporated as a town, and on the 6th day of May, 1805, the first corporation court met in the Masons' Hall, situated on the corner of Ninth and Church streets, which was for the time the court-house of the place. In 1805, 1813, 1814, 1819, and 1826, the Legislature enlarged the corporate limits of Lynchburg, and on June 5, 1827, by act of Legislature, three commissioners were appointed—Thomas Dillard, D. G. Murrell, and Ralph Smith, Jr.—who made a survey and report, by which the limits of Lynchburg were laid off to the river, extending from the mouth of Blackwater creek, at the toll-bridge, to the mouth of the Horseford branch, at Hurt's mill. The plat of this incorporated extension is now extant, and can be found in the first deed-book in the corporation court clerk's office. In 1830 the first reservoir was constructed, and a general gathering of the citizens celebrated that event, who thought their water supply amply sufficient for any future needs, but afterwards found out that another reservoir would have to be constructed.

But the year 1849 seems to have inaugurated a new era for Lynchburg. A subscription of $500,000 was made to the Virginia and Tennessee railroad, and a charter was granted the same. In 1852 the town of Lynchburg, by act of incorporation, stripped itself of the title town and adopted that of city, having over five thousand inhabitants. In 1857 both the Southside and Virginia and Tennessee railroads opened up, and Lynchburg possessed the fertile grazing section of Southwest Virginia and the tobacco region of Southside to draw from, besides the succulent valley of the James, with all its agricultural resources, reached by the James River and Kanawha canal.

The city improved until the civil war came on, and during that ordeal Lynchburg was patriotic and true to her trust, and after it ended the soldiers returned to their home on the James, and again Lynchburg began to grow. Nothing daunted by the reverses met with, this city opened up an enviable tobacco business and wholesale trade, and in 1871 subscribed $200,000 to the Lynchburg and Danville road, without which subscription we doubt if that undertaking could ever have succeeded. Manufacturing industries began to be erected. Tobacco factories, iron works, nail works, and various kinds of other enterprises sprang up, until the place subscribed $250,000 to the Lynchburg and Durham railroad, which was completed in 1889, rendering Lynchburg one of the greatest railroad centres in the South. At this period the city had become a place of commercial interest, a manufacturing point, and a centre of about twenty thousand people.

Commercially, this city necessarily occupies the most prominent position of any other in this part of Virginia. It lies 204 miles from the sea-coast at Norfolk, and the same distance from Bristol, the southwestern terminus of the Norfolk and Western Railroad Company. It is within a short ride of Baltimore, Philadelphia, New York, and other northern cities, while the Richmond and Danville and the Lynchburg and Durham place it in direct communication south. Through this place the supplies going east, west, north, and south have to pass, as well as the vast quantities of mineral ores and manufactured iron coming from Southwest Virginia. At present, for this country, it possesses the most direct outlet south, having equally as superior eastern, western, and northern outlets as any other city we can think of. On the whole, it has almost every railroad facility which one could desire, and the result has been that, commercially, it has reached a prosperity second to no city in Virginia. The place has a State reputation for wealth, and as a trading mart its manufacturers and jobbers, both wholesale and retail, are extending their various channels all over the South. A New York salesman, in any line of goods carried by Lynchburg, has no advantage whatever in quality or price—in consequence of which Lynchburg holds her own against any market. The result of this commercial basis is, that many of Lynchburg's citizens are among the leading merchants in Virginia, and a large number have amassed a competency which they are richly entitled to enjoy.

With good transportation facilities, in the midst of a fine agricultural region, and on the borders of a rich mineral section, there is but a step from commercial enterprises to manufacturing industries. This step Lynchburg has taken, when we turn to her various manufacturing establishments of tobacco, as well as other products, now. For a number of years much money has been made in the place through buying and selling tobacco, as well as the manufacture of the article itself. Some people have contended that the city has declined as a tobacco mart, but an examination into the statistics themselves concerning this staple of Southside and Eastern Virginia controverts any such suggestion. We herewith submit a table which gives an idea as to the immense amount of tobacco handled and manufactured at this point. The tobacco year ends October 1st, the time when the old crop is disposed of and the new one placed upon the market:

Amount sales of leaf tobacco for year ending October 1st,
1885, was . . . . 29,495,758 pounds.
For year ending October 1st, 1886 . . . . 37,462,979 "
" " " " 1887 . . . . 28,517,670 "
" " " " 1888 . . . . 24,806,725 "
" " " " 1889 . . . . 23,769,200 "

And, notwithstanding the drought of last season, the place has held her own. In this business, concerning tobacco, the city has twelve manufacturers of tobacco, twenty-four dealers in leaf tobacco, twelve exporters of tobacco, five warehouses for the sale of it, commission merchants, manufacturers of cigarettes, snuff, smoking tobacco, and cigars. This staple, in passing from the crude leaf into chewing and smoking tobacco, cigarettes, and snuff, gives employment to many thousand people, when we enumerate the families all employed who derive their subsistence from the necessary labor expended in the manufacture of it.

But the wisdom of Lynchburg has long since taught it that no place can become a city from dealing in tobacco alone; so she has turned her attention towards the manufacture of other products. The proximity of the place to the ore and coking fields of Southwest Virginia has naturally led to the establishment here of furnaces, iron works, and other metal industries, which are now in extensive operation, and among which may be mentioned two blast furnaces, two machine shops, one pipe works, nail works, merchant bar-mill, two iron foundries, zinc reduction works, and gas and water main foundry. These are all busy and prosperous, with every prospect of success, and are beneficial in every way. Pig-iron of the most approved quality is made here from the ores around, while the rails, bars, spikes, and iron of other varieties forged are well thought of and command a ready market. Iron piping of all kinds and castings for agricultural works are made and have a good market throughout the country. The means of supplying, running, and repairing is thus brought within the reach of all who employ engines and other mechanical machinery, either upon railroads, mills, and tobacco factories, or in the simpler, but no less essential, operations of the farm. The zinc works here have proven of great benefit to the city, and use much material from the southwest of Virginia. The extraction of the zinc will be made by the new patented process, by which the ore is made soluble. By applying a strong electric current the zinc is extracted from this solution, and the advantages of this latter over the old methods are marked. In addition to these manufactures, Lynchburg abounds in many others, comprising minerals, wood, stone, and clay. The natural consequence of such manufacturing power is that a large amount of active capital is employed and distributed among the people.

This city justly has the reputation of being one of the wealthiest in the South to its size, and so great is the amount invested within her borders that an account of it is well worth mentioning. Its mercantile establishments are upon the soundest basis; its manufactories have all their capital stock paid in; its commercial dealings honest and prompt; its banking institutions have always the largest kind of deposits, and its private citizens generally have good incomes. There is a solid, conservative air of financial soundness which impresses itself upon even the stranger sojourning within its gates, and the residences themselves betoken the fact that plenty reigns within their walls. We give below a table of figures carefully compiled, which shows the financial standing of this city up to 1890:

Value of real estate as assessed	$ 8,154,218 00
Value of personal property as assessed	2,198,311 00
Value of property on which license is paid	2,232,500 00
Amount invested in land companies	2,675,000 00
Amount on deposit in banks	2,714,428 72
Amount value personal property in surplus of assessment	732,770 00
Amount value real estate in surplus of assessment	1,630,843 60
Total capital invested, with value of property	$20,338,072 32

Considering the number of inhabitants, the foregoing estimates will give some idea of the wealth of the place, which is claimed by some very prudent persons as even less than the real values. With this amount of capital at its disposal, Lynchburg has not made the rapid strides which it ought, nor fully imbibed that spirit of progress exhibited by many of its sister towns in the Southwest. The reason of this may be attributed to two sources. First, the manufacture of tobacco has been for many years the chief industry, and a great deal of capital bound up in that; and many having made fortunes by it, others were loth to give it up until the success of other manufacturing industries convinced them of their error. Again, the manufacture of iron, zinc, and other products from the raw material of ores were new industries to the people of this section, and they were unwilling to embark in what were uncertain seas concerning these, or risk their capital in them. The result was that for some time Lynchburg held back from investing in manufacturing industries of minerals until the test made by foreigners coming within its borders allayed its fears, and showed that the profit was well worth the risk. In addition to the want of knowledge of these new classes of industries fast developing in the Southwest, some of the largest capitalists of the city appeared to view all innovations with more or less suspicion, and carried to a detrimental extent this conservative spirit, which, in its proper sphere, has such a salutary effect upon the community. This was to be deplored in this instance, because the want of that spirit to grasp hold of the things held out because they were new undoubtedly prevented Lynchburg from advancing with that rapidity which its position and means would have caused it to do had her citizens not been governed by that conservative spirit which objects to advances except in a certain well-known and beaten groove. But for the future good of the city, it is with pleasure that we are able to say candidly that the people are laying aside a great deal of that old spirit of sameness and taking hold of the developments around, and forming joint-stock companies for the material advancement of the place. Several development companies, with ample capital, are taking hold and making improvements, which evidence the fact that Lynchburg will not stand still, but press forward. If she does so, with her facilities and the nucleus she has already for a city, it will be but a short time before it will increase to a place of considerable size and magnitude.

At the present time Lynchburg is steadily increasing in a business way. There is no better evidence of this fact than by an inquiry into the sale of stamps at the post-office. The sales for Lynchburg show the following amount:

First quarter	$9,710 12
Second quarter	9,570 66
Third quarter	9,647 17
Fourth quarter	10,243 42
Total	$39,171 37

In proportion and ratio with the increase in the sale of stamps we find the manufacturing and commercial interests advancing and other industries coming in. Improvements, too, are being made in the way of grading streets and building handsome bridges and public buildings well worth seeing. Particularly in the West End are extensive additions being made, which will add greatly to the business capacity, as well as the beauty of the city.

The location of this place, with reference to agricultural resources and climate, is unsurpassed. Almost at its door lies the great granary of the James River Valley, while the rich country bordering Shenandoah river is but a short distance off. The tobacco region of the Southside, Piedmont, and Eastern Virginia sections all throw this staple into her lap, and the trucking tide-water country is in direct communication, with its wealth of vegetables, fish, and oysters. Transportation facilities extend in every direction into the various sections we have named, giving Lynchburg rare opportunities from which to draw the comforts as well as the luxuries of life. Nor is there a more salubrious climate anywhere than the one in this place. Situated in the mountains, yet far enough south to possess a balmy temperature, it is free from the heat of the latter and the blizzards of the north. The nights even in July and August are pleasant and agreeable, while the days have a temperature comparing favorably with any location. The mean temperature, as shown by the United States Signal Service, which office is stationed in the city, is as follows for the last five years:

January	37.17°	July	75.18°
February	41.17	August	
March	46.16	September	69.11
April	56.03	October	60.17
May	67.17	November	46.14
June	75.05	December	40.05

Mean temperature for the year, 57.09°

It can be readily seen that such a temperature not only insures a pleasant climate in which to dwell, but one perfectly free from all malarial troubles of every nature whatever.

When we turn to the religious privileges, educational facilities, and the social status of Lynchburg, we cannot speak with too much praise concerning the place. The moral sentiment of the community, as well as religious observances, stand pre-eminently forth in a marked degree. Churches of all denominations are here, and are sustained and supported in the best manner possible, having as pastors the best men and most able talent. Comparing the number of church members, members of the Sunday-schools, and the number of those in some way connected with the religious bodies, with the population as a whole, Lynchburg occupies a most enviable position. The number of people, as we have said, in this city is nearly twenty thousand. The number of church and Sunday-school members are as follows:

Number white members of churches	5,470
" of Sunday-school scholars	3,357
" of colored members	3,500
Total connected with church	12,327

More than one-half of the population is in some way connected with the churches of Lynchburg, which speaks well for the tenets of Christianity there. While Lynchburg has no great number of private schools, still educational facilities are undoubtedly good, and one of the best public graded schools is in existence here that we know of. The curriculum is unusually good, and languages taught in conjunction with the highest grade of English. The faculty is composed of highly-educated persons, and the patronage of the school by the children of the best people in town shows that it is held in high repute. The number of scholars in attendance is extremely large, being 3,350, while the teachers number 62—8 in the high school, 20 in the grammar, and 34 in the primary department. The course of instruction is high, including Latin, French, and German. It is but natural to expect that the parents of these children should compose a state of society most desirable in every respect, and such is the case. The social features of Lynchburg have a reputation for gentility and refinement which extend beyond its borders, and society there is delightful. Whether we take the class moving in the highest circles on account of their money and position, or the working class of merchants and traders, with their families, all have their share of refinement. This causes the young ladies working in stores for a daily subsistence to possess that class of bearing and manners which would become the rooms of a cottage or adorn the halls of a palace; and people are to be deemed peculiarly fortunate when they can combine the occupation of gaining a livelihood with true culture and grace, which is so necessary for congenial intercourse. Taking this city as a whole, we know of no place which presents superior social attractions.

We cannot close this imperfect sketch of Lynchburg without a remark or two upon the place generally. In many respects its superiority must be seen taking it as a whole. Some of its buildings are not only very stately and costly, but ornamental to the town. The Post-Office, the First Baptist church, the numerous handsome residences, add greatly to its beauty. The Law Building, on Main street, in which Kirkpatrick and Blackford, Thomas N. Williams, John E. Lewis, and other noted lawyers have their offices, is undoubtedly one of the handsomest buildings we know of, from the well-appointed *café* on the first floor to the rooms upon the seventh. The mosaic tiling composing the floors and wainscoting is beautiful in both design and execution.

The complaint that Lynchburg is a city of hills will soon pass away, for it is destined to grow until the hills will soon seem lost in the vales it will occupy. Time will as surely prove this as it has already shown that forty years ago the place was but a small town with only four thousand inhabitants, while now it is a city with twenty thousand.

The financial condition of the city is upon the healthiest basis possible, as can be easily shown from the revenue and expenditures. For the year ending January 31, 1889, the receipts from taxes, licenses, fines, and other sources amounted to $307,661.55. The disbursements during the same time were $298,238.96, leaving a balance in the treasury of $9,422.59, to be expended as the authorities saw fit for the improvement of the city. It is not often that cities present such a financial showing, for often appropriations have to be made to defray the calls of expense. The mayor and common council are generally composed of the most substantial citizens of the place, who look after its affairs with that prudence and care which characterize them in the government of their individual concerns.

One cause of Lynchburg's good government and peaceful, moral character is the admirable police for the protection of the place, under the guidance of Chief Irwin and Sergeants Pendleton and Seay. The shocking murders and highway assaults of various desperate characters so often committed in cities generally are rarely if ever heard of in Lynchburg. This staunch police force, composed of sober, upright gentlemen, gives a tone and dignity to the law of the land that awes people into an obedience and submission which all the brute force in the world can never do, and has a wonderful efficacy in establishing peace and quiet. At all times in this place, full of business and energy, there is a peacefulness and security which larger and more rapidly-growing cities cannot claim. And yet it is a kind of blessing which people rarely recognize until they are placed in rough and disorderly places. Lynchburg's future, to a certain extent, is necessarily an assured one. With her many railroad facilities, her commercial and manufacturing enterprises, her capital and wealth, the spirit of development which is fast becoming infectious, with those at the helm who will take hold and not look back, the place must continue to go forward until her true position is fully asserted and it becomes a city of magnitude and importance.

CHAPTER IX.

Roanoke—Derivation of the word—Big Lick—Its inception—Original owners of the soil—Its inhabitants—Its sudden progress—Change of name to Roanoke in 1882—Roanoke's rapid growth—The causes of it—The Shenandoah Valley Railroad—The Roanoke Machine Works—Incorporation of the place as a city in 1884—Its manufacturing industries, commercial enterprises, and joint-stock land companies—The peculiar patriotic spirit of its inhabitants—Their pluck and energy in a material way—The laboring population—Strikes—Present number of people—Capital and financial condition of the city—Its churches, schools, and journals—Some general remarks about the city—Its probable future.

THE name of Roanoke throughout Southwest Virginia is as synonymous with the term rapid growth as the region we have just named is throughout the rest of Virginia. So quickly has it become a commercial mart and manufacturing centre that it is known almost everywhere as the "Magic City" of Virginia, and some account of its birth and wonderful progress is fraught with unusual interest. The name of this city of which we are now writing is not less romantic than the development of it is marvellous, being derived from the Indian word Raw-re-noke, or precious money, an appellation formerly bestowed upon the valley. Almost in the centre of this valley, in Roanoke county, on Roanoke river, rests the place which is fast growing to be a city of large dimensions, and a railroad centre second to none in our State.

The original soil on which this city rests, which was formerly known as Big Lick, was granted by royal personages to one Thomas Tosh, an old settler in this county, which at that time was known as Botetourt. From the original map and grants now in the possession of Colonel Thomas and Andrew Lewis, descendants of Mr. Thomas Tosh, we find that in the year 1747, and thence on until the year 1767, grants were made of some sixteen hundred acres to Thomas Tosh lying in that section of country from near Tinker creek to Roanoke river, south of the city, and across, bordering the lands of the Tayloes and others.

This land included what was known as the Terry place, the Rorer tract, and what is now called the Carr farm. The land covering these particular tracts named was granted Thomas Tosh in 1767 by George III, while the balance was granted during the years previously named by both George II and III. It fell to the heirs of Thomas Tosh, and a portion afterwards was conveyed by the latter to Ferdinand Rorer, and at the time of Big Lick's incorporation, in 1874, the land around was possessed by Peyton L. Terry, William Carr, John Trout, S. M. Fergusson, Mrs. Jane Lewis, Colonel Thomas and Andrew Lewis, and B. T. Tinsley. The latter owned all that ground between the Carr property and Franklin street, and sold Peyton L. Terry his farm, a large part of which the latter disposed of to the Roanoke Land and Improvement Company when that was first organized. This particular piece of land was that owned by William L. Peyton, an old Virginia gentleman as noted for elegance and refinement as his hospitality.

Prior to the year 1874, a small little village lay in a "Sleepy-Hollow" kind of way on the Atlantic, Mississippi and Ohio railroad, containing some three or four hundred people, known as Big Lick. It derived its support from the rich surrounding agricultural country and some tobacco trade, and had for its amusements old-time Virginia customs, entertainments, and "fish-fries"—the latter of which is so beautifully delineated by the pen of Mr. George P. Button, the graceful and fluent writer, of Virginia. In 1874, on the 28th day of February, the town was incorporated as "Big Lick," with John Trout as mayor, Ferdinand Rorer, John M. Fergusson, Peyton L. Terry, James M. Gambill, Dr. James G. McG. Kent, and William Raines as councilmen. These gentlemen were staunch citizens, and in every way administered the affairs of this village with care and prudence, while time rolled on nearer to the day when the place would suddenly grow into a city. The country surrounding this town had been richly blessed with the gifts of nature, and when formed had the most substantial blessings poured upon the face of the soil, from which the village drew its support. It literally flowed with milk and honey, and no country in the New South could boast of more prodigal gifts in a natural way than this lovely valley. The truth is best stated when we say that for health of climate and diversity of soil, for lovely mountain scenery on every side, from green foliage to blue mist, for every kind of agricultural pursuit, from wheat-growing to sheep-raising, Roanoke can have no superior and but few equals. It is watered by rivers and mountain streams, affording abundant water of the best type. From the year 1874 until the sudden rise in 1880, Big Lick gradually grew and moved peacefully on, its inhabitants slowly increasing and following the various pursuits of life, enlivened by innocent occasional amusements already noticed, to which may be added Queens of May and strawberry feasts. A portion of what was once Big Lick is still in existence north of the city of Roanoke, and is a rambling, hilly place of two hundred people or more. Some of the buildings originally composing the town south of the railroad are remaining, although there are but few left to tell the former existence of Big Lick, so completely are they absorbed by Roanoke. On Salem avenue two or three of Samuel Grigg's buildings remain, while on Commerce street Startzman's house still stands, and the store occupied by Kinnear was formerly the Farmer's Bank, over whose counters many a dollar passed from the plethoric pockets of the farmers around. Some "Old Lick" buildings, as they are called, remain on Commerce street, between the large brick wholesale house of P. L. Terry & Co. and Salem avenue, while the old Trout house is back of the new Ponce De Leon Hotel. Rorer Park Hotel, old with many memories, was first a mere log building, and afterwards was added to until it has become a long, rambling house, looking like a fit residence for bats and owls. But these relics of this place heretofore existing, now almost historical, are fast becoming things of the past—forgotten in the bustle and rush to found a mighty city. And the location geographically of this town was a fortunate one for the foundation of a place of magnitude. Some of the best counties in the State surrounded Big Lick. Botetourt, Franklin, Montgomery, Craig, Bedford—all rich in agricultural resources—lay with hidden trophies for the future city, and even now pay their tribute to Roanoke. Another feature which was of immense value to this locality, and has been an important factor among the original causes of Roanoke's progress, is the fact that the place was almost the centre of what is known as the "springs region of Virginia." This point is but seven miles distant from Coyner and Botetourt Springs, ten miles from the Blue Ridge, thirteen miles from the Roanoke Red Sulphur Springs, twenty-five miles from the Craig Healing, thirty-five miles from the Craig Alum. The Alleghany, Montgomery White, and the Yellow Sulphur Springs are but an hour's ride, while half a day's journey by rail will reach many others so familiar to the travelling public. Nature, so far as it was in her power, smiled in the most pleasant manner upon the country which was to support the place about to spring into existence.

During 1881 Big Lick seemed to suddenly cast off its lethargy and awake from its quiet repose with the avowed purpose of astonishing the world. All at once it began to lay off lots, the sound of the hammer and saw could be heard on all sides, and on February 3, 1882, the Legislature of Virginia changed the name of Big Lick to that of Roanoke, enlarging its territorial limits. During this year the Roanoke Machine Works were placed in course of erection, and various other enterprises began—dwelling-houses, stores, and warehouses; contractors, artisans, mechanics, and laborers came in to construct and build them, while dealers, merchants, and suppliers followed the latter. This year was a memorable one for Roanoke, and will long be recollected as the beginning of an end which has not been reached as yet. But notwithstanding what wonders were performed during that memorable period, the place, to what it is now, was a mere nothing. Creditable information, derived from the accomplished architect and engineer, Mr. Charles Jacobsen, now at Pulaski City, reveals the fact that Salem avenue was then a marsh, and was filled up later on in the fall of 1882 and the winter of 1883. This gentleman, with other friends, hunted rabbits where Hotel Roanoke now stands, and picked up genuine Indian arrow-heads. In going from his room to the office Mr. Jacobsen waded through mud, and rubber boots were the order of the day. The first house constructed on Salem avenue, as well as we can gather, was the grocery stand formerly occupied by Page, and at that time was the Star saloon. Grant occupied the first store on Salem avenue, and Rorer Park Hotel was the first boarding-house known in the city, except the Trent House, kept by John W. Ryal, and the Neal House was the first hotel proper. The old Lutheran church on Bunker Hill was turned into a boarding-house, and afterwards sold to the Colored Baptist Association, who are still in possession of it. During this year of 1882 there was a large influx of people, and improvements advanced rapidly. Things continued on a progress until about April, 1883, when, the machine works being completed and the railroad offices built, there was an almost magical growth until January 1, 1884, when, by act of Legislature, the place Roanoke shed its youthful name of town and took the full-fledged title of city. People stood aghast and wondered at the cause. The intersection of the Shenandoah Valley railroad with the Norfolk and Western at this point was the reason. Why did they happen to intersect here? An answer will assist in elucidating the wonderful start of the magic place, as well as its subsequent growth.

It is asserted that prior to the construction of the Shenandoah Valley railroad the Chesapeake and Ohio Company made many promises as to traffic arrangements if the former would construct its line to Waynesboro Junction and intersect the latter there. It is further said that the Shenandoah Valley company did not rely upon these promises, but for other reasons pushed the route forward to that point. We are inclined to think the latter solution is correct, for early in 1881 the Norfolk and Western was purchased by Clarence H. Clark and *his associates*, and at that time it is but reasonable to suppose that a route to the Flat Top coal field was the object, for even then the controlling interest in the coal options were held by Philadelphia parties—presumably the same who purchased the Norfolk and Western Railroad Company, since the latter, in its first annual report for the year 1881, makes this statement on page 15:

"The Norfolk and Western Railroad Company has acquired the control of the various roads in the States of Virginia and West Virginia which, aggregated, constitute what is known as the New River Railroad Company."

As Mr. J. D. Sergeant, by his proffered contract to Roane, showed that he treated this road and these options as his property, then the Norfolk and Western, which afterwards controlled it, must have had an idea of reaching the coal lands by an extension of the Shenandoah Valley* railroad, for a short time after, the Shenandoah Valley railroad was controlled by the same parties who governed the Norfolk and Western. At all events, in April, 1881, the Shenandoah Valley railroad was completed to Waynesboro Junction, and when the Norfolk and Western was purchased, in May, 1881, by the Philadelphia parties, an intersection was determined upon. Roanoke (or Big Lick then) was the point chosen, and in June, 1882, the Shenandoah Valley railroad was completed to Roanoke, and a new era dawned for this place as well as Southwest Virginia. From this on the town seemed to be an assured city in the future.

The incorporation of the town of Roanoke as a city, in the year 1884, was an epoch in the history of the place which marked a forward movement in a material way. The inauguration of a hustings court, under the executive ability of that cultivated gentleman, accomplished scholar, and eminent jurist, William Gordon Robertson, had a salutary effect upon the new city, and law and order was brought out of chaos as quickly as possible. A disciplined police force, with municipal law brought to bear upon the people, assisted in materially advancing them, as well as the interests of the city.

In the meanwhile the Crozier iron and steel furnace was completed, which gave an impetus, too, to the city, and the Roanoke Land and Improvement Company, pursuing a conservative policy, assisted in advancing the interest of the town.

But though Roanoke commenced a new era in 1884, that year was not without some drawbacks, which are still within the recollection of many people here. During this time a fearful depression prevailed, and to Mr. S. B. Haupt's superior management is due the fact that Roanoke weathered the storm. The prosperity of the place then was mainly dependent upon the Roanoke Machine Works, and when it was thought that they would stop work, Mr. Haupt, in conjunction with Mr. D'Armond, captured the contract for the building of five hundred cars for the New York, New Haven and Hartford railroad at a reduced price, and started the shops with renewed energy and vigor. Nor was that contract secured without trouble, because the competition of other works was so great that the utmost delicacy was required to secure it. This temporary depression retarded the growth of the city for a short time only, since during the latter part of 1884 everything continued to progress and move forward. It was during this year that the city was wrapped in gloom by one of the foulest murders ever recorded. We allude to the killing of Lizzie Wilson, a bright young lady of some seventeen summers. Everything was done that was possible to bring the guilty parties to justice, but all without any effect. The officers of the law as well as citizens united in their efforts to satisfy justice, but the criminal escaped, only to meet another and worse fate in all probability.

From 1885 on, Roanoke rapidly increased in every way. We often see towns spring up and grow as if by the stroke of some magic wand, but they soon fall into decay and become, as it were, dead, resulting from the fact that the necessary industries to support them do not keep apace. On the other hand, we find places which have gradually grown, and commercial and manufacturing enterprises supported them; but Roanoke is unique in this: not only has its growth been marvellously rapid, but its commercial and manufacturing industries have kept ahead of the wants of this phenomenal growth. Following the two large industries we have already named others came in train—valuable ones, too, such as the American Bridge Works, the rolling mills, the Rorer Iron Works, the Bridgewater Carriage Works, the West-End Furnace, the Virginia Brewing Company, tobacco factories, planing mills of every description, and almost every other kind of manufacture that can be imagined. The necessary result of these industries was the establishment of a good commercial basis, which has been of infinite service towards upbuilding the place. Solid mercantile firms, both wholesale and retail, opened up to supply not only the wants of the people at home, but to enlarge the borders of their trade into foreign territory. The mercantile interests of the people at large throughout the great Southwest, and the mineral counties of Mercer and McDowell, West Virginia, can testify to the fact that, from the year 1886 and on, this place has made fearful inroads on the wholesale trade of other surrounding cities. Her commercial interests in this branch compare favorably with even the more experienced efforts of the Northern States. The banking system and institutions are on a first-rate footing, and while not having the same large deposits which older ones of larger capital may boast, still they compare well with any that we know of. In fact, taking the Commercial National Bank, the existence of which is mainly due to the efforts of J. W. Coon, now president, we scarcely know of an institution which has accomplished more than this in the same length of time. From Mr. J. C. Davenport we obtained the following statistical information: The bank has now a paid-up capital stock of $100,000, with an undivided profit and surplus of $22,000. It has only been in existence a few years.

But it is mainly to the joint-stock land companies that Roanoke is indebted for its rapid development. The Roanoke Land and Improvement Company, the Home Building and Conveyancing Company, did wonderful work towards inducing capita and labor to locate in the place. These companies may be said to be the pioneers in the Southwest of all others which have pursued their course in locating industries and developing the resources of the country. From these companies in Roanoke have sprung many others, such as the Virginia Land Company, the Virginia Development Company, the Creston Land Company, the Belmont Land Company, the Melrose Land Company, the Fairview Company, the Hyde Park Land Company, and numerous ones to mention which we have not the space. These not only brought in outside capital and manufacturing industries, but stirred up the citizens within. Almost every one in Roanoke has an interest in one of these companies, and thus every man is more or less on the order of a land agent, and through the untiring efforts of all millions of dollars of capital has been brought in, either by way of public industries or private enterprises, which have really caused a continual boom. Numbers of manufacturing concerns owe their existence to these companies, which seem determined to allow nothing to pass the borders of the Magic City. These have all been conducted on the very safest financiering policy; for no stockholder has ever lost by investing in their shares, and persons buying their real estate have all turned a handsome fortune in accordance with the amount invested. Even the Hebrew race, who generally turn their attention to mercantile pursuits, finding that money was to be made otherwise, formed a joint-stock land company known as "The Phœnix Land Company," and have done well. By its manufacturing powers, its commercial interests, and these joint-stock developing companies, Roanoke has grown since 1884 from a town of five thousand inhabitants to a city of eighteen thousand people in 1890, and at present is rapidly increasing in every way and extending its limits out in all directions. From Roanoke to Vinton is almost one continual city, while the West End is fast encroaching to the railroad between this point and Salem. The amount of capital invested in the manufacturing enterprises will range from five thousand to one million dollars, while that of the commercial interests goes from one to one hundred and fifty thousand dollars. The capital invested in the land companies ranges from ten thousand to one million dollars. It is not hard to see that with all this capital Roanoke was obliged to advance. The peculiar patriotic spirit of the inhabitants of this city is proverbial in every way. To any one dwelling here the material advancement of the best interests of the place is the first consideration. If any enterprise is to be founded or industry started, then no question is asked farther than the fact whether it is to be located in Roanoke or not. If it is, then a liberal subscription is donated and every impetus given to forward the undertaking. This patriotism has been exhibited from the start—almost in the inception of the place. The Palace Hotel, erected by S. W. Howerton when Roanoke was almost hanging in a balance, is one of the instances, for though small now in proportion to others, at that time it was evidence of Mr. Howerton's faith in the place, and not a few predicted that he was going too far. Then it was a spacious structure, and the patriotism of such men towards the city in those early days goes far towards showing why Roanoke improved rapidly. This gentleman has been here from the inception of the place, and comes from an eminently respectable family in Halifax county, Virginia, noted for their Episcopalian proclivities. If our Roanoke friend's cousin, Captain Phil, could rise from the grave and know that this patriotic son of Roanoke had departed from the Episcopal faith and gone into another sect, he would usurp Mr. S. W. Howerton's place in the justices' court, sit in judgment upon him in the sternest manner, and wonder at the change in this "new era." The "Wright Block," on the corner of Jefferson and Salem avenue, was one of the earliest substantial buildings in the city, and still bears testimony to the founder's faith in Roanoke, for it was constructed in those times when faith in the city meant something. But perhaps no people deserve more credit for their patriotism in this way than Messrs. D. C. and W. P. Moomaw, originally citizens of this county, and descendants of the Moomaw family of Botetourt. Block after block of handsome brick buildings testify to their faith in and patriotism to their native heath, and some were constructed in the earlier days of trial and tribulation. The material necessary for the construction of these, with the money paid the artizans who constructed the buildings, forged strong links in the chain which holds the complete fabric of the city's progress together. To all such men—and there are many more coming afterwards—Roanoke is deeply indebted for her rapid material advancement. The Norfolk and Western Railroad Company has done all in its power for the development of the town. The principal office being here, with its hundreds of employees, who have invested and built their homes, is another strong link in the chain of Roanoke's prosperity which should not be omitted. We can all remember a short time back, when the question was mooted as to the Roanoke and Southern railroad not running into the place, that just such a subscription as the road required was promptly made and the right of way secured into the city for it as demanded. R. H. Woodrum, Simmons, Grey, Boswell, Powell, Wingfield, Pugh (editor of the *Herald*), Nicholson (editor of the *World*), Brown (editor of the *Times*), and many others too numerous to mention, worked and engineered in every way until the road was secured and a route into the city an assured fact. Such earnest zeal must build up any place, and in this the citizens of the town have made a pathway which the neighboring places may well follow. And while these men by their untiring efforts have done much towards advancing the city, they have in no small measure carved out their own fortunes.

In every new place where the manufacturing interests are large and the population a cosmopolitan one, the best interests of the city depend more or less upon the class of labor which resides there. Whether the city advances or is retarded depends very materially upon whether there is a quiet, orderly set of laborers, or a turbulent, agitating one. In this respect Roanoke has been particularly fortunate. The place has treated the mechanical and laboring part of the population well, and in return the latter has been peaceful and quiet, making good, faithful, and efficient citizens. This city has a peculiar charm for the man who has to earn his bread by the sweat of his brow, for two reasons: wages are remunerative in almost every calling on account of the demand for labor, and the mechanic who earns two dollars a day can sit under his own vine and fig tree, on account of the instalment plan here. Houses may be purchased for the sums of $15, $20, and $25 per month—as cheap almost as the rent of a house. East Roanoke is the dwelling-place of many of these workmen, and they live in comparative ease, enjoying their own firesides and many of the comforts, and not a few of the luxuries, of life.

The logical result of all this is, that disturbances and agitations have been almost unknown on the part of the laboring population. In 1884 there was some talk of a large strike, but owing to the united efforts of Dr. H. A. Sims and James A. McConnell the calamity was averted, and things flowed on in their usual channels. Afterwards the men at the rolling mills went off on a short strike, but the differences they had with their employers being soon adjusted, they returned to duty. No place, for the number of workmen, has been freer of this nature than Roanoke, and it may be reckoned as one of the causes of its prosperity.

The present population of Roanoke, after a patient investigation, numbers some 18,742 people, with an increasing tide all the time. This estimate does not include those visiting, but the actual residents of the city. The people of the place as a whole are cosmopolitan in the extreme, and on that account interesting in the highest degree. They are all busily engaged in the pursuit of their various occupations, and in this, as in all new places, are laying the foundation for the development of the city, which is yet in its infancy. In speaking of the people of the place it is not amiss to quote from a letter writen by the Rev. W. C. Campbell, the learned, cultivated, literary gentleman who fills the pulpit in the Presbyterian church. He says:

"To me Roanoke and its people compose one of the most interesting places I have ever seen, and certainly the city is unique in the history of Virginia."

All thinking people who stay in Roanoke become convinced of the same thing, and so express themselves. One peculiarity concerning it, which is rare, is that the people have less to do and say concerning their neighbors' affairs than in any other place that we know of, and this is attributable to the fact that the population is extremely cosmopolitan, and the rapid development and influx of strangers prevent such inquiries. It is a state of affairs for which the place should congratulate itself.

When we consider the short time in which the "Magic City" has grown, its financial showing is undoubtedly a good one, and the rapid increase in values great. The statement which we now give, with a comparison of former years, will assist in showing the marvellous advance:

In 1885 the assessable value of real estate was $1,481,632 25
In 1890 it was 6,750,884 00

giving an increase of $5,269,251.75 during the period named. The values of property upon an equitable basis in Roanoke is as follows:

Value of real estate, as per assessment $6,750,884 00
Value of personal property, as per assessment 1,715,642 00
Value of capital in business on which license is paid . 1,600,000 00
Amount on deposit in banking institutions 1,671,760 67
Surplus on personal property not given in 571,880 66
Amount surplus on real estate, assessment not given in, 675,088 40

Total value of property in the city of Roanoke . . $12,985,255 73

In the calculations above the greatest care is taken, and, whilst there may be some variations, on the whole it is a correct statement of Roanoke's values. Where a place increases over a million in values every year it is a difficult matter to arrive at an exact valuation any time you may desire. For ten years it is a showing of which the people of Roanoke may well be proud.

When we turn from the manufacturing, commercial, and financial view of Roanoke to its religious aspect, educational facilities, and journalistic features, the place shows a good condition in these respects. And our inquiry has been a careful one along this line, because we do not desire to misrepresent anything in any way. When an examination is made of any one of these particulars of which we are writing the facts must necessarily be gathered from the heads of each department. From completed statistics we find these facts concerning the churches:

Number of members of churches 3,320
Number of members of Sunday-schools 2,240

Total connected with religious denominations 5,560

This does not include the colored people, who number some 2,740. Almost all the denominations are represented here, including Roman Catholics, Episcopalians, Presbyterians, Lutherans, Christians, Methodists, and Baptists. The community is a liberal one, and the churches—some of which are very handsome edifices—are always crowded.

Educational facilities in the city are good. In addition to the high-graded schools there are some excellent private and public ones. The Alleghany Institute, situated on an eminence north of the city, is a large, five-story brick building, with a capacity of accommodation for several hundred pupils. The free school system is a graded one, under the charge of Rush U. Derr, superintendent. The attendance numbers some eighteen hundred pupils, with a constant increase. Mrs. Gilmer's private school for young ladies has gained quite an enviable reputation, and its roll is now large. While we readily see that educational facilities here are good, on the other hand the attendance is not what it should be. This is a fact to be deplored, as every place should give every possible attention to education of the young people. The habit of withdrawing boys from school at the early age of fourteen or fifteen years, in order to obtain some situation in an office or store, can neither be too much decried nor severely criticised.

The journals of Roanoke have done a good service in developing the resources and good interests of the city. Among the earlier ones published was the *Saturday Review*, with Oscar D. Derr as editor. The *Leader*, published in the earlier days of Roanoke, was under the management of Colonel S. S. Brooke, the now efficient and able popular clerk of the hustings court. To an article in one of his files we are indebted for much valuable information concerning the earlier history of Roanoke. The *Daily Times*, inaugurated and founded by M. H. Claytor, a gentleman of ability, passed into a company's hands, which has given it a new garb in the shape of an eight-page paper, and it has the press dispatches. The editorial department is under H. E. Brown, who governs that part well. The *Daily Herald* has the largest subscription, and is the leading advertising medium in the city, and is under the business management of Mr. J. W. Camper, to whom it is indebted for much of its success. J. A. Pugh, who is president of the Virginia Press Association, is editor, and C. E. Herbert, formerly with the Baltimore *Sun* and *Manufacturers' Record*, is travelling correspondent. The *Evening World*, founded by J. P. Ackerly and W. H. Dooley, is under the editorial control of H. Q. Nicholson, who is from Baltimore, a gentleman of unusually fine journalistic parts as well as high literary attainments. The *World* is advancing rapidly, and is a good journal in every way. All of these publications can well be commended, and are doing a wonderfully good part in advancing the interests of the community. The *Daily Herald*, under Camper's management, has become a large advertising sheet. Mr. Pugh, the editor, is very careful in dealing with every side of any case, desiring to do full justice to both, never allowing personal prejudice to influence him. The *Evening World* is both nice and discriminating in the same manner, and, while fearless in the discharge of its duties, never allows a single personal feeling to become mixed with its printer's ink. Would that we could say the same for all journals, which have the public more or less in their power.

As time advances over the Magic City we are glad to be able to write that hotel facilities here are sufficient now. And sufficiency is not all, for we scarcely know of two more commodious and handsome buildings than Hotel Roanoke and the Ponce de Leon, recently opened to the public. The former had an addition made to it which places it second to none. Too great credit cannot be given to the Smith brothers, among the most respectable citizens here, for their pluck, energy, and wisdom in the conception and erection of their mammoth building. The service and *menu* is in keeping with the house itself, which is handsomely ornamented and finished. Just such buildings add more to the value of a city than one can well imagine, and the projectors of them are entitled to its thanks.

Other handsome buildings have been constructed, among which is the court-house, fire department, and private blocks, and there is a marked improvement in every way, particularly in the class of architecture now being erected. The streets and drives are being looked to, and the boulevard by R. H. Woodrum's handsome residence is becoming a favorite resort for pleasure-seekers. Such improvements are always welcome, and it is to be hoped that they may continue until the beauty and adornment of Roanoke equals its material advancement. Many lovely residences are being erected, which not only gratify the taste for the beautiful, but renders the city so much more attractive. The city government is well conducted, and considering that the place is new, with such a heterogeneous population, it is both orderly and quiet. Some people are disposed to cavil as to Roanoke's health, but we who have lived and resided here enjoy the same health as other people. Of course people die here, but not in greater numbers than elsewhere, and considering the number of excavations going on for new buildings in the city, we wonder that, without a proper sewerage system, it should be so healthy. No place advancing like Roanoke can perfect everything in a moment, so patience must be called in question to bear the few ills along with the many blessings of the Magic City.

What is Roanoke's probable future? In reply we cannot do better than to quote from "Historical Sketches of Roanoke," so ably revised by H. Q. Nicholson, editor of the *Evening World*, which says:

"With the gigantic corporations we have discussed; with her public enterprises, in which millions are invested; with her steady, sober, and honest class of labor; with her private undertakings and mercantile pursuits; with her hotels, journals, churches, and schools; with her thoroughly organized city government, Roanoke is destined to become one of the largest, wealthiest, and most prosperous cities south of Mason and Dixon's line. *Sic transitur.*"

CHAPTER X.

Salem—Its name—Surrounding country, scenery, and climate—A summer resort—The seat of learning, refinement, and culture—Manners and character of the people—Epoch of 1889 to the town—The land companies—D. B. Strouse, A. M. Bowman, J. W. F. Allemong, J. T. Crabtree, Dr. Dreher, George Allen, William M. Nelson—Industries and manufactories—Mineral resources and F. J. Chapman—Wonderful growth—Number of inhabitants—Financial status—Religious, educational, and social features of the place—Something concerning its future.

WHEN nature, clothed in the garb of beauty and plenteousness, cast her countenance over this section she smiled first with joy upon that part of the valley where rests a town which used to bask in the sunlight of its own name—Salem, or Peace. This place occupies something of a central position between the ranges of mountains known as the Alleghany and Blue Ridge, amidst a land of beauty and delight, ever satisfying to every sense of taste and sight. Look as we may around the lovely valley stretching away to the everlasting hills, and naught but sublimity and grandeur greet the eye, from the succulent green pastures and foliage to the ethereal blue of the peaked Blue Ridge or the rugged Alleghany. The serene calmness surrounding all, the lovely varying scenery in perfect view on all sides, the level outstretching landscape sweeping away, blended with a balmy atmosphere, gives a surrounding air impregnated with peace and contentment found only in Salem. The climate is all that can be desired, as can be seen from the average temperature for fifteen years, observed by the late Dr. Griffin, which is as follows: Spring, 56°; summer, 76°; fall, 61°; winter, 41°; average for year, 58°.

It is distinguished for the equability of its climate, being seldom too warm in the summer or cold in the winter. Storms, tornadoes, and cyclones are never known here, and rarely does one hear of a case of sickness, except that kind of disease which providence has provided to gradually remove people from this world, termed by us in plain *parlance*—old age.

Logically, with such a climate and surroundings, Salem could but be a famous summer resort. Not only the town, but Lake Spring, near by, and the Roanoke Red Sulphur, nine miles off, have been taxed to the utmost to sustain the swarms of people longing to summer in this Eden of the Valley. When persons used to travel the macadamized road from Lynchburg to Salem *en route* for the Montgomery White and other places west, before the days of steam, the town was then a place of a thousand or more, and a noted summer resort, as well as the county-seat of the rich county of Roanoke. The society of the place has ever been celebrated for culture and refinement, an impression of which charmed and followed the visitor even after he had left the place behind and turned his face homewards.

Since 1853 this town has been a seat of learning. From that year until now the classic shade of Roanoke College has thrown its mantle of culture over the place, and the walls of the building not only enclosed the grand library of seventeen thousand volumes, but learned professors, and students groping after that most satisfying yet unattainable elixir of life—the forbidden fruit—knowledge. Its *alumni* have branched all over the land, first shedding its light in Salem, then casting maturer rays elsewhere. The families of many of the students lived in the place, who, with the households of the professors, caused it to be *par excellence* one of learning and culture indeed. The natural consequence of this was the formation of a *status* of society for refinement and native elegance scarcely to be surpassed. An air of gentle breeding and ease settled over the place which always impressed itself upon every one entering the gates of the town.

The manners and character of the people residing in Salem were moulded in the highest type, amid the influences of this nature, and developed a race of people peculiar unto themselves. Of all the places in Southwest Virginia along the line of the Norfolk and Western railroad, there is no town whose inhabitants are characterized more fully by honesty, probity, and uprightness in all their dealings than the people of Salem. The social feature presents a distinct feature in the make-up of the place, and the original inhabitants were composed of the best people in the Southwest of Virginia, and the many inducements offered as a summer resort insured always a state of society at once conservative, elegant, and refined. For a number of years Salem existed with her college and this state of affairs. Yet it was by no means a stagnant place during this period, for in 1880 there were some eighteen hundred people, and the placed contained, perhaps, more wealth and business calibre than any small town in the Southwest. From 1880 to 1889 it progressed very slowly, but the time had now come when Salem was to discard the long-worn robe of peace and quietude in order to adorn that of material prosperity.

Touching the development of most of the towns in Southwest Virginia, the causes generally rise from situation, railroad intersections, or some chapter of events suddenly springing up, unknown before. But not so with Salem. From 1880 until 1889 the place stood at one thing almost, while towns around rapidly advanced. Towards the latter part of 1889 the place shot up like some meteor, and from that time until January 1, 1891, its growth and development for the time being excelled any place in Southwest Virginia, Roanoke not excepted. No railroads ran past her doors suddenly; no chapter of events appeared upon the scene; no bonanza that had hitherto lain dormant was found; no sudden placing down of any large manufacturing plant was seen. What, then, was the cause? The formation of joint-stock land companies, and placing the natural and manifold advantages of the town before the public. Salem owes her development to the united efforts of D. B. Strouse, A. M. Bowman, J. W. F. Allemong, J. T. Crabtree, Dr. Dreher, George Allen, Wm. M. Nelson, T. J. Shickel, and F. J. Chapman, all gentlemen of the best business qualifications and of indomitable pluck and energy. On October 2, 1889, the Salem Improvement Company was organized with an authorized capital stock of $1,000,000, of which $300,000 was issued. J. W. F. Allemong was made president, and D. B. Strouse, who had been prominent in originating the move, with T. J. Shickel, were placed upon the Board of Directors. The company purchased about nine hundred acres of land in and adjoining Salem, and laid off streets and avenues sixty to seventy-five feet wide, with other improvements. The first sale of lots took place on December 11, 1889, and within ten days $300,000 worth were sold. This was virtually the beginning of the development of Salem, and manufacturing industries began to be located at once. On the twenty-seventh day of January, 1890, the Salem Development Company was organized with an authorized capital stock of $1,000,000, with A. M. Bowman as president. He is of the Palmer-Bowman Company, of Saltville. Mr. Bowman, originally from the Shenandoah Valley, has done a great deal for Salem, and the policy adopted by his company was an aggressive one in the extreme concerning the material advancing of the place. Eight hundred acres were purchased by this company for business and manufacturing purposes, and improvements of the most substantial kind were inaugurated, among which was the construction of the two iron bridges across the river, with both a drive and a walkway, at a cost of $18,000. The company also put in water-works at a cost of $8,000, conveying the fluid from Mountain Spring, 307 feet higher than any point in town, and put under construction fifty dwelling-houses suitable for mechanics. The concern is interested, like the rest of the development companies in Salem, in various enterprises in the city, and owns stock in many companies. Not less than thirty dwellings and a handsome hotel and office were constructed by the Salem Improvement Company, which also took stock in almost every industry securing a location in Salem and desiring to operate there. On January 6th the West Salem Land Company was organized with a capital stock of $500,000, issued in series or classes, based upon property which supports each series distinctly. Mr.

George Allen is president, whom we have already mentioned in connection with joint-stock land companies in another chapter. This company has in course of construction a number of houses, market-house and four stores, and other improvements. The South Salem Land Company organized in March, 1890, with a capital stock of $300,000, and elected J. T. Crabtree as president, who is better known as a former professor of Greek at Roanoke College, which position he resigned with honor to himself and the sincere regret of the college faculty. This company began its operations by the purchase of 318 acres of land around Salem. Negotiations were set on foot by the company for two manufacturing plants which they secured, and plans were laid out for the erection of residences and other improvements. During the month of February, 1890, the Lake Spring Land Company was organized with a capital stock of $100,000, M. M. Rodgers being president. In March, the Glenmore Land Company came into existence, with E. S. Strayer as president; while in this same month the following companies were organized: The Creston Land Company, capital stock $200,000, G. J. Ligon, president; the Central Land Company, capital stock $80,000, C. M. Killion, president. The Glenmore Land Company (mentioned above) was capitalized at $250,000. In April (the following month) the Steelton Land Company, capital stock $500,000, with J. C. Langhorne as president, Arthur T. Powell (brother of L. L. Powell, of Roanoke, and son of D. Lee Powell, the accomplished educator of Richmond, Va.) being made secretary, was organized. In this month, also, the Hockman Land Company was formed with a capital stock of $100,000, and W. M. Nelson, an able financier, formerly from the Valley of Virginia, was declared president. From October, 1889, to May, 1890, ten reliable, strong land companies were organized, with authorized capital ranging from $80,000 to $1,000,000 and unlimited chartered powers.

The men who took the helms of these various organizations did not start out with any purpose of bare speculation, but with the avowed object of building up Salem, and the results crowning their efforts almost immediately proved the fact that to their industry the development of Salem was due. During the year 1890 these companies brought in a number of enterprises and industries that caused the town to double its wealth and population in the space of one year. Every undertaking or commercial pursuit which was located at Salem had a free donation of site, and the companies subscribed liberally to the stock of these industries planted there. As we have previously stated, the inducements offered by them to foreign capital were simply irresistible. The logical consequences of such patriotism and energy were soon experienced. By August 22, 1890, a number of large and small industries had been secured and located, and 228 houses of all kinds had been constructed or were in course of erection, including 159 residences, 35 for stores, offices, and other business purposes, and 34 for manufacturing enterprises. A scarcity of material prevented further construction, and how many were then under contract is not definitely known. By a fair, reasonable estimate, there was expended during the year about $870,000 in buildings for residences and business purposes. Among the many industries may be mentioned: The Salem Furnace Company, Salem Car and Machine Company, Holstein Woollen Mills Company, the Salem Tanning Company, the Flynn Wagon-Manufacturing Company, the Salem Gas-Heater Company, the Salem Building and Investment Company, Salem Folding-Chair Company, the Conrad Chair and Manufacturing Company, candy factory, Camden Iron Works, sash, door, and blind factory, the Crystal Ice Company, the Gravely Foundry and Machine Works, brick and tile works, carriage factory, grain cradle works. These industries include only those which are in operation and secured, and which have been located during the year 1890. The list, with the old enterprises of Salem, will employ not less than 2,000 or 2,500 mechanics and laborers, and notwithstanding the number of dwellings constructed during the year there is a pressing demand for house room. In addition to the enterprises named, the principal offices of the following large industries are located in the city : The Bonsack Machine Company, $1,600,000; the Carper Spark-Conductor Company, capital $1,000,000; the Universal Long-Filler Cigarette Company, $300,000, and the Comas Machine Company, $100,000. These land companies subscribed $250,000 to the capital stock of $1,000,000 of a basic steel plant, to manufacture steel rails, plates, and the like. The matter was placed in the hands of Charles G. Eddy, vice-president of the Norfolk and Western railroad, and the Improvement Company of Salem states that it was at his solicitation that this subscription was made. He has a high opinion of this place, and is one of the directors, with Clarence M. Clark, in this Salem Improvement Company. The fact that the Clarks, and Denniston and Brock, and other Philadelphia parties, have an interest in Salem augurs well for the place, since they have shown a wonderful financiering capacity for stocking companies, ranging from the howling wildernesses in the rugged mountains to the level lands in the fertile valleys, and also the greatest ability for building towns.

People heretofore have been in the habit of speaking of the climate, rich country, and lovely scenery with which Salem is blessed. She has all those and something else equally as valuable almost at her doors—mineral resources. So far as we can see, this was the cause of a furnace being located there. To the untiring efforts of F. J. Chapman is due the fact that people knew of minerals being immediately in the vicinity of the town. Visionary as Mr. Chapman was deemed when hunting minerals, it seems now that his opinion was correct in thinking that the embedded wealth of Southwest Virginia would "make us all rich some day," as he termed it. He is now a resident of the town which he has seen grow so rapidly, and, with his sons, manages the Roanoke Red Sulphur Springs, Lake Springs, and Hotel Lucerne. Some of the iron ore around Salem is highly spoken of by Edmund C. Pechin, general manager of the Virginia Development Company, and one of the most consummate judges of such property in this country. In his report, made April, 1890, he says:

"After considerable negotiations, the furnace has secured the lease of the Bott property, about seven miles from Salem. * * * * Not only is the amount of ore apparently very large and of good quality, but it lies in the foot-hills and on the mountain side in such a shape as to allow easy opening up and cheap mining. The washing plant and machinery are now being built."

In 1875, Mr. Chapman began taking options on mineral lands between Salem and the Peaks of Otter, and there was scarcely a mountain or hill which he did not explore, and it must be a source of gratification to him to know that opinions which he then expressed, though deemed visionary, have been literally verified by results, even if they were accomplished by means not then thought of—in fact, not even within the borders of his native State at that time.

The growth of Salem for the past fourteen months has been simply marvellous. All of the level plateau east of the old town has become a lively scene of activity in the way of erecting hotels, banks, offices, and residences. All have a substantial look, and the placing of the new handsome passenger depot by the Norfolk and Western Railroad Company in this eastern part of the place will make a lovely town. Pretty villas, cottages, and brick buildings are going up, while south of the railroad is the great blast furnace, now in operation for the manufacture of pig-iron. The whole surroundings have put on the air of activity, and so rapidly has building increased that it is almost impossible to keep apace with it. South of the river, on the development company's land, quite a village is springing up, and the large brick woollen mill now erected will soon pour forth its products from the raw material, worked up by numerous operatives for wholesale use. Forty or fifty houses are now being constructed on the plateau around, while some handsome dwellings are being finished on the brow of the hill above. About the whole place there is an air of rapid progress and growth which impresses one very decidedly on viewing the city even from a passing railroad car. That this improvement will continue there is every reason to believe, from the fact that in the near future the place will have railroad facilities which it does not possess at present. The Valley branch of the Baltimore and Ohio Railroad Company is partly graded from Lexington to Salem, some fifty-four miles, and the construction of a branch line by the Roanoke and Southern to Salem will almost insure the building of the Baltimore and Ohio branch. With such railway facilities the place would breathe with renewed energy, if such a thing were possible.

The increase in the population of Salem has been in keeping with her other improvements. From the best evidence upon the subject which we could gather we are satisfied that in October, 1889, there were some 2,500 people in Salem. About January 1, 1890, there were some 4,350, as near as we could arrive at the matter, which shows that in fourteen months the place has almost doubled in inhabitants.

It is a difficult matter to give a correct statement of the financial worth of a place that is growing rapidly, for the reason that between assessments there is such a marked change as does not justify one in adopting any past computation by which to reckon present value; so the values we give are estimates based upon the fairest calculations we could obtain at the end of the year 1890. But one thing is true—Salem has been, and is now, a wealthy place. From the best light upon the subject we should say her values were:

```
Real estate . . . . . . . . . . . . . . . . . . . $1,856,493 10
Personal property . . . . . . . . . . . . . . . .    769,380 96
Value of capital invested, including various enterprises
    and stock companies . . . . . . . . . . . . .  2,375,000 00
                                                  ─────────────
        Total values . . . . . . . . . . . . . . $5,000,874 06
```

The foregoing, we are sure, is as fair an estimate as can be given under the circumstances which we have named. There has been a wonderful increase of values in the space of twelve months—probably a larger amount in value than any place we know of in the same length of time.

The religious, educational, and social features of the place are all that could be desired. The whole community is a correct, moral, and upright one, besides attending faithfully to the outward forms and ordinances of religion. Five denominations—Baptist, Episcopal, Lutheran, Methodist, and Presbyterian—throw open their doors for the worship of God every Sabbath, and hold divine service. The Sunday-schools are well patronized and excellently supported in every way. The town is absolutely free from open violation of the code of morality, and drunkenness is rare.

The educational facilities are unexcelled. There are two good public and several private schools fully equipped in every way, while a handsome building for a good graded school is now going up. This is one of the finest school buildings in the South, and will be handsomely supported in Salem. Roanoke College, as we have seen, is located here, and has attendance from many States, Indian Territory, Mexico, and Japan, while the graduates from this institution of learning can be found scattered over twenty-eight States and Territories, and some on foreign shores. Dr. Dreher is president of the college, and its standard under his management is of the highest type. The buildings of the school are spacious and handsome, and the library an extremely valuable one. The grounds are beautifully laid off, and, with their canopy of shade, afford a cool resort to pleasure-seekers in the summer months, of whom there are generally large numbers in this charming town.

For many years Salem has been, and is now, noted for its cultivated society and cultured people. Happily, the rapid material development of the place and influx of strangers do not seem to have altered its standard or changed its aspect in this respect. The same culture, refinement, and high standard are preserved, and characters who are not in keeping with sobriety, honesty, and probity are not welcome in this retreat, nor are they wanted. The influence of education and intellectual culture is undoubtedly a refining process, for while it may not eradicate vice, it will always suggest a guise for it which will not shock the finer taste of society. This influence is strong in Salem, as elsewhere where colleges are in existence, and exerts a powerful lever in preserving a higher state of society. The influx of visitors every summer from all parts of the country, of the best class, has its influence too; it tends to preserve the best order of society for congeniality, if nothing else. On the whole, the social scale is charming.

That Salem will grow into a city there can be no doubt, and many think that it will eventually meet Roanoke, forming a second edition of St. Paul and Minneapolis. The extension of Roanoke west and Salem east, which is the tendency now, would seem to be some ground for the assertion. Colonel C. G. Eddy is reported as having said that a union of the two places was inevitable. While we are sure from the reasons we have given that Salem must continue to grow and become larger, yet what will be in the future we cannot say. It is the duty of the chronicler to record past events, and deal no farther with the future than the former by actual experience will justify. Certain it is, that for natural surroundings and climate, social and other privileges, its present resources—agricultural and mineral—its many commercial and manufacturing powers, Salem has no superior that we know of as a place of residence or business centre.

CHAPTER XI.

Radford—Situation of the town—Formerly known as Central—Original owners of the soil—Inception of the place—Its gradual growth until construction of the New River Railroad—Incorporation of the place as Central in 1887 — Purchase of the Wharton and Radford farms by the Radford Land and Improvement Company—West Radford—Development of the same—Its enterprises and industries—The Radford Development Company—Growth of East Radford—Spirit between East and West Radford—Resources of the town — Its financial status — Its population, schools, churches, and hotels—Improvement and growth of the place—The Radford "Enterprise"—Future of the town as an iron centre.

RADFORD, one of the coming cities of Southwest Virginia, is situated on New river, in Montgomery county, 301 miles from Norfolk, and about 100 miles from Bristol, Tenn., the western terminus of the Norfolk and Western Railroad Company. With reference to the Pocahontas Flat Top coal region, it is most happily situated, since it is at the junction of the New River division of the Norfolk and Western with the main line of the latter. This fact, and the further statement that New river is some 500 feet wide at this point, and amply sufficient for water-power, gives the place a prominence at once in the eyes of any one at all acquainted with the topography of the country. Its proximity to the coking fields at Pocahontas and ore region of the Cripple creek-New river mineral territory is pregnant with significance as to the future of the place. Some inquiry into its past is by no means uninteresting.

The place known as Radford now was at one time called Central. Long before the civil war, and sufficiently far back for the purposes of this sketch as to the original ownership of the soil, it appears that it was owned by John McCandless Taylor, Colonel Hamet, and the Ingles family, the latter of whom were descendants of Mary Ingles, who figured so conspicuously in frontier warfare with the Indians, as we have already seen.

John McCandless Taylor's daughter, Elizabeth, married Dr. John B. Radford, and in the year 1840 the former gave the latter a thousand acres, situated on both sides of the river, which property was given by Dr. Radford to Mrs. General G. C. Wharton, the charming and cultured Mrs. Adams, and his son, J. Lawrence Radford—all of whom reside at Radford, except Mrs. General Wharton, who is dead. Colonel Hamet's property passed into the hands of Stockton Heth and his wife, the latter of whom was the daughter of Colonel Hamet. The Ingles property descended to Captain William Ingles, now living at Radford also. Most of this land, as we shall see later on, passed into the hands of the development companies now located at the place.

This point being equi-distant between Lynchburg and Bristol, in 1856 the Virginia and Tennessee railroad concluded to have machine shops started here. At that time the place was a mere railway station, with three railroad companies' tenement houses, a temporary hotel, depot, and store-house, with some half a dozen families. On the 15th day of October, 1856, W. B. Ransom, now a resident of New River, landed there with engines, tools, and machinery, and four apprentice boys, with a journeyman, for the purpose of opening a shop for the Virginia and Tennessee Railroad Company. On the 10th of December, 1856, the machine shops started under supervision of Samuel Peters, master mechanic at Lynchburg, with W. B. Ransom as foreman. In 1858 the latter was made master mechanic, with charge of the shops at Central for the western division of the Virginia and Tennessee railroad. In 1860, at the commencement of the civil war, there were some twenty families in the place, the population numbering about one hundred people, composed principally of railroad men. The town did not progress at all during the civil war which raged, and the railroad did but little except to transport troops over its line; so Central came out of the struggle in rather a dilapidated condition. At the close of the civil war the road was soon gotten into a condition to pass the trains over, and Central began to revive and build up slowly. At this time the town of New River, across the river at Radford, had four houses and a sawmill, and the property was purchased by General G. C. Wharton. Subsequently the General was elected to the Virginia Legislature, and while there obtained a charter incorporating the New River Railroad, Mining, and Manufacturing Company, in 1872—a history of which we have already given. The inception of this regenerating scheme for Southwest Virginia was, as we have seen, due to General Wharton, and many subsequent acts of his to aid and assist it place the people of this section in his debt for the conception, birth, and construction of the New River railroad, which regenerated Central and was the beginning of the wonderful development of the Southwest. There is nothing which he might reasonably demand of the people that should not be acceded to by them with gratitude.

Upon completion of the New River railroad and commencement of the coal traffic in 1882 and 1883, Central began to improve, and in 1887 the place was incorporated, with a population of five hundred or more. In this same year the Radford Land and Improvement Company purchased 585 acres of land from General and Mrs. Wharton, and 970 acres from J. Lawrence Radford. The organization of this company and the purchase of this property was the beginning of the west portion of the town called West Radford. From this period on industries, such as the stove foundry, brick-works, and plant for an iron furnace, came in, and the place grew rapidly and increased in population until in 1890 there were about 3,000 people in both East and West Radford.

The policy of the Norfolk and Western Railroad Company of making frequent divisional stops for the purpose of building towns was one of the reasons of Radford's former growth. The construction and operation of the machine-shops and round-house at this point gave a decided impetus to the place. The shops consist of a brick building 200x50, with an annex for the smith's department of 40x60. Eighty-five hands are employed regularly in the shops proper, with twenty on the car-repairing and inspecting force. There is a round-house with twenty-four stalls, and the crews running the trains for both passenger and freight traffic change here. The result is, most of these workmen have homes, while part of the money made by the train employees is spent in this place. The office of division superintendent for the Western division of the Norfolk and Western Railroad Company is located here, with its employees and clerks. The pay-roll for the shops, offices, and yard force amounts to some $7,000 per month. The situation of this shop here has been very material in advancing the growth of the town.

Subsequently to 1887, when the Radford Land and Improvement Company begun their operations, other joint-stock land corporations were formed, which were as follows: The West End Land Company, the West Radford Land Company, the New River Land and Improvement Company, the River View Company, South Radford Land Company, and the Radford Development Company. These companies, with an authorized capital stock of $1,915,000, purchased lands from William Ingles (property northwest of Radford, over the river—land belonging to Stockton Heth and wife), and by a donation of lots, the natural advantages of the town, and a liberal subscription to undertakings and plants located there, many valuable industries were brought in, which gave the place a material move forward.

Some very important manufacturing plants were secured, among which may be mentioned the Radford Brick Works, East Radford Brick Works, the Townsend and Hooper Manufacturing Company, the Radford Stove and Range Company, the Crane Iron Works and Furnace, sash, door, and blind factory, knitting company, dwelling-house company, Radford Lumber Company, water company, electric light company, street railway, stone quarry, Radford Bank, Exchange Bank, and the trust company. Of the industries we have named many were in operation, some under construction, but all secured. The majority of them are situated in West

Radford, the rest in East Radford and New River, across the river.

The natural result of all these industries pouring in between 1887 and 1890 was the place became a business town, and began to be spoken of abroad as one of the coming cities of Southwest Virginia. The erection of the cosy, commodious inn by the land company and the lovely new passenger station by the Norfolk and Western Railroad Company added materially to both the comfort and beauty of the town. Where in 1887 we saw only fields rich with cereals and grass, we now see a town with broad, well-graded avenues; huge industries, either in operation or in course of construction; rows of beautiful residences and cottages, and the imposing Radford Inn, the trust company's offices, and other attractive buildings. This is West Radford of 1890.

Nor is the east portion of the place (formerly Central) behind in this spirit of forward movement which has characterized the west portion of the town. The organization of the Radford Development Company by Lieutenant-Governor J. Hoge Tyler was a new era to the place which had grown so slowly as Central. This concern was formed on the 25th day of March, 1890, with a capital stock of $200,000, and purchased three hundred and eighteen acres of land from Stockton Heth and wife, one-third of which was laid off into lots and broad, long streets, properly graded. This property lies north of the town, directly upon the railroad, and east of that part of the place located upon the eminence south of the railroad. The situation of this part of the company's property on the eminence is beautifully located for residence purposes, while the portion lying between the railroad and river is admirably situated for business houses and manufacturing sites. In order to fully appreciate the east portion of Radford it is necessary to go on the hill, or rather gentle acclivity, around by Captain Heth's lovely residence, and then the residence part bursts upon the view, adjoining which lies the lands of this company to the east. One of the improvements inaugurated by the company was the construction of "La Belle Inn," which lies east of the beautiful grove surrounding Captain Heth's. Lots and sites are donated by this concern for all manufacturing purposes, and it is thought by some that the railroad will consume a part for extension of their yard and shops.

In addition to the railroad shops in this portion of Radford, there are several other enterprises, such as brick works, wood and lumber manufacturing concerns, and a substantial banking and commercial business, supported not only by the people of the place, but by others from the surrounding country. Much of the trade which used to go to Christiansburg, the county-seat of Montgomery, now comes to this town, owing to the fact that its rapid development and influx of manufactories have created a demand, and supply invariably follows the former. Radford is now taking much of the trade of Montgomery and Pulaski, which was not so formerly, and a further inquiry has developed the fact that it is making inroads into Giles county, west of the place.

Considering that East and West Radford are but one place, and that there is a unity of interest between the two, there should be complete harmony and a purpose of determination to advance the interests of each as if they were a whole. But such is not the case. Each place seems to possess a desire to help and assist the other no farther than their individual welfare requires. Necessarily such conduct injures Radford as a town, and this kind of spirit cannot be too strongly decried nor severely condemned. With all the advantages, both natural and artificial, which the city possesses, it does seem wrong for any one part to hold back on account of another when all is at stake. Both have the same unexcelled agricultural and mineral resources, which, after all, are the substance of every town's growth in this section, and each could advance and assist the material prosperity of the other without injuring or affecting its own.

When we come to speak of the resources of this place we more or less give an insight into its advantages, with which we know of but few places that compare so favorably. In the first place, its situation seems to have been formed by nature for the purpose of making it an iron centre. It is peculiarly fortunate in having unusually fine railway facilities. Located on the great thoroughfare east and west, it has the certain probability of an outlet northwest by way of the New River branch into Ohio, and a southeastern one by way of the extension from Ivanhoe into North Carolina, to connect with the Cape Fear and Yadkin Valley railroad. It has almost unlimited waterpower running at its borders, and that is a material item in the make-up of a city. Its surrounding country is one of the finest agricultural regions in this whole section, having on the east the grain-growing counties of Montgomery, Roanoke, and Botetourt, while on the west it possesses the splendid grazing and stock-raising country noted throughout the whole State for its productiveness. By reason of its lying on New river, which flows from North Carolina in a northwesterly direction into the Ohio at Point Pleasant, and its railroad communications, it is the natural outlet for all the agricultural and grass productions of the rich Southwest. Its immediate surrounding country is extremely rich in all the natural fruits of the soil; and although it lies on an elevated plateau, the land possesses all the fertility and beauty that is seen in the rich valleys of Pennsylvania and Maryland. As a place of residence it has no superior, because, being elevated some 1,800 feet above the sea, it is free from all malaria, and possesses an atmosphere at once pleasant and invigorating.

When we turn to mineral resources, this place occupies a pre-eminent position above every one that we know of, if we except Pulaski City. As we have stated before, it is situated at the junction of the main line of the Norfolk and Western Railroad Company with the New River division of the same. This latter branch leads directly to the great coal and coking fields of the Flat Top region, some seventy miles off. The value of this coke for blast furnaces manufacturing pig-iron has already been alluded to, and virtually the material in this part of iron making may be said to be at Radford's doors. Only a few hours run places coke of the best quality and in unlimited quantities at its furnaces, giving the city a rate as to freight which others farther off cannot hope for except through railroad manipulation, which is now a violation of law. In respect to ores the town is equally as fortunate. Only twenty-five miles away are the celebrated New river-Cripple creek regions, containing large quantities of the best iron ore, which can be reached now by rail. The quality and character of this ore have been referred to already in a former chapter, and a full analysis given. But Radford may, and has it in its power to come nearer still to the ore section than at present. At the last session of the Legislature Mr. J. Lawrence Radford, the representative from Montgomery county, obtained a charter incorporating the Radford and Little River railroad, which in time is obliged to be constructed, and when it is, the ore fields of Carroll and Floyd will be but a matter of eighteen miles away. The construction of furnaces for reduction of the raw material will cause the Radford and Little River railroad to be built. So the natural position of the place is that of Pittsburgh and other iron centres—a junction of the ore and coking regions.

The financial condition of Radford has a fair showing, and gives evidence of the capital invested in the place since 1887. Inasmuch as the land companies own a greater part of the real estate, this property is classed with the amount represented by them. While there may be some slight variation from the statement we give, in the main it will be found to be a fair epitome of the values in the place:

Value of property owned by the land companies, and real estate,	$1,950,000
Amount of capital invested in other enterprises of every description	2,250,000
Value of personal property	486,200
	$4,686,200

This estimate includes everything in the nature of property, real and perishable. The values may seem large on the first blush; but it must be remembered that Radford, as delineated by us, extends from East Radford to New River town across the river, including that. The amounts, upon investigation, will be found to be a fair representation as of the year 1890.

The population of the place has increased greatly since 1887. At that time there were some five hundred people, and the town was slowly progressing, but now it is claimed by the people of the place to be four thousand. From an investigation on this score we are safe in saying that in January, 1891, the town had about 3,700 people—may be a fraction over. The last census did not show so many, but since that was taken there has been a considerable increase. The inhabitants as a whole are good and clever people, and, considering that the place is new, there is an absence of those rough, *quasi* criminal characters which usually infest a town just beginning to grow. A great many of the descendants of the original people of this Southwest section are there, among whom may be mentioned General G. C. Wharton and family, Captain R. H. Adams and wife (*née* Radford), J. Lawrence Radford, the Goodwyns, Kearsleys, Barclays, Crockets, Ingleses, Heths, Tylers, Hoges, and some others, all of whom compose a social status extremely pleasant. In New River (the upper part of the town) live some persons who have been at the place for many years and know each and every step of its progress. Educational facilities in the town are good, and there has been an increase in the attendance of scholars since the town was incorporated. There are two schools in the place, one of which is known as the "Belle Heth Academy," which is in East Radford, and a fine building in West Radford. These schools are under the charge and control of Professor Gunn, who has an able corps of assistants, and the grade of scholarship is fair. The usual attendance of scholars number up to five hundred. Christian privileges are ample and sufficient in every way, there being Methodist, Missionary Baptist, Christian Baptist, Episcopal, Presbyterian, and Northern Methodist churches in the place, and divine worship is held in each one respectively every other or every Sabbath day. The pastors are men of both high moral character and theological culture. In West Radford a lot has been donated, and an Episcopal church will be erected, not far from where the present rector (Mr. Robert Goodwyn) resides with his charming and cultured family. In addition to school facilities and religious privileges the stranger can always find in Radford pleasant hostelries in which to enjoy the comforts and luxuries of life. The Radford Inn, in the west part of the town, is one of the number of hotels managed by Fred. E. Foster, and its service and *menu* is good. Several others are in East Radford, among which may be mentioned, in addition to "La Belle Inn," the Commercial and Hoffman houses, both comfortable places.

In many places the growth of a town into 3,000 or 4,000 people in three years would be considered quite rapid. but in Southwest Virginia it is what is termed a sound, healthy progression. Radford has never been advertised to any considerable extent until the latter part of the year 1890, yet its improvements resulting from natural advantages have been marked. Three years ago Captain Barclay, of Kearsley, Barclay & Crocket, a real estate firm in the place, and a gentleman originally from Lexington, walked through the mud from East Radford to West Radford to sell the lots laid off by the Radford Land and Improvement Company. He was a pioneer real estate agent there, and then there were neither houses, streets, nor sidewalks, and no bridge was in existence to connect the two places. Now a well-graded street, with sidewalks, can be seen, and substantial residences, business-houses, and manufacturing enterprises greet the eye on every side. And so it is with East Radford, where the development company's property is situated, which has done so much in every way for the growth of the city. The improvement in every way has been a marked one, extending even across the river as far as the property known as "Brooklyn Heights," a beautiful site for resident purposes, and which belongs to A. Robinson, of West Radford, one of the leading real estate men in the place. Among the improvements in Radford, and one which has done its part in the development of Southwest Virginia, is the Radford *Enterprise*, published by Wardle & McGregor. It has always been a beautiful sheet, and well edited in every sense. The special issue prepared by them in October, 1890, was a monument to their taste, energy, and mechanical genius, and its portrayal of the advantages and resources of Southwest Virginia should enlist the gratitude of the people and insure the paper a handsome support. In the selection of all material there is a perfect freedom from all bad taste and *double entendre* which sets an example that other journals in this section might well follow.

The future of this place, so far as we can see, is undoubtedly a bright one. With its natural situation and water-power, its position with reference to the coal and coking regions, its rich surrounding agricultural country, its climate and health, its manufacturing and commercial interests, its upright and honest class of people, Radford is sure to be one of the coming cities of Southwest Virginia, and an iron centre of no small magnitude.

CHAPTER XII.

West of New river — Stock-grazing section — New river plateau — Pulaski county—New river-Cripple creek mineral region—Cripple Creek extension of the Norfolk and Western Railroad Company—Martin's Tank—Beginning of its development—Growth of the place, and change of name to Pulaski City—Bertha Zinc Works — George T. Mills — L. S. Calfee—The furnaces and other industries and enterprises—Population, schools, churches, and social state of the town—Pulaski City as an iron centre—Probable future of the place.

WE will now conduct our reader into that productive, charming, and beautiful country west of New river, and known as the blue grass section of Southwest Virginia. Near Pulaski City, and adjoining the county by this name, lies the counties of Floyd, Grayson, and Carroll, composing the celebrated region known as the New river plateau. This country, as well as the counties west and southwest, is the home of cattle, sheep, and all classes of stock, the raising of which has been so remunerative in days gone by, and which still constitutes one of the chief agricultural pursuits in these counties of which we are writing. A lovelier country than this, or a richer or more productive one, it would be hard to find, and the climate is more salubrious, if anything, than the places we have been writing of hitherto. The reason for this difference we have already explained, which arises from the fact that the farther west we go after reaching the summit of the Alleghanies the milder it becomes, which accounts for the delightful temperature around Wytheville, Virginia. The finest bred herds of cattle are raised in this section, which not only assist in supplying the Northern markets, but are shipped to Europe; and horse-breeding has become quite popular with many of the people of the country. Pulaski is one of the counties composing this favored section, and was cut off from Montgomery and Wythe in the year 1839 to administer its own affairs, with Newbern, one mile from Dublin, as the county-seat.

This county composes a portion of the celebrated "New river-Cripple creek mineral region," of which we have already spoken, and which contains an area of some 300 square miles in this and Wythe county. This country is rich beyond conception in ore-bearing properties, and the quality of the very best. Limestone iron ore and mountain ore lie in vast quantities, while in the county of Carroll adjoining has been discovered what is known as the "gossan ore," which not only makes a splendid class of pig-iron by itself, but gives a decided character to the iron manufactured from ordinary ores mixed with this. This ore-bearing section has long been known, for charcoal furnaces have been in course of operation for years, hauling their products by wagon over the mountains to the nearest station on the railroad, before the erection of the Cripple Creek extension. Along the lines of this last branch of road may be seen the remnants of these old furnaces, which were fed with coal burned from the trees of the forest. Having given in a previous part of this work an analysis of these ores, we will not attempt another here, but simply say that a richer and better ore-bearing territory does not exist than the one we are attempting to describe. And not only iron, but both zinc and lead, have been worked with profit, and the largest zinc works—the Bertha Zinc Works—in this section draws its raw material from this ore-bearing territory. The Claytons, of Baltimore, own and are developing this gossan ore, which even impressed Mr. Edmund C. Pechin so favorably as to cause him to report especially upon it to the stockholders of the Virginia Development Company. The Pulaski Iron Company at its furnace used some of this gossan ore with the ordinary ores, and the result from the reduction was a superior quality of pig-iron. All of this valuable ore-bearing country is but a few miles from Pulaski City, the town which we now propose to describe; of which Colonel Eddy says, in "Reference Book of the Norfolk and Western Railroad Company," for which he deserves special credit in compiling:

"An additional iron furnace is now being erected, and the promise of Pulaski becoming one of the most important industrial cities in Southwest Virginia is now becoming a fact." (Description of Pulaski City, page 39).

There is an amusing tradition concerning the ground on which this place rests, which we have determined to give, because it may have been true. In fact, the weight of the extrinsic evidence in its favor leads us to credit it at least. We give here a statement of Mr. Robert L. Gardner, in his own language, who resides in this place, and is a prominent attorney and a gentleman of unquestionable veracity. He writes:

"Tradition has it that some time back—very early—in the present century Robert Martin traded an old flint-lock rifle gun to the two Montgomery boys for a large, wild boundary of lands located in the county of Wythe, near where a tank, familiarly known as 'Martin's Tank' now lies. However that may be, the records of Pulaski make no mention of anything of the kind, inasmuch as this county was established from portions of Wythe and Montgomery in 1839. The records of Pulaski county do show that the said Robert Martin departed this life leaving a will of date June 26, 1854, and which was admitted to probate on the 5th day of May, 1859, wherein he devised a large body of arable lands to his son, Robert D. Martin.

"Also, the large tract of land owned by John Montgomery was purchased from him by John Floyd, ex-governor, and father of John B. Floyd. The tract consisted of 2,000 acres of land. John B. Floyd subsequently sold to James N. Pierce and Dr. Watson, said Pierce coming into possession of that portion of the tract now known as the 'Litchfield and Bohanon properties.'"

Martin's Tank, the name of the railway station which stood where Pulaski City now stands, doubtless took its name from the family of Martins who formerly owned the soil. Near the spot where the development company's furnace is now being erected under the supervision of George T. Mills, the president, and successful railroad contractor, stands the frame house in which Governor Floyd once resided, after whom the county of Floyd was named. This property passed out of the hands of that family, being subsequently owned by Mr. Pierce and Dr. Watson, from whom the development companies purchased.

Martin's Tank was but a flag-stop prior to the commencement of the development of the place, and its subsequent growth and change of name to Pulaski City may be attributed to the building of the Cripple Creek extension of the Norfolk and Western Railroad Company into the rich ore-bearing country we have described. This place gradually improved from 1883, during the construction of the Cripple Creek extension from Pulaski City through Wythe county, by Allisonia, Reed Island, Barren Springs, Foster Falls, Austinville, and on to Ivanhoe, which point was reached late in 1886 or early in 1887. From this time the town commenced to improve, and the industries springing up was the cause. The first and largest, probably, of any other manufacturing enterprise in this section at that time was the Bertha Zinc Works, located at this point. This wealthy company was first organized in 1879, and reorganized in the year 1886, with a capital stock of $3,000,-000—George W. Palmer, of Saltville, being president, Thomas Jones superintendent, and G. M. Holstein local treasurer and paymaster, as well as general manager of the office. The grounds of these works occupy ten acres of lands, and they have the most approved methods for manufacturing pure spelter. The coal, ore, and all material used by this company comes from their own property, and they have a department to manufacture their own pottery, such as fire-brick, pots, and pipes used for the reduction of the raw material in the furnace. The company works about eight hundred men at the furnace, mines, and in all the occupations connected with the zinc manufacture, with a pay-roll of $20,000 per month. The product of this company's works is said to be as pure spelter as any made in the United States, and possesses a fine reputation in Northern markets. The result to Pulaski in having such an enterprise was that the place began to grow at once, and people came from a distance to seek knowledge concerning it. This company has its narrow-gauge road running from Pulaski City to its coal mines, the construction of which assisted the town materially, and the number of laborers employed gave an impetus to the commercial interests of the place which produced a marked change in this line at once. Stores, dwellings, and improvements began to be erected; the town was named Pulaski City, and we hear of Martin's Tank no more except as a thing of the past. Branch roads to the mines were built in 1886 or early in 1887. Since then this extension has been pushed to Speedwell, while the proposed line into North Carolina branches off at Ivanhoe. The completion of the road to Ivanhoe, in the year 1887, inaugurated a new future for Pulaski City, which in 1883 was known as Martin's Tank, and was the dwelling-place of three or four families, as well as a watering station for the Norfolk and Western Railroad Company's engines.

Probably no two men have played a more important part nor done more to develop the country and city than George T. Mills and L. S. Calfee, who now reside in the place. George T. Mills first saw this portion of the country when he passed through with Cooke's raid in 1863 and engaged in the fight at Cloyd's Mountain, subsequently striking this immediate section at Dublin, which was burned. After the cruel war was over he became engaged in railroad contracting, and gradually worked his way until in 1883 he became a wealthy man, and reached Pulaski City (then Martin's Tank) for the purpose of grading the Cripple Creek extension. He, in conjunction with L. S. Calfee, obtained possession of several large bodies of mineral lands, which subsequently were the basis of formation of two or three large joint-stock companies. Lee S. Calfee was born in Pulaski county, and merchandised up to 1882, when he began to take a part in the development going on, and afterwards became connected with the various enterprises for the advance of Pulaski City.

In the year 1887 the Pulaski iron furnace was constructed, being the property of the Pulaski Iron Company, organized in the same year with a capital stock of $450,000. This concern also owns mines at Patterson, on the Cripple Creek extension, from which point much of the ore used by them is brought. The capacity of the furnace is one hundred and twenty tons *per diem*, and it made a two-year run before going out of blast, producing 100,000 tons of pig-iron. As may well be seen, the establishment of such an industry gave the town an impetus in a business way which can be well imagined. This furnace has been eminently successful, especially under the management of Mr. George Echman, who has charge now, and whose knowledge of the reduction of iron ore, coke, and limestone to pig-iron is of the most intelligent and varied order. The organization of the "Pulaski Land and Improvement Company," in 1887, was another enterprise which assisted this young town. With a capital stock of $250,000, this company purchased a lovely tract of land north of the railroad, and its policy to sell lots cheaper to those who desired to erect houses, and a requirement that only brick houses should be built in a certain part of the town, resulted in some very handsome dwellings in the way of banks, stores, and other buildings now under the ownership of various people. Mr. Dinges is president of this company, but the well executed management devolves upon Mr. Taylor, who has charge, and resides at Pulaski City. During the same year the Hematite Iron Company, capital stock $100,000; the Martin Land and Improvement Company, capital stock $150,000; the Swansea Land Company, capital stock $100,000, were formed, which did good work towards the development of the city of Pulaski. The two latter companies constructed a number of houses, which added greatly to the beauty of the place and are a source of revenue to the company. George T. Mills and L. S. Calfee were the moving spirits in these developing concerns which assisted so materially in building up the town.

The year 1890 saw Pulaski City a place of some 2,500 people, with an increasing population to three thousand by now. Good, solid, substantial buildings can be seen on all sides, while some lovely residences adorn the place. The character of the architecture of the place is unusually good, seeming to be constructed with a view towards the town becoming a city. In this year the Pulaski Development Company was organized with a capital stock of $500,000, which subscription was made principally among the people at home, Messrs. Mills and Robinson taking the principal part. This concern began at once the erection of a large furnace, with a capacity of one hundred and fifty tons *per diem*. This huge plant is placed in a bottom to the east of the town, on the old Floyd place, while the offices and dwellings connected with it are located on a lovely eminence above, commanding a fine view of the surrounding country and mountains. Following this great enterprise others came in rapidly, and now the future of the place as a city is an assured fact. The enterprises under construction, and those to be built which have been secured, will create a demand for employees enough, with families, to double the present population. The place is constructing a water-works which will supply the town with an abundance of the fluid from a mountain side near the lower furnace. The mercantile interests and banking facilities are admirable, and the place as a whole seems to be both prosperous and happy.

The inhabitants of this place are composed of the best people in the section of which we are writing, and considering that it is in part an iron-manufacturing centre and a mineral region, they are remarkably quiet and well behaved. That part of the city where the employees of the Bertha Zinc Works live and the furnace hands reside is picturesque, comfortable-looking, and quiet. Riots, agitations, and rows are unknown among this class, who quietly pursue their occupations and amusements. Religious privileges are good, as churches of the Episcopal, Methodist, and other denominations are there to hold worship every Sabbath. Educational facilities are unusually well provided, since they have the finest school building and one of the best graded schools that we know of in Southwest Virginia, the regular attendance of scholars being some 350 children, exclusive of colored.

The hotel accommodations here are of a superior order in every way conceivable, as the Maple Shade Inn, known far and wide, is still in existence, and being enlarged under Fred. E. Foster's management. Of all the well-known hostelries controlled by the Norfolk and Western, which are all admirably conducted, Maple Shade is the most superior, resulting from Mr. Hayes' management, who has a genius for the business. On the shaded avenue near the railroad Mr. Richard B. Roane has an excellent house. He is the same who played an important part in the New River railroad, and who did so much for the development of that road in its earlier history.

The social features of Pulaski are good and interesting. Whether we take the inn or go into town, there is always a genial, intelligent set of people with whom one can while away the time. The Browns, Moores, Calfees, Taylors, Joneses, Langhornes, McGills, and others equally as pleasant, compose a delightful circle in a social way, and one of which Pulaski City may well be proud.

The situation of this city with reference to the ore and coking fields render it, as it is already beginning to be, an iron centre. True, there are furnaces on the Cripple Creek extension, but hey have a haul on coke, and the furnaces east and west of Pulaski have a haul on ore, which gives this latter place an unquestionably good position as an iron centre. Here, too, are the supplies and the necessary sites for both residence and business purposes. Furnaces are going up, and a plant for a rolling-mill and bar-mill established. With its present industries, its near situation to the ore regions, its natural advantages, Colonel Charles G. Eddy was not wrong in saying in the reference book, page 39:

* * * " And the promise of Pulaski's becoming one of the most important industrial cities in Southwest Virginia is now becoming a fact."

CHAPTER XIII.

Wythe County—Max Meadows—Wytheville—Crockett and Rural Retreat—Washington county—Glade Springs—Saltville—Future of the cities and towns of Southwest Virginia.

LEAVING Pulaski City, in going westward we soon come into Wythe county, whose name is synonymous with agricultural resources and mineral wealth. This county plays an important part in the make-up of the New river-Cripple creek mineral region, as we have seen, and is noted for the fine stock raised within its borders. Some of its lands have been long celebrated for their productiveness, while years ago iron was made from its charcoal furnaces, and lead manufactured at Austinville. We know of no country which has a finer mineral territory, and why its towns have played so small a part in the recent development we cannot imagine for a moment. But this section is fast progressing now, and the day is not far distant when Wytheville will redeem itself for past errors in this respect and take its proper place as the county-seat of one of the wealthiest counties in Southwest Virginia.

Max Meadows a year or two ago was a station on the Norfolk and Western railroad, at which point iron from the furnaces on the Cripple creek region was hauled in wagons for a distance of ten miles. Capitalists, recognizing the vast mineral deposits near this place, purchased these ore banks and, forming a land company, bought the ground around the station, and now it has become quite a village, with every mark of improvement. A large furnace is in course of construction, built by the "Max Meadows Iron Company," with a capacity of one hundred and thirty-five tons *per diem*. This furnace draws its ores from lands of the company, some four miles away, or less. The company also constructed a handsome inn, which is now open to the public, and is a model of elegance and comfort. This place, for many reasons, has a future before it, two of which we need only mention—its natural advantages in reference to climate and agricultural resources, and the further fact that it is supported and controlled by the Virginia Development Company. The capital stock of the Max Meadows Iron Company is $400,000, and the shares owned by the Virginia Development Company in this amount to $75,000. In the Max Meadows Land and Improvement Company it owns $75,000 of its stock, and practically controls it. These facts lead us to naturally suppose that the place which in the last few months has developed so rapidly will grow into a town, or perhaps a city—who knows? The position of Max Meadows is a central one for its supply of coke and ores, as well as for the shipment of manufactured products to the northern and northwestern and eastern markets. The section around is one of the finest live-stock countries we know, and Fort Chiswell stock farm is but a short distance off. Throughout this whole productive country there will be a home demand in a few years for the supplies raised which will place the farming community upon a much sounder basis. Max Meadows is three hundred and twenty-nine miles from Norfolk and seventy-nine miles from Bristol. Its development and improvement is mainly due to the efforts of the Virginia Development Company, which is playing such an important part in the progress of the extreme Southwest that at this point in our work it deserves some notice.

On October 1, 1887, the Virginia Steel Company was organized under a broad and liberal charter of the Legislature of Virginia, and until 1889 confined itself to operations in the mining of ore. In May, 1889, desiring to extend the operations of the company by building blast furnaces, rolling mills, foundries, and other enterprises, and to develop in particular the resources of Southwest Virginia and Shenandoah Valley, the company increased its capital stock from $100,000 to $5,000,000, and the name was changed to that of the Virginia Development Company, with the following officers: President,

Richard S. Brock; First Vice-President and Treasurer, Clarence M. Clark; Second Vice-President, S. E. Chauvenet; Secretary, E. J. Collins. This company has a cumulative, full-paid, preferred stock of $1,000,000, and $4,000,000 of common stock, 20 per cent. of which is paid with provisions that not more than 15 per cent. can be called in any one calendar year. By liberal subscriptions on the part of this company industries and enterprises, by way of furnaces, land improvement companies, and other operations, have been put on foot and brought to completion in Radford, Max Meadows, Graham, Salem, and Pocahontas, in Southwest Virginia, giving an almost invaluable assistance to this section in developing its resources and utilizing them. Mr. Edmund C. Pechin, whom we have quoted frequently on the subject of ores, is general manager, and a gentleman eminently qualified to fill the onerous and important duties of this post. It has done more than any other joint-stock company that we know of for Southwest Virginia, and on that account is entitled to the thanks and gratitude of the people. As an engine of development it has struck telling blows, and wherever it touches progress comes as if by some magic hand. So we may well understand that when Max Meadows was centred upon as one of the points of investment for this company, it was but natural that it should make rapid strides materially.

Wytheville, the county-seat of Wythe, is situated on a beautiful plateau, slightly depressed, on the summit of the Alleghany mountains, 133 miles west of Lynchburg and 71 miles east of Bristol, the western terminus of the Norfolk and Western Railroad Company. Owing to its position in a country of unexcelled productiveness and charming scenery, and with a climate that is almost perfect, this place for many years has been a noted summer resort for people from many other States in the Union, particularly the Southern States. The place is 2,300 feet above the level of the sea. There is always a refreshing breeze, which not only relieves depression and debility, but gives an invigorating, healthy buoyancy to the system so pleasant to wearied humanity. The climate compares favorably with that of Turin and Geneva, in Europe, as can be seen from the following comparative temperature for some years:

	Spring.	Summer.	Autumn.	Winter.	Year.
Turin	52.2	70.3	54.2	34.0	52.07
Geneva	53.7	71.5	53.8	33.5	53.1
Wytheville	52	70.6	53	32.3	53

The thermometer is rarely above ninety degrees in summer or below zero in winter, and in the warm months of July and August the evenings are delightful, and the nights so cool that a blanket becomes comfortable.

This place is one of the oldest towns in Southwest Virginia, being over a century in years, and is very conservative in all its ideas and views. The place is one of the yearly circuits of the Court of Appeals of Virginia, which sits there every June for this section of Virginia. The town is well laid off, with broad streets, the main one being the old macadamized road which ran from Seven-mile Ford, in Smyth county, to Staunton, in Augusta county, Virginia. Standing at the upper end of Main street and looking down through the place, a beautiful vista is presented between the sidewalks, which becomes almost sublime when seen at night under the rays of the electric-lights, which the town has the good fortune to possess. From the earliest years of this century Wytheville has been a trading centre for the counties adjoining Wythe, and from this source principally it drew a support, and a handsome one, too. The past days of covered wagons, loaded with produce of every description, coming in from the country to get their supplies, are still within the memory of some of the inhabitants of the place, who deem railroads an invasion and regard the continued triumphs of science as a sign of the demoralization of these days in which we live.

Wytheville, owing to the demands of this trade of which we have just spoken, has always been something of a manufacturing place in order to supply them as far as profitable and practicable. A furniture establishment, carriage and wagon manufactory, a machine shop and foundry, a flouring mill, several cigar factories, a canning establishment, are in operation, all of which add materially to the welfare of the place. But now Wytheville is throwing off her lethargy and recognizing her vast agricultural and mineral resources, and is determined to take advantage of them. Capitalists are seizing hold of these; a development company has been organized, and new hotels are to be erected and a general improvement inaugurated. The construction of Jackson Park Hotel in the beautiful woodland west of the place will result in the erection of a building which will eclipse any other we know of in the way of natural scenery and beauty of situation. There is no reason that can be possibly assigned to show why this place should not become a great manufacturing centre and still retain its prestige as a summer resort and an educational point of celebrity.

Wytheville is certainly a seat of learning, if the number and good reputation of its schools constitute it. A great many institutions of learning are here, both male and female, among which may be mentioned Wytheville Male Academy, A. A. Campbell principal; Plummer Memorial Female College, Rev. S. R. Preston principal; Wytheville Seminary, Mrs. Thomas R. Drew principal. All of these schools are conducted upon the best possible educational principles, while moral and physical training are strictly attended to, and the comforts and pleasures of the students considered. These establishments have developed the minds of many a man and woman who have played no small part in the development of Southwest Virginia. Co-existing with these fine scholastic advantages are the best possible religious privileges, which have a material influence upon the place. The Roman Catholic, Episcopal, Presbyterian, Methodist, Christian, Lutheran, and Baptist denominations are here, all of which have churches, and divine worship is held every Sabbath; and Sunday-schools are in a flourishing condition. These educational facilities and Christian observances have not only a salient effect upon the residents of the place, but impress the minds of the visitors more or less.

The result is a state of society which is admirable and charming in every way, and which gives the place the reputation of being the most elegant and refined one in this section of country. Amusements are plentiful, and the German club, organized by the young men of the place, and which meets once a week at each of the hotels, is a distinctive feature in the make-up of the pleasures of the town.

While Wytheville has grown slowly, there has been an increase all the time in its population, for in the year 1860 there were only fifteen hundred people in the place, while now there are three thousand; and with the many natural advantages it possesses in the way of agricultural resources and mineral wealth almost at its doors, it should continue to increase—only more rapidly—than it has done hitherto. It is surrounded with the best type of ores, and a soil on which nature has expended her utmost force to render it rich and productive. The United States fish hatchery is near this town, and is an object of no small amount of curiosity.

Passing westward from Wytheville some thirteen miles, we arrive at Rural Retreat, which is 2,500 feet above the level of the sea, being the most elevated place on the line of the Norfolk and Western Railroad Company. Near this place is Crockett, which has been, and is now, a shipping point for the iron manufactured at the charcoal furnaces near by. Both this place and Rural Retreat are the centre of a section of country which is growing financially well off from the production and sale of cabbage. Large quantities of this succulent vegetable of the finest quality are produced and shipped South annually from these places. The cultivation of fruits, vegetables, poultry, and eggs is always a sign of prosperity among the farming community, and with a home demand, which they are fast gaining, to consume their supplies, they must necessarily become a rich and independent class.

Glade Springs is located in Washington county, one of the wealthiest and loveliest counties in Southwest Virginia. This thriving town, though small, has a future, and is the native heath of blooded horses shipped everywhere, and finely bred cattle. The place takes its name from the point known as Old Glade Springs, on the wagon road between Baltimore, Maryland, and Knoxville, Tennessee. Its situation is in the richest blue-grass section of Washington county, agriculturally one of the best in the State, and possessing the same mineral traces running through the county to Damascus which we find on the Cripple creek region. In 1865 there were five residences only at this place, and it drew its support from the rich agricultural region, where stock-raising and grazing constitutes the chief pursuit. Now the town has a population of six or seven hundred people, and is on the increase. It lies at the junction of the Saltville branch with the Norfolk and Western Railroad Company, and on that account possesses some importance, while Washington Springs—quite a summer resort—as well as the Glades, is only some two miles and a half distant. In this place is a large agricultural machinery company, which has the supply of the territory of the States of Tennessee, Kentucky, North Carolina, and Virginia, and which does a handsome business. The situation of the town is in a beautiful country, directly upon the line of the railroad.

Besides being the junction of the railroads already named, Glade Springs has become quite a school centre, at which the Glade Spring Academy for young men is situated, and a school for young ladies, conducted on a system of the utmost economy consistent with the acquisition of knowledge, health, and true comfort. This college is known as the Southwest Virginia Institute for young ladies, and was first opened for the reception of pupils in 1884, and since that time, under the executive management of M. M. Morriss, D. O. Beatty, and others, has succeeded admirably. The peculiar object and intention of the promoters of this school were worthy in the extreme, for they proposed to found an institution, not for the purpose of making money, but to give ladies in straightened circumstances the best possible culture at the least possible cost. Through the aid of philanthropic persons sums sufficient were obtained to erect the buildings and have sufficient grounds. These were placed in charge of some capable person, *rent free*, which enabled the principal to take the young ladies at much less than ordinary schools are in the habit of doing. The buildings are increased as the occasion may require by the board of trustees, and kept in thorough repair without expense to the principal. At the last session the faculty was composed of seventeen officers and teachers, while there were one hundred boarders and some forty day pupils. This plan for assisting in the culture of poor young ladies is worthy the highest commendation, and Mr. M. M. Morriss and Rev. J. R. Harrison, who labored so hard to make it a success, and did so, deserve to have their names carved in the historical niche of education, for we know of no other place formed of this nature in the section of which we are writing. The result is that at this school a young lady can obtain a course in English language and literature, Latin, German, French, mathematics, natural science, mental and moral philosophy, history, medicine and medical attendance, board, tuition, and calisthenics for the small sum of one hundred and fifty-five dollars. The success of the institution already proves that it is highly appreciated.

Glade Springs does now, and will in the future, derive an importance from Saltville which, casually looking at, one would not observe. It is the junction, or virtually the shipping point from the latter place, on the main line of the Norfolk and Western. Saltville is eight miles distant, and takes its name from the salt works located in Washington county, and which have been in existence for over one hundred years. The brine from these salt works is stronger in saline matter than that of any other situated in the United States that we know or have heard of as yet. The place, with the works, employees' residences, and other dwellings, make a population of some five hundred people, located on a lovely plateau of some one thousand acres of indigenous blue grass.

In 1869 the present company, with W. A. Stuart as president, and George W. Palmer as secretary and treasurer, was organized, a capital stock of $1,000,000 being paid in, and since then the operations have been on the broadest scale, resulting in the employment of over two hundred laborers, clerks, and mechanics, and an output of ten thousand tons of fine salt, which is shipped East and South. Such industries as this are of the most material advantage to any country, and deserve the highest credit. The prosperity and development of not only the immediately surrounding community, but Glade Springs as well, is traceable to this source. George W. Palmer, originally from Syracuse, New York, and W. A. and H. C. Stuart, of Russell county, have played steady, important parts in developing this section and giving employment to hundreds of laborers.

Near this place is the celebrated herd of short-horn registered cattle belonging to the Palmer-Bowman Company. It is said to be the largest herd in the world, and great numbers of them have been shipped to foreign countries as breeding cattle, for which purpose alone are they sold. The Clydesdale and Denmark horses of Mr. Palmer's stock farm have gained quite a reputation for draft and saddle purposes. Saltville, in every way, is a place of unusual interest, with its salt and plaster works, its lovely scenery, and splendid turf for grazing, and the stock farms of Mr. Palmer. It must necessarily have a good effect upon Glade Springs, and be a potent factor in the development of all around, into which our inquiry has been especially directed.

In giving an account of the cities and towns of Southwest Virginia we have of course confined ourselves to those places which so far have aided most materially in the development of this section, an inquiry into the causes of which has been the object of this imperfect work. But before closing these sketches we desire to say a word or two on the subject of these places, and others which are in this country playing their part, the description of which we cannot undertake for the want of space, however much we might desire so to do.

That this whole valley of Southwest Virginia, with its great agricultural resources and mineral deposits, is but in its infancy, is an undeniable fact. All thinking people, business characters, and foreign capitalists are of the same opinion, and at no far off future date, in this very section, there will be cities almost anywhere numbering from five to twenty thousand, and may be more. In advancing this opinion we are not alone, and we now quote that of others on this score. George W. Palmer, of Saltville, who has been living a long time in this section, says this:

"Whoever lives twenty-five years from to-day will see a town from here (Glade Springs) to Lynchburg, almost as thickly settled as Pennsylvania. The soil, climate, and mineral wealth are not surpassed by any other country under the sun; for coal, iron, zinc, lead, gypsum, salt, and copper abound throughout the section."

This opinion is re-echoed by many of the best people in the Southwest; nor is the picture an overdrawn one. The resources of this section only partially developed are of that character which warrant these assertions. Lehigh Valley, in Pennsylvania, dotted every few miles with towns and cities, is neither as prolific in natural, agricultural, and mineral resources, nor blessed with so salubrious a climate, as the Southwest. Then, with capital and energy pouring in, what is to prevent the development of our riches and the building of towns as well as cities? Many gentlemen now residing here are from the mineral district of Pennsylvania, and all admit the superiority of this section both as to climate and minerals; so it is but natural to suppose that these places in course of time are obliged to become cities. One of the best articles which we have ever seen bearing upon this subject is in the report of the president and directors of the Virginia Development Company to its stockholders, made in April, 1890, in speaking of investments made by that concern. On pages 26 and 27 the language is as follows:

* * * "It must be borne in mind, also, that in Virginia values of farms and town lands, with one or two exceptions, have not increased during the past twenty-five years. The attention of the public had not been generally attracted to the great natural advantages of that section (Southwest Virginia) until within the past six months. During this time there have been very great activity and increase in values, and large amounts of outside capital have been invested. The only real foundation for this is the large number of new industries which are now in course of construction and in prospect. These new industries have already brought and will continue to bring a large population to the towns where they are located. The people of Virginia, moreover, who heretofore have lived in towns distant from the railroads, are moving into the new industrial towns, located on lines of railroad, where there is ample opportunity to invest money advantageously that has been gradually accumulating and lying idle, or to get work at good wages. All this change in population justifies an increase in values of real estate at the favorable places. There are to-day in Southwest Virginia very few towns of 3,000 inhabitants. *There is no reason why there should not be as many towns of from 3,000 to 10,000 inhabitants* as in most parts of Pennsylvania, New York, and New Jersey, and if this district is to become the iron centre which is confidently expected, it is only a question of a few years when, to the traveller, this section will more nearly resemble the active industrial districts of the North than the quiet farming country he has hitherto seen." * * * *

The italics in the above are our own.

From this will be gathered the fact that Pennsylvanians themselves are confident that these places will grow to be cities, and nearly all are supporting that confidence by investing largely of their capital in the resources of the country to which they so favorably allude. With the embedded wealth of the country but in its infancy, upon which the welfare of these places depend, we have every right to expect that when the resources are fully matured that many of them will cease to be towns and become cities.

PART II.

SHENANDOAH VALLEY

WITH SKETCHES OF THE PRINCIPAL TOWNS

ALONG THE LINE OF THE

SHENANDOAH VALLEY RAILROAD.

INTRODUCTION.

AN inquiry into the causes of the growth of this wonderful section of country will necessarily be much less than the one concerning Southwest Virginia, for two reasons : First, two of the causes which played the same part in the progress of this country that affected Southwest Virginia have already been discussed—the abolition of slavery and the development companies ; second, we have no long histories of railroads to detail, as in the case of Southwest Virginia.

The causes which led to the wonderful growth of this section may be said to be five, two of which we have previously discussed. The remaining three are : First, the natural resources of the country—its climate, scenery, agricultural productiveness, and mineral wealth ; second, the Shenandoah Valley railroad ; third, the discovery and opening up of the wonderful Caverns of Luray and the Grottoes of the Shenandoah.

In writing of Shenandoah Valley, it can be readily seen that we will confine ourselves to those counties through which the Shenandoah Valley railroad runs, beginning at the West Virginia line, and following the main line until Front Royal is reached. From there on we follow the south branch of the river until Shendun comes upon the scene, when our labors are ended, after a sketch of the remaining towns which have been instrumental so far in the development of the Shenandoah Valley.

CHAPTER I.

Territory traversed by the Shenandoah Valley railroad — Early settlers of this country—Indian warfare—Peace—The growth of the country—The civil war—This country part of the battle-field during the war—Climate, scenery, agricultural and mineral resources—Manufacture and cost of making iron—These natural advantages original cause of the development of the country.

IN the year 1716, Governor Alexander Spotswood penetrated the Blue Ridge mountains at Swift Run Gap, in company with his knights of the "Golden Horseshoe," and after casting his eyes over the lovely valley of the Shenandoah, returned, and he is reported as having said: "I have discovered God's country."

We can scarcely blame him for this accredited utterance, because whoever casts his eyes upon this exquisitely lovely habitation of man feels the same—that so superior is it to the usual possessions of men in the shape of soil, climate, and scenery that it does not belong to man, but some supernatural being who should have the fairest of all the fair earth as his dwelling-place. There is a sublime beauty in the broad plateau and gently-rolling hills which charm the eye, while the rugged mountains in the distance give a variation just sufficient to break the sameness without destroying a scintilla of its beauty. The very breezes which softly stir over the land seem laden with plenty and impregnated with peace and contentment, while the rays of the sun appear to shine with a clearer brightness and embody every color of the rainbow. Truly this is a beautiful land, literally *running* with milk and honey; and he who could not be happy in Shenandoah Valley would be happy nowhere. Had Rasselas, Prince of Abyssinia, in his wanderings reached this country, his restless, perturbed spirit would have been satisfied, and that charming work of Dr. Samuel Johnson would never have been written to illustrate the fact—

we cannot be satisfied on earth, it matters not where we go. We never seem tired of gazing on this land: the rich, broad fertile fields of waving grain, or thick, soft grass; the green foliage stretching here and there; the meandering streams, flowing on with an almost musical sound, charm the most wearied existence into a feeling of peace and produce the impression that after all God's world is fair. Such is the face of the country which the Shenandoah Valley railroad traverses.

As we have seen before, as early as the year 1734 the county of Orange was formed, and at that period embraced all the indefinite claims of the Colony of Virginia west of the Blue Ridge, which included this section of country. In 1738, the counties of Augusta and Frederick were cut off from Orange, and this portion west of the Blue Ridge in Shenandoah Valley was included in Frederick. The earliest reliable evidence we have as to the disposition of land in this country of which we are writing was the grant to Colonel Carter, in 1730, for sixty-three thousand acres of land, commencing a short distance below the forks of the river, running down a little below Snicker's Ferry, about twenty miles. This land lies in the south of what is now known as Clarke county, and was afterwards owned by Colonel Carter's sons, who derived their title by devise from their father. Subsequently it was carved into smaller estates, passing into the hands of the Burwells, Pages, Nelsons, and others, whose descendants still reside in Clarke county, and preserve the inimitable prestige of gentle birth, culture, and refinement possessed by their ancient sires—worthy scions of a noble stock.

The next grant of land in the Valley that can be relied upon was that made by the throne of England, in 1733, to one Jacob Stover, an enterprising German. This grant was not obtained by him without some trouble, for then a man was obliged to have a requisite number of families to settle upon it, which he did not possess. Being unable to give the governor of Virginia satisfactory evidence on this score, he passed across the waters to England, and to insure success informed the court that he had the requisite number of settlers. He accomplished this by giving his dogs, horses, cows, hogs, sheep, and mules human names, and succeeded in persuading the court to direct the governor to issue his grant for five thousand acres of land on the south fork of Gerandos (Shenandoah) river near Messinetto creek. On this ancient grant are some of the best farms in Page county, owned by descendants of the early settlers.

The land lying in Clarke county, next to Colonel Carter's original grant, is the next that we have any evidence of. This was a body of thirteen thousand acres, which was purchased by Ralph Wormly, prior to the Revolutionary war, at an auction sale. Wormly bought this when he was excited from several bottles of port wine, and when he became cool regretted it extremely, until General Washington consoled him by offering to take the purchase off his hands. It afterwards became a magnificent estate, and passed from his children's possession, reaching the ownership of the firm of Castleman & McCormick, Hierome L. Opie, Esq., Judge Richard E. Parker, and several others. This country about Bullskin, Long Marsh, and Spout Run was settled after the lands near the larger watercourses and the mountains, and lies in the immediate neighborhood of that inimitable, charming, and delightful spot over which the lovely young ladies of Berryville now tread.

The lands upon the south branch of Shenandoah, around about the western portions of Rockingham and Augusta, were originally granted to Lord Fairfax. This august personage was in England on a visit when one Howard arrived there from the Colony of Virginia with a glorious description of these lands along the south branch of the Shenandoah. His lordship immediately took up a grant of them, which at first he leased to certain persons, who, on account of the fertility of the soil, emigrated at once there.

About the year 1736 William Miller and Abraham Hite settled in the valley about Moorefield, and Miller, becoming somewhat dissatisfied when the Indian wars broke out, sold out his interest in five hundred acres of land, and all his horses, cattle, and stock for £25, and removed to the south fork of the Shenandoah river, near the spot where Front Royal now stands. Historically this is the first evidence we have of any settlement of Warren county. Soon afterwards others came in until the country around there was gradually settled and cleared up.

About 1740, John Lindsey and James Lindsey, two brothers, removed from a Northern State, and settled on the Long Marsh, between Bullskin and Berryville, in what was then the county of Frederick; and in 1743 Isaac Larue removed from New Jersey, settling on the same marsh. About this period Christopher Beeler removed and settled within two miles of Larue, while in 1744 Joseph Hampton and two sons came from the Eastern Shore of Maryland, and located on Buck Marsh, near Berryville, and dwelt the greater part of the year in a hollow tree. Finally enclosing a piece of land, they made a crop preparatory to the removal of their families. From every satisfactory source that we can gather, these were the first settlers in and about that portion of Clarke county around Berryville.

From the year 1744 the emigration into the Valley was very much increased, and, for those times, the country began to be tolerably thickly settled. People in the lower country, learning of the fertility of this lovely land, sought homes in it, and endeavored to make a permanent residence. As a great many of these settlers were from Pennsylvania, the Indians credited them with the virtues of the mild Quaker, John Penn, and for twenty years after the first settlement did not molest any of the whites. This enabled the settlers to clear lands, accumulate stock, and make arrangements for a permanent home, since, having been unmolested so long, they scarcely dreamed of any trouble with the Indians; but in this they were mistaken, as we shall now see.

In the year 1753 emisaries from the Indian tribes west of the Alleghanies invited the Indians in the valley to cross over the mountains and join them in Ohio. In 1754 the Indians, in response to this invitation, departed unexpectedly, and all left the country east of the Alleghany range. It has never been definitely stated why these red-skins departed west, but after a careful investigation upon the subject we are inclined to think that the Indians west of the Alleghanies were resisting the encroachments of the settlers over there, and desired assistance, for only a year or two after this invitation was extended the Indians in Shenandoah Valley, we hear of a long series of massacres and incursions on the part of the Indians west, beginning with the Draper's Meadows settlement in Montgomery, and not ending finally until the memorable battle of Point Pleasant. The year 1756 opened up by attacks from the Indians on the inhabitants of Shenandoah Valley, and from that time on we hear of numerous massacres on the part of the redskins, in attempting to destroy the settlements of the whites. This grew out of General Braddock's defeat by the French and Indians at Pittsburgh. The French had always instigated the Indians to resist the encroachments of the white settlers west, and the war between the French and English, which grew out of a squabble over territory, gave the Indians ample opportunities to harass the English; so, when Braddock was defeated in 1755 at Pittsburgh, the Indians, believing their friends (the French) to be invulnerable, began to attempt an extermination of the settlers and their homes. For ten years—from 1756 until 1766—there was a continual feudal warfare carried on by the Indians and whites, resulting in loss of life and destruction of property to both races, and the white settlers hailed with delight a cessation of hostilities in 1766, which lasted until 1774, when what was known as Lord Dunmore's war broke out, an account of which we have already given. After this latter war the Indians, with the exception of a few attacks, gradually disappeared, leaving the whites in undisturbed possession of the soil and their settlements.

Subsequent to hostilities with the Indians the people enjoyed tranquility and repose, and the country settled and increased with great rapidity as new settlers from many different quarters poured in. Some families of distinction came in from the lower country, who were the ancestors of the Washingtons, Willises, Throckmortons, and Whitings. Later on the Lewises took up their possessions, and the descendants of those old people still reside in a portion of Jefferson county and Clarke. The lands taken in the neighborhood of Long Marsh by the latter people are in the possession of Major H. L. D. Lewis, Colonel Washington Lewis, Mr. Edward Lewis, and others.

After the Revolutionary war, with which we are so familiar, the inhabitants of this country increased considerably, and for nearly one hundred years the entire land enjoyed universal peace—with the exception of the short war of 1812—and the Valley gradually became one of the most productive and advanced portions of Virginia. Great attention was paid to the cultivation of mind, heart, and manners, which gave the people decidedly a caste character, especially in the lower part of Warren and the county of Clarke. Living upon soils which produced everything that the wants of man could suggest, and that in the most abundant profusion, they became as independent and sturdy a race of people as could be found anywhere. As time rolled on and their means increased from the fatness of the land, they erected finer houses and paid more attention to the refinements and arts of life, until the whole fabric in a social way reached a high state of existence. Another thing which caused some parts of this valley to maintain a set distinct unto itself was the fact that, in a portion, clans, or relations, settled a particular country, and their descendants questioned the rights of outsiders to intrude themselves unless invited so to do. To give a faithful portrayal of these people who played such an important part in the subsequent development of the country, we cannot do better than quote the words of Mr. John Y. Page, who lived among them, and who is an intelligent, high-toned gentleman. He says:

"This portion of the Valley (Clarke county) was pretty well settled by a few family connections, especially in the southern part, in the neighborhood of Millwood. Under the will of Robert Carter, formerly known as 'King Carter,' of Lancaster county, Virginia, some fifty-one thousand acres of lands were divided among his sons, grandsons, and other relatives. Descended from these were the Carters, Burwells, Nelsons, Pages, and others, many of whom are still in the county, and some killed during the war. From this settlement grew a habit of country life which made the social feature of the county an admirable one in some respects. They did not care what they ate, or drank, or wore—the most prominent characteristic being an indifference to the future, with a determination to enjoy the present. Being all related or connected, they visited and mingled freely in every way—dropping in to dine, spend the night, or a day or two, without ceremony. A very sincere religious feeling prevailed of unquestioned faith, without an inquiry as to knowledge, showing itself principally among the females of the families, while men believed as much as their mothers and wives, but practiced it a great deal less. The result of all this was a society of families very exclusive among themselves, and thought by strangers to be two exclusive. This was the prevailing tone of the Lower Valley socially. Among the older people, the descendants of whom are still here, are the Lewises, Clagetts, Taylors, William P. Smiths, the Pages, Boyces, Wheats, Pendletons, Allens, Carters, Halls, Nelsons, Whitings, Burwells, Castlemans, McCormicks, Moores, and many others."

Mr. Page's clear-cut ideas are right, and his conception of the people in full keeping with their characters, manners, and customs, which even to this day retain odors of the old habits and charms which will never wear away. The marked difference between the people of this lower portion of the Valley and those residing upon the south fork of the Shenandoah, in Page, Rockingham, and Augusta counties, is completely elucidated by Mr. Page's account. Those in the upper part were settlers of German, Dutch, and Scotch-Irish extraction, who, being strangers, were different from the English colonist settlers below, and not so exclusive in the social bond formed among themselves. The good people of this lovely section, from one end of the Valley to the other, cultivated their estates, increased in every way, grew well off, and became an independent class, and were as happy on the whole as people could be, until the flames of a civil war devastated in a great measure their homes, and, after four years of fighting, left them like their forefathers, with nothing but the naked soil on which to contest the battles of life for a daily existence.

During the late war the Valley was a continuous battle-field for the contending armies in this section of Virginia, and very naturally so, too. The agricultural resources were extensive in every way, and foraging for supplies much easier here than elsewhere. At Antietam, in Maryland; Shepherdstown and Charlestown, in West Virginia; Berryville, Shenandoah, and Waynesboro, in Virginia, the artillery played, and human blood was shed regardless of consequences. It was in the county of Clarke that Mosby's force was raised, and they pursued their guerrilla warfare, keeping the Yankees in a continual turmoil. This hitherto peaceful country was laid bare, and when the Confederacy grounded arms at Appomattox, and Lee surrendered, these brave men returned to their devastated homes, with scarcely anything but the native soil, as we have previously said.

But this was a rich inheritance. Previously, from the counties of Augusta and Frederick had been taken Rockingham, Page, Warren, and Clarke, the country traversed by the Shenandoah Valley railroad. These, with Augusta, have no superior in climate or scenery. The winters are neither extremely cold nor the summers very hot, for the mountains not only protect from the chilling winter blasts, but furnish the cool nights so delightful in July and August. The average mean temperature campares favorably with the rest of the valley reaching from New York to East Tennessee, of which this is a part, and cyclones, storms, and tornadoes are rarely if ever known. The scenery all along the winding Shenandoah is grand in the extreme. Whether we take the rugged mountains in the upper part, or the level plateaus about Shendun, or the sweeping vistas around Luray, or the gently-rolling lands of Warren and Clarke, fringed by mountains, all are beautiful and capable of satisfying the taste of the most fastidious.

In every way that part of Augusta and Frederick from which was taken Rockingham, Page, Warren, and Clarke composed almost the fairest, if not the largest, part of those counties. The agricultural and mineral resources of this part of Shenandoah Valley, from Basic City to the West Virginia line, are as fine and varied as those of any county under the canopy of heaven. All of the cereals—wheat, corn, oats, barley, rye, and buckwheat—grow in profusion, while as grass lands they have no superior. The soil is of a chocolate loam, or red clay in most places, and is unexcelled in productive capacity. The average yield of wheat is from twenty to forty bushels per acre, and the planters fallow wheat and small grain after corn with impunity, which is a severe test as to character and quality of land. The lands are easily cultivated, and not steep enough to wash, being, generally speaking, of a rolling character. It is a great country for stock, and the horses of Shenandoah Valley command a premium on account of their superiority. Sheep-raising is a pursuit largely followed, and has proven highly remunerative, and the cattle are of a superior kind, especially for dairy purposes. The number of live stock in the counties of Clarke, Page, Warren, Rockingham, and Augusta are: 26,796 horses, 59,513 cattle, 27,102 sheep, and 42,683 hogs.

This section has the finest agricultural showing of any other in Virginia, and far exceeds the Southwest in this respect, or the Tidewater or Piedmont regions. When this wonderful section is in full bloom with its various productions, nature itself seems to blush at the profusion and wonder at her own handiwork. The great waving fields of corn, and wheat, and oats, and hay present a scene of agricultural wealth which it is almost impossible to describe—certainly not to be appreciated properly until seen. Surely, in all productions of the soil, Shenandoah Valley stands pre-eminently before any section that we know of or have ever seen.

In addition to the wealth which exists on the surface itself, the Valley is rich in hidden treasures but lately discovered, in speaking of which we allude to the mineral resources. These are found to be in large quantities, and in some places of most excellent quality. Iron, manganese, umber, ochre, brownstone, sandstone, fire-brick, and china-clay, limestone, and tin ore have been discovered all along the Valley, and pronounced superior, both as to quality and quantity. In days gone by, before the many mineral resources were developed at all, there were charcoal furnaces about. There is a remnant of one at Luray, on the north side of the town, which at one time was in blast. Another was at Milnes, but has been replaced by a superior coking furnace. And now new furnaces are being constructed in many places in the Valley to utilize these deposits of iron ore, and at no place that we know of can limestone for fluxing purposes be gotten so cheaply as in this valley. The construction of the Washington and Western railroad, now being surveyed and located, will throw the coal and coking regions of West Virginia right at Shenandoah Valley. The quality of the ores as analyzed are given, in order that every one may see exactly what is in each county. From McCreath's Mineral Wealth of Virginia we find that the ores from Clarke analyzed as follows, from ninety-two pieces taken from A. Mason Moore's property (Mineral Wealth, page 19):

Metallic iron	49.875
Phosphorus	.146
Silicious matter	11.430
Phosphorus in 100 parts iron	.292

This is a fair comparison of other analyses made in the same county.

In Warren county an analysis of eighty-five pieces taken from the Overall property, near the station of the same name, shows:

Metallic iron	56.375
Phosphorus	1.275
Silicious matter	1.890
Phosphorus in 100 parts iron	2.261

—(Mineral Wealth, page 21).

In Page county several analyses of various openings are given, from which we select an average sample. Mineral Wealth, page 23, shows, from an analysis of ore taken from Rust's property, one hundred and fifty-three pieces:

Metallic iron	50.950
Metallic manganese	1.455
Phosphorus	.442
Silicious matter	9.780
Phosphorus in 100 parts iron	.867

In Rockingham, from Wilmer and Jackson's property, the following is given, taken from one hundred and forty-five pieces of clean lump ore:

Metallic iron	50.450
Phosphorus	.217
Silicious matter	14.360
Phosphorus in 100 parts iron	.430

—(Mineral Wealth, page 33.)

In Augusta county, samples from the Cotopaxi Furnace property yielded on analysis (Mineral Wealth, page 40):

Metallic iron	49.400
Phosphorus	.062
Silicious matter	14.260
Phosphorus in 100 parts iron	.125

From the foregoing, it is not difficult to form an idea as to the quality of the ores. In speaking of this section as a point for manufacturing iron, the same work from which we have already quoted, on page 143, says, in allusion to the territory traversed by the Norfolk and Western and Shenandoah Valley railroads:

"The advantages which the territory traversed by your several lines of railroad offers to the iron master may be summed up in a few words: the ores are abundant and generally of good quality; they can be economically mined, for the country in many localities is broken up by numerous ravines, affording natural openings for mining operations; most of the deposits are within convenient distance of the railroads, with easy down grades; the water supply for either washing ore or for manufacturing purposes is ample and permanent at all seasons; limestone for fluxing purposes exists in unlimited quantities; coke of the finest quality for blast furnaces can now be obtained at a reasonable cost, and the railroad facilities for reaching markets in every direction are unusually good, thus forming a combination of favorable circumstances rarely equalled."

Nor are iron ores the only valuable mineral properties in this section. The Virginia Manganese Company, near the mouth of Turk's Gap, in the Blue Ridge, at Crimora, has the most valuable manganese mines that we know of, and the shipments run over a thousand tons per month at times. Near Marksville are the ochre mines belonging to the Oxford Ochre Company, which ships large quantities of this mineral. In May, 1886, the shipments amounted to one hundred and twenty tons, which shows the amount that is sold. The Virginia Fire-Brick and China-Clay Company are making over three thousand brick and washing about eight tons of china-clay *per diem*, and at the time this estimate was made the output was expected to be larger. In mineral resources the Valley is rich, and not completely developed as yet. The cabinet of minerals displayed at Basic City, Marksville, Luray, Front Royal, and the samples seen at Berryville, place the question at rest as to the ore-bearing territory of this rich agricultural country.

The actual cost of manufacturing iron in Shenandoah Valley has been practically known for some time, and we furnish a statement which was made for Andrew S. McCreath by L. S. Boyer, secretary of the Shenandoah Iron, Lumber, Mining and Manufacturing Company, in his official capacity. It is as follows:

COST OF MAKING IRON AT MILNES.

Ore, 2¼ tons at $2	$4 50
Coke, 1¼ tons at $4.20	5 25
Limestone	30
Labor	1 50
Incidentals	1 00
Total	$12 55

The companies at various places claim that iron can be manufactured cheaper than the above figures indicate, which may be true, because the freight upon coke and quality of ore, as well as cost of labor, might make some little difference; but this cost is nearly four dollars cheaper than any iron has ever been manufactured in Pennsylvania. Even in 1884, when the reduction in fuel and ore took place in that State, the cheapest estimated cost was $16.01 per ton. This difference necessarily gives the iron manufacturer a wonderful lever power in Virginia over the one in Pennsylvania. A simple glance at these facts must clearly demonstrate that Shenandoah Valley will put on the manufacturer's garb at no long future day, and draw the same wealth from the bowels of the earth which is yielded by its surface.

With these natural advantages, with the agricultural and mineral resources within its borders, we can readily perceive that the Valley has all that nature could bestow as a firm foundation for its future development. We cannot wonder that it recuperated rapidly from the effects of the war and improved, until 1881, when a progress commenced which has since caused people everywhere to turn their eyes towards this rich and lovely county.

CHAPTER II.

The Shenandoah Valley railroad—Organized in 1867—How constructed—Dates of construction of the various parts of the road—Completion to Waynesboro Junction—Tripartite agreement between the Shenandoah Valley railroad, the Norfolk and Western railroad, and the East Tennessee, Virginia and Georgia, which constituted the Virginia, Tennessee and Georgia Air Line—Issue of new mortgage by the Shenandoah Valley Railroad Company—Interest of the Norfolk and Western in this company — Receiver appointed — Purchase of this company by the Norfolk and Western—Some general remarks as to effect of this purchase upon Shenandoah Valley.

THE construction and completion of the Shenandoah Valley railroad was a new era for Shenandoah Valley, or at least that portion of it through which the road ran. Nearly all the towns along its line seemed to put on a new life, and grew larger from that date. Railroad facilities meant the establishment of industries, and as these were most likely to locate their plants at places where supplies and the like could be obtained, the values in property at the towns through which the road ran advanced in price. There is scarcely a town along the lines of this company that will not tell you that the first progress of any note occurring within their borders dated from the time of the construction of this road in their midst. We are sorry that a full history cannot be given, owing to the destruction of the records by fire at Charlestown, West Virginia, where the general offices were kept in its earlier days. Many accounts have been given concerning it by several persons, but in giving the corporate history of these concerns which have played so important a part in the development of the country, we desire to use their own reports and records, or only such extrinsic evidence as bears the truth intuitively upon its face.

This company was first organized on February 23, 1867, under the laws of Maryland, West Virginia, and Virginia, the

States which it traversed. Notwithstanding the fact that its organization dated back so early, twelve years elapsed before the first forty-two miles were constructed as far as Riverton; nor did this become completed until, in the year 1878 (the same year in which J. Dickinson Sergeant sent Roane the contract to sign concerning the New River railroad and options on mineral lands), Mr. Frederick J. Kimball became actively engaged in the construction of it. In December, 1879, the first part to Riverton was opened up and traffic begun over it; in September, 1880, seventy-nine miles more were finished, and on April 18, 1881, the line was completed as far as Waynesboro Junction. It is further known that the road was built partly by construction companies, partly by private individuals, and partly by the company itself.

In February, 1881, at the time that the Atlantic, Mississippi and Ohio railroad was purchased by Clarence H. Clark and *his associates*, there were some kind of relations existing between these gentlemen and the Shenandoah Valley Railroad Company, since in the first annual report, pages 12 and 13, we find the following announcement:

"The relations between the Norfolk and Western Railroad Company and the Shenandoah Valley Railroad Company contemplated at the time your road was purchased and reorganized are still kept in view, and negotiations are in progress looking to the consolidation and merger of the two corporations so soon as proper legislation can be had. Very favorable results are anticipated from the completion of the connections of the two roads at Roanoke Junction."

That these relations were of the most friendly character there can be no doubt, and the object of extending the Shenandoah Valley railroad on to Roanoke was to bring the mineral traffic from the New River railroad north, and to form a connection with the East Tennessee, Virginia and Georgia railroad. So in the latter part of September, 1881, a tripartite agreement was entered into between the three companies, which secured to these systems for a term of years a unified general management, and what is known as the Virginia, Tennessee and Georgia Air-Line burst into view. Work upon the Shenandoah Valley railroad was pushed forward, and in June, 1872, the line was completed to Roanoke, where it connected with the Norfolk and Western.

On the 15th day of February, 1882, a committee was appointed, by virtue of a resolution of the Board of Directors of the Norfolk and Western Railroad Company, to consider the relations existing between the two companies, and to make a report to the board as early as practicable upon a plan by which the purposes of the tripartite agreement and traffic contract of 1881 would be more effectually carried out. Under these instructions the committee proceeded to work, and pending their action, questions were raised by the Shenandoah Valley railroad as to the true intent and meaning of certain clauses in the traffic contract of September 27, 1881, respecting the establishment of freight rates and a division of the revenue derived from this joint arrangement. The Norfolk and Western Company, well knowing the advantages of an all-rail route *via* Hagerstown, and fearing this company as a competitor, determined to adjust every difference possible and get control of the road if practicable. Yet this must be done on the most advantageous basis for the Norfolk and Western Company, as is shown in their second annual report, page 21, which says:

"Whilst, therefore, in the development of new business your company would have *direct* advantages through the interchange of traffic between the two companies, *indirect* advantages almost equally important would accrue through the ability of your company to direct and control the distribution of through business in such a manner as will earn the most money for both companies."

The only possible means by which the distribution of through business could be controlled by the Norfolk and Western Railroad Company was by owning a majority of the shares of the Shenandoah Valley Company, so the result of the traffic-contract investigation by the committee was, the Shenandoah Valley railroad mortgaged its line for $2,500,000 for the purpose of finishing its road to connect with the Norfolk and Western railroad at Roanoke, and the former company subscribed for thirty thousand shares of the common stock of the latter, and paid this subscription with twenty thousand of its own shares of stock, virtually giving the Norfolk and Western the controlling interest in its thirty-seven thousand six hundred and seventy-four shares—the total capital stock of the Shenandoah Valley Railroad Company. In the annual report for 1883 the Norfolk and Western states, on page 25, that:

"The share value of the capital stock of the Shenandoah Valley Railroad Company is 36,962 shares, of the par value of 100 each, representing $3,696,200, of which 30,506 shares have been acquired by your company in accordance with the terms of the contract dated December 29, 1882, and referred to fully in the last annual report, and which were received in payment of subscriptions for 40,506 shares of the common stock of your company."

The Norfolk and Western now held a complete controlling share in the Shenandoah Valley railroad, giving the former the *indirect* advantages arising through the ability to direct and control the distribution of through business between the two companies—just what the committee deemed most advantageous for the interests of the Norfolk and Western. What was the actual cost to the Norfolk and Western Railroad Company to obtain this control? The second annual report of the Norfolk and Western railroad, page 25, after setting forth the traffic contract—the financial bargain and all—says:

"A contract on these terms was executed under the direction of your board on the 29th of December, 1882, and it is believed that the important advantages which it contemplates will be secured with but little, if any, actual cost to this company."

The report of the Shenandoah Valley railroad for the year 1883 was a very flattering one as to its condition, and so forth. In accordance with the terms of the contract the Norfolk and Western agreed to advance it two hundred thousand dollars per annum, and from this source and from the sale of its bonds the Shenandoah Valley Railroad Company was enabled, in addition to meeting all its fixed charges, to make many desirable improvements and pay for rolling stock urgently needed. Its net income was $192,257.58, and the prospects for another year much brighter. The result of its operations since it was opened on June, 1882, were mentioned as very flattering and encouraging.

But the year 1884 brought a different state of affairs, for the depression in business and want of traffic so reduced the income of the company at the end of the year 1884 that upon January 1, 1885, default was made in payment of the interest, and a like result in April and July. The Fidelity Insurance, Trust, and Safe-Deposit Company, of Philadelphia, being the trustee of a general mortgage issued to secure the indebtedness of the company, upon default in payment of its interest, filed its bill for the appointment of a receiver, which was done by order of court, and Sidney F. Tyler was appointed to that post, and duly took charge. The road was operated by the receiver until October, 1890, when, under decree of court, a sale was made, and the Norfolk and Western Railroad Company became the purchaser of the Shenandoah Valley Railroad Company for $7,100,000, with all its roadway, equipments, property, rights, and franchises. Although the company was in the hands of a receiver for five years, yet that did not affect the advantages derived from the construction and operation of it to the country through which it ran, and the towns along its lines continued to develop.

The purchase of the Shenandoah Valley railroad by the Norfolk and Western has already had a good effect along the line of the former company. The developing policy of the Norfolk and Western, and its interest in the general welfare and progress of the towns and country along its route, cause these to hail its advent with delight, and there was a general spirit of joy pervading Shenandoah Valley when it was announced that the road through the Valley had been purchased by the Norfolk and Western. Already many enterprises are springing up and industries coming in, feeling a spirit of confidence in their future since this company, which has done so much materially for the Southwest, has charge. The connection of the Washington and Western railroad—now being located—with the Shenandoah Valley branch in this country not only secures a long-coveted entrance into Washington by the Norfolk and Western railroad, but will give a new impetus to the whole country, and be of infinite advantage to the connecting point. The charter of the former road further gives power and authority to this company to locate, construct, and equip a railroad from some point on the Shenandoah Valley railroad into the coal regions of West Virginia, which road will be of more importance to the iron interests of the Valley than can be well calculated, as it will place the coking fields almost at the feet of Shenandoah Valley. In all of these undertakings the people will be glad to know that the Norfolk and Western is the prime moving power, so great is its effect upon the country through which it passes.

The whole country traversed by the Shenandoah branch of the Norfolk and Western company is one capable of the highest state of development. The road starts from Hagerstown, Maryland, connecting there with the Cumberland Valley road for Philadelphia and points North, and with the Western Maryland for Baltimore. Coming south, it passes the lovely rich valley bordering the Potomac; crossing into West Virginia, it connects with the main line of the Baltimore and Ohio at Shenandoah Junction, pursuing then its line through the charming Shenandoah Valley by Charlestown, Berryville, Front Royal, Luray, Shenandoah, and Basic City, terminating its route at Roanoke city, a distance of 239.3 miles through as productive and beautiful a country as ever the sun shone upon. This road has been most beneficial in its results towards developing the whole section, and all along the line people acknowledge it.

Notwithstanding the fact that the road was placed in the hands of a receiver, it has been a great success, and has certainly been conducted well under the management of D. W. Flickwir, superintendent, and O. Howard Royer, general passenger and freight agent. Its equipment is good and the service all that could be desired. Had the road been opened up in the past four years, and not when it was—during a period of depression—it would never have passed into the hands of a receiver, but would have met its liabilities promptly. Within the past four years there has been a marvellous increase in the passenger and freight traffic. There is no doubt that it has played a very important part in not only the development of Shenandoah Valley, but Southwest Virginia as well.

CHAPTER III.

Effect of the wonderful Caverns of Luray upon Shenandoah Valley—Luray—Derivation of its name—Its gradual growth—Discovery of the caverns by B. P. Stebbins, Andrew J. Campbell, and W. B. Campbell—Purchase of Cave Hill by these parties—Litigation over the same—Decision of the supreme court against the purchasers—Sale of the property to a Northern syndicate—Description of the caverns—Advent of Shenandoah Valley railroad—The Defoard tannery—Rapid growth of Luray—The Valley Land and Improvement Company—Manufactories and industries of the town—Population, schools, and churches—Luray Inn—General remarks upon the place.

THE discovery and opening up of the Caverns of Luray and the Grottoes of the Shenandoah had such a marked effect upon the development of Shenandoah Valley that they may be assigned as one of the causes of its recent growth. In giving an account of these wonderful underground passages, we deem it but just to also give a sketch of the town of Luray, now one of the most important points along the line of the Shenandoah Valley railroad, or in this charming valley of which we have been writing.

Luray is situated directly on this railroad, in Page county, one hundred and fifty miles from Roanoke and eighty-nine from Hagerstown, Maryland, in the middle of the charming Luray Valley, celebrated for its beauty of scenery, salubrious climate, rich agricultural lands, and mineral resources. Ever since the formation of the county of Page, in 1831, the place has been the county-seat, and is an old town. The general impression that it takes its name from Lorraine, a French settler, is erroneous, for, after a patient investigation, the extrinsic evidence, as well as internal facts, substantiate the position taken by Judge Alexander Y. Brand, who states that its name was taken from that of one Lewis Ramey. This latter person was one of the oldest settlers in the county, and the log cabin in which he resided was located at what is now the corner of

Main and Court streets. He was called Lew Ramey; then, for contraction, was spoken of as Lew Ray, from which source of sound the name of Luray is undoubtedly derived.

From 1831 the town, as a county-seat and a kind of trading centre for the valley of its name, gradually increased, deriving its support from the surrounding agricultural productions and profits from the sale of its wares, until, in 1869, the place had some five hundred people. From this on the progress was still scarcely perceptible; for in 1878, almost ten years afterwards, there were only about six hundred and forty-two people, pursuing the even tenor of their way, not dreaming of the wonderful revolution through which their quiet place would go in the next succeeding ten years. On August 13, 1878, the wonderful caverns were discovered, which subsequently played such an important part in this whole section of country by drawing visitors from all parts of the country and giving everything an impetus never before known at Luray.

It was due to the efforts of B. P. Stebbins, Andrew W. Campbell, and W. B. Campbell that the caverns were first discovered. B. P. Stebbins, a photographer, who came to Luray in 1878, from certain external indications became satisfied that caverns were somewhere in the vicinity, and persuaded the Campbells to join him in the search. This "cave company," as it was jocularly termed, was subject to much ridicule from the people of the town. They were called "cave rats" and "searchers after mares' nests"; but, nothing daunted, they continued their explorations until, on the date above mentioned, their labors were crowned with success, and A. J. Campbell was lowered by means of a rope into what is known now as Entrance Hall. This discovery was fully appreciated by the parties, for that night they returned with candles and explored Stebbins Avenue, Entrance Hall, and Entrance Avenue as far as the lake, which then prevented a farther insight into the most wonderful parts, which were first seen after the lake was drained. At the very time of this discovery proceedings were pending in the circuit court of Page by creditors against the bankrupt estate of Samuel Bueracher, and, in 1878, Cave Hill, containing twenty-eight and one-half acres, was sold, and Messrs. Stebbins and Campbell became the purchasers at a price considered extremely high for the land. Their discovery had been not only concealed, but every means to prevent discovery used, by placing brush, earth, and rubbish over the entrance of this cavern after their exploration that night. A few days subsequently, however, the town was startled and astonished at the news that a wonderful cave had been found. The commotion and excitement was intense, and on learning the nature and value of the property sold the relatives of the original owners instituted suit for its recovery. The lower court sustained the sale to Stebbins and the Campbells; but, in 1881, the supreme court set it aside on the ground of fraud, and there was another sale, at which W. T. Briedler, a son-in-law of Samuel Bueracher, purchased the property, afterwards disposing of it to the Luray Cave and Hotel Company, a syndicate from Philadelphia. From this on Luray began to improve, when the caverns were opened up and the inn erected, which has won since such an enviable reputation as a hostelry.

Owing to the importance of these caverns a description of them may not be amiss, for it is acknowledged by all that in the way of cave scenery they are fully equal to the Grottoes of the Shenandoah, and superior to any other known underground passages. Subterraneous passages are one thing, but it is quite another to have them beautifully and richly decorated with exquisitely formed growths of stalactites and stalagmites, composing columns, figures, folds, draperies, and statues, illustrating the fact that caves are common anywhere, but beautiful caverns rare. Large caverns are found in limestone regions only, and a cave is but an underground valley caused by erosion—a gorge or ravine roofed over with stone—a repetition under a lightless sky of limestone formations above the earth on its surface. Luray Caverns are a system of large ravines, such as Entrance Hall, Entrance and Stonewall avenues, Pluto's Chasm, Giant's Hall and its ramifications, which are the dominating lines.

As we have stated, these cavities are formed by erosion. With carbonic acid as an active agent, and water as a carrier, we are able to account for the disappearance of strata, however thick either above or below ground. Above, the result is a lowering of the general level and formation of valleys, where causes favor the disintegration of stone. " Hard " water flows away, and a clay soil is left behind. Below ground, the result is a cave, if there be a vertical fissure in the strata through which the water charged with carbonic acid makes its descent. In course of time these fissures are worn larger, and the water entering forms pools, which by and by causes disintegration of the softer horizontal strata with which it comes in contact, and, finding an exit at last, bears away the minerals little by little, leaving the clay behind to cause the adventurous cave-hunter no end of annoyance. Wherefore, it is not incorrect to assert that a cave is a fissure widened by the combined action of carbonic acid and water disintegrating and carrying away the softer strata around. But how about the lovely cave formations which appear so weird and sublime that it is but natural to suppose they were made by hobgoblins or ghosts, or some supernatural agency? Nature created them, too, but from a mere view of them it appears as if she not only set aside her own code of laws, but defied those of all gravitation as well. The folds and drapery; the figures, some lovely, some grotesque; the curtains, frozen cascades, columns, shields, fish, and many other representations are the result of the stalactite formations on the roof and the stalagmite on the floor of the cavity, with the lateral or helictite growth from the sides. These come together in every imaginable shape and form, producing pictures of beauty and sublimity impossible to conceive unless seen. These stalactites are made from the water percolating through strata of limestone above, which, being charged with carbonic acid, on reaching the ceiling evaporates, leaving the carbon of lime, which, on account of the continued dripping of the water, gradually forms the hanging stalactite. At first this has a minute tube through which the water trickles, but which becomes closed after a while from deposits of carbon of lime; then the water drips down on the outside of this formation, leaving the same deposits we have named, becoming in the course of ages much larger. The drops of water which percolate with force enough to leave the ceiling reach the floor and build up the stalagmite, which often joins the stalactite above, forming the columns and drapery which we see. Some of these formations are white and others of a brown color, which difference some geologists explain by stating that age causes the discoloration; but this theory will not do, for there are stalactites and helictites scarcely half an inch long which are brown, proving that age has nothing to do with it. The difference in color comes from the fact that when the water percolates through the pure limestone untouched by oxide of iron or clay, the pure carbon of lime is made, which is perfectly white. Whether we visit Entrance Hall, the Amphitheatre, the Fish Market, Elfin Ramble, Pluto's Chasm, the Crystal Spring, the Mermaid, the Cascade, the Ladies' Toilet Table, Giants' Hall, Proserpine's Column, the Grotto of Oberon, the Bridal Chamber, the Fallen Column, the Cathedral, the Organ, the Ball-Room, and other points of interest in the Caverns of Luray, we find everywhere these beautiful, exquisite, and supernatural formations which cause one to feel as if he was in the realms of ghosts, gnomes, and fairies, who flee when the flood of brilliant electric light is poured into this grand region. To go through these caverns is well worth a trip across the Atlantic ocean. The entrance to them is but a short distance from the inn, and conveyances are always on hand to carry visitors over. Good, stout shoes are all that is needed in the way of foot-gear, and no extra raps, as the temperature is always pleasant and the same.

The discovery of these caverns and the advent of the Shenandoah Valley railroad gave the town of Luray an impetus that stimulated the place into immediate growth almost. In September, 1881, the inn was constructed, and cement walks and electric lights placed in the caverns, and the continued increasing number of visitors caused Luray to be known from home, and its many attractions, natural advantages, and agricultural resources led people to look at the town in other lights than as the resort for visitors to the caverns. The timber district around drew in a manufacturing plant, which is the largest of any that we know of in this section, or in Southwest Virginia, except the Roanoke Machine Works. We allude to Defoard's huge bark-grinding company and tannery combined, which has a capital of $800,000 employed in its operations, and works about two hundred and fifty men in the tannery and bark works also. The pay-roll amounts to some $40,000 per month, a greater part of which is spent in the town. The result of this was, the place grew rapidly, and with other plants that came the town increased to about twenty-five hundred people by the year 1888 or early in 1890. It became also quite a centre for education, several schools being located there.

While Luray was improving by reason of the resources we have named, others began to be developed in the vicinity of the town in the shape of a variety of minerals, such as iron ore, zinc, lead, ochre, slate, and copper, samples of which are in the cabinet of minerals belonging to the development company there. Owing to the naturally fine agricultural resources and the varieties of minerals found, an organization was formed in 1890 for the development of these resources, as well as those of the place, called the Valley Land and Improvement Company, with an authorized capital stock of $2,000,000, a great deal of which was at once taken, and D. F. Kagey, from one of the oldest families in the county, was made president, with C. G. Marshall, from Uniontown, Pa., as vice-president and general manager. This company purchased the caverns, inn, and all the land surrounding the town, and considerable bodies of fine timber and mineral lands in addition. This concern inaugurated a spirit of material progress for the place which resulted in marked improvement almost immediately. Several valuable manufacturing plants were secured through the patriotism and public-spirited policy of the company that enhanced the values in Luray at once. The financiering qualities of D. F. Kagey, with C. G. Marshall's knowledge of minerals and ores gained in Pennsylvania, inspired a confidence in the public which greatly assisted the company in carrying out its various undertakings for the benefit of Luray. Now the place is quite a manufacturing centre, with its tannery, Luray Manufacturing Company, wagon works, flouring mills, cigar factory, and several other minor undertakings. Commercially, the town is upon a good basis, having a trade that has always branched out very considerably into the surrounding country, and every possible care is taken by the merchants to foster the same.

The policy of the Valley Land and Improvement Company is not only a liberal one, but very conservative where the interests of the town are concerned. C. G. Marshall's wrestles with miners in Pennsylvania, among whom he battled, not only gave him a good physical training, but placed ideas in his head of the fitness and conservativeness of men and things which have been of immense value in conducting the affairs of the company. While he is willing always to give every possible inducement to industries, in the way of subscription, donation of lots and free sites, he is not going to start an enterprise, place an outsider at the head of it, and say: "Look what we have brought in!"

The result is, what Luray has it has, and if employees and pay-rolls are taken as an evidence of manufacturing power, we know of no place superior to Luray on the line of this railroad. The company has some two thousand five hundred acres in town lots and eight thousand acres in mineral lands, which sooner or later will be the foundation of considerable manufacturing power at this place.

The Mountain Park Springs Company, headed by Walter Campbell and Judge Alexander Y. Brand, is not less unique than worthy in the purpose of its organization. The concern has a capital stock of $50,000, and has purchased a lovely mountain site not far from Luray, where a neat, commodious hotel will be erected, with a number of cottages, for the purpose of furnishing a summer resort to people of limited means who are not able to pay the higher prices. All success should attend every undertaking inaugurated to relieve the ills of humanity, whether of a mental, moral, physical, or pecuniary nature. No man is more capable of conducting the enterprise properly than Judge Brand, a gentleman of humane temperament, genial, kind manners, and a fund of anecdote and pleasantry only acquired by having seen much of humanity through the glasses of kindness of heart and charity which so few people wear in this day and generation. We cannot doubt that the liberal support which this company will have will make it a complete success.

The population of Luray amounts to about 2,500 people—may be more now—and is composed of a fine class of upright, sober, and, in the main, refined people. The influence of the schools over the town is easily seen, and some artistic talent resides in and around Luray, which is being highly cultivated. The schools, of which there are several here, advance the town in every way, for many of the pupils are boarders from a distance, and their means are more or less expended in Luray. The Von Bara College is a good institution, capable of accommodating some seventy or eighty pupils, and is always filled. It is under the management of J. I. Miller, a gentleman of varied experience and much culture. The Luray Female Institute for young ladies, on account of the homelike appearance and neatness of the school, the sweet, airy, pleasant rooms, often filled with flowers, the unity existing among the pupils and teachers, the high grade of its curriculum and scholarship, the refined, honorable treatment given the pupils and ideas of honor instilled in them, is one of the best places for the training and education of female minds and character that we know of. From high intellectual cultivation to Christianity is but a step, and, therefore, Luray, with the influence of such schools as Mr. Miller's and Professor Hargrove's, is a church-going, religious place. The Episcopal, Presbyterian, Lutheran, Methodist, and Baptist all have their religious houses, where divine worship is held every Sabbath, and the attendance invariably good.

It would not be justice to Luray to close this sketch without some description of the inn there under the incomparable management of Mr. Freeman, which has done much towards the development of the town and given so many strangers a pleasant, never-to-be-forgotten impression of Shenandoah Valley. Whether we take the inn from the railroad, or glance at it from the town, the eye meets a view which satisfies every craving of the human sense in the way of sight, taste, and beauty. It is situated upon an eminence approached by a well-laid walkway, amid soft, cool-looking grass turf, flower *parterres*, shrubbery, and rare plants. The building is constructed in Queen Anne style, the lower portion being of stone and the upper part of ornamental wood work, shingled down to the stone. An annex has been added, giving this structure accommodation for four hundred people, while a vine-covered piazza fronts the entire length. The appointments, cuisine, and service are all that can be desired, and everything is conducted on a homelike principle which robs the entire establishment of that sting of hotel publicity so often unbearable. All of the surroundings, from the pages seated in the office to the damask curtains, suggest ease, comfort, refinement, and culture, and the very acme of human existence physically can be obtained at this charming retreat, while socially it is always delightful, from the artistic touches of Colonel Lee's sketching pencil to the young ladies who waltz in the air of Luray Inn, always ladened with culture and elegance. It is a credit to the place and a delight to visitors who come in quest of pleasure.

Taking the place as a whole, with its many advantages and resources—both in an agricultural and mineral sense—its wonderful caverns, its scenery and admirable climate, its educational facilities and Christian principles, its beautiful surrounding country, we feel safe in saying that its future as the "Saratoga of the South" and a manufacturing town can scarcely be controverted, although by some enemies it may be denied.

CHAPTER IV.

Shenandoah—Formerly Milnes—Centre of a mineral region—Some of its advantages—The railroad shops—An iron-manufacturing point—The furnaces—Its advantages as a divisional point—The Shenandoah Land and Improvement Company—Capitalists connected with it—Something as to the future of the place—The Grottoes of the Shenandoah—Weyer's Cave—Fountain's Cave—Madison's Cave—The place now called Shendun—The Grottoes Company—Jed. Hotchkiss—Improvements made there—Its future as a business centre and summer resort.

GOING south from Luray we pass several stations, and after travelling some sixteen miles reach Shenandoah, a divisional point between Hagerstown and Roanoke, where shops of the company, as well as divisional offices, are located. This place lies in Page county, almost on the borders of Rockingham, and is one hundred and seven miles south of Hagerstown, and one hundred and thirty-two miles from Roanoke. It is located in a fine agricultural region, and surrounded by bodies of unusually valuable timbered lands. Formerly the town was called Milnes, taking its name from the Milnes who was at one time actively connected with the construction of the Shenandoah Valley railroad. The town is situated in one of the finest mineral regions in the Valley, and for a number of years has been an iron-manufacturing place, formerly engaged in making iron when its charcoal furnace was in blast. The ores (iron), of which we have already given an analysis, are remarkably fine, and from these banks the charcoal furnace drew its supply, as well as the coke furnace completed seven or eight years ago.

The advantages which Shenandoah has are manifest in every way. Immediately adjacent to it are immense tracts of land known to be very rich in iron, manganese, copper, and lead ores of the best character, together with asbestos, slates, ochres, fire-clays, and limestone of the best quality. Vast bodies of the best timber lands are here, and furnish in almost endless quantity the very best of oak, hickory, poplar, ash, maple, walnut, birch, chestnut, and pine, which answer equally as well for manufacturing as for decorative purposes; and near here is also found an abundance of bark for tanning purposes, thousands of tons being shipped annually within a radius of five miles from around Shenandoah. On account of which advantages in the way of timber it can be readily seen that a better point could not be selected for manufactories of various kinds of woodenware. A finer agricultural region from which a city could draw its supplies does not exist than that around this place, for the lands are noted for their versatility of productions, as well as rich productiveness. And not the least of Shenandoah's advantages is the prospect of the place being at no great future day a railroad centre. The terminus of the Washington and Western railroad will doubtless be here, while the road projected from Ceredo to Quantico is most certain to pass this way. If such reasonable hopes are fulfilled, then Shenandoah can point with pride to her northern, southern, eastern, and western outlets.

The fact that Shenandoah was made a divisional point, and the shops and round-houses erected there, was the cause of the growth of Milnes, afterwards called Shenandoah. As the railroad has some permanent interest at this point, it is but natural that they will do all in their power to promote the interest of the place and enhance its value in every way. Already these shops have been long in operation, and employ a large force of hands in the repairing of engines and on the yard, while the employees in the offices are there, too, both going far towards swelling the pay-roll to that amount which is doubtless of great assistance to the town. It is further claimed, too, by the people of Shenandoah that these shops will be enlarged now that the Norfolk and Western Railroad Company has gained possession of the Shenandoah Valley railroad—a claim which is not without hope and reason.

For some years past this place has been quite an iron-manufacturing point. The Shenandoah Iron Works had some reputation even before the erection of the Gem furnace, which uses coke instead of charcoal. The former iron works consisted of a charcoal blast furnace with a stack 33x8½, with Player hot-blast attachment, a forge and refinery, all of which had the capacity to turn out some sixty tons a week of warm-blast charcoal iron, which was worked up into blooms at the company's forge. These works were situated about five miles from the station on Naked creek, at the end of the branch road from Shenandoah. Prior to 1883 the new coke furnace known as the "Gem," with a 70x16 stack, and a producing capacity of seventy to eighty tons of iron *per diem*, was built, and during the years of 1883 and 1884, up to February, its output was 16,585 tons of foundry and forge iron. The above was really the product of a ten months' run, as two months were taken in repairing the old hot-blast stoves. The iron from these works has been shipped to Harrisburg, Philadelphia, and Baltimore markets, and gave universal satisfaction on account of its purity and character. The following analysis of a bloom fully substantiates this claim:

```
Carbon . . . . . . . . . . . . . . . . . . . . . . . . . .  .042
Silicon . . . . . . . . . . . . . . . . . . . . . . . . . .  .008
Sulphur . . . . . . . . . . . . . . . . . . . . . . . . .  .001
Phosphorus . . . . . . . . . . . . . . . . . . . . . .  .074
Manganese . . . . . . . . . . . . . . . . . . . . . . .  .003
Iron by difference . . . . . . . . . . . . . . . . . . 99.872
```

The advantages derived by the place from being a divisional point can be readily appreciated. In the first place it caused the erection of the shops there, and brought in a certain number of people whose interests became more or less identified with the place. The natural development and increase of every kind of resource in this wonderful country will necessarily create a demand for increased railway facilities, which upon its face means an enlargement of the railroad plant there. The capitalists and officials of the railroad company being interested, have taken stock in the future of the place, and the result was that on May 9, 1890, a development company was organized which having already a good nucleus for a town proceeded to develop it.

The Shenandoah Land and Improvement Company, organized with a capital stock of $300,000, has C. Powell Nolan as president and J. F. Wheelwright as secretary. The formation of this developing scheme is fraught with more than ordinary meaning, on account of the persons who are interested in it. These men are: F. J. Kimball, president of the Norfolk and Western Railroad Company; Jas. Sands, general manager of the same; D. W. Flickwir, superintendent of the Shenandoah Valley Railroad Company; Mr. McDowell, Mr. Armes, Mr. Robinson, Clarence H. Clark, and P. L. Terry. There is no doubt of the fact that these gentlemen have it in their power to either make or unmake towns at present, and if they are greatly interested in Shenandoah then the natural and logical consequence is that it will soon grow beyond the dimensions of a town. This company, which has some seven hundred acres of land in and adjacent to the place, is offering every possible inducement to manufacturers to locate, and have some lovely residence sites situated on a commanding, rolling eminence. The business and manufacturing lots, which are donated free, lie upon the river, which is capable of furnishing all necessary water power. Through the ingenuity of the company the manufacturing plants which locate there are exempt from all municipal taxation, and a perfect system of gas and water works has been inaugurated, without which every town is more or less imperfect. Every conservative, prudent step possible is being taken by this company for the future development of the place.

The outlook for the place is undoubtedly bright. The furnace company intends enlarging its plant, and already a payroll of $20,000 is monthly distributed among the railroad employees and furnace men, the latter of whom, including the quarrying men, now make some three hundred and fifty employees, who, together with their families and other citizens, number some eighteen hundred people, and may be more.

On the most careful, painstaking grounds, one would not err in predicting that Shenandoah will in course of time become a city of no small dimensions.

Grottoes of the Shenandoah.

Leaving Shenandoah, and proceeding southward again, we pass Elkton and Port Republic. At the latter place, in June, 1862, one of the hardest-fought battles took place that was engaged in during the war, and of which General Jackson said: "The dead seemed to be more numerous than the living." Two miles south of this place we come to the most beautiful spot in all Shenandoah Valley—Shendun, or what was formerly called the "Grottoes of the Shenandoah," which really means Weyer's, Fountain's, and Madison's caves.

The town of Shendun, comparatively speaking, is a new place, and occupies that broad, sweeping plateau south of Port Republic. The natural location of the place is beautiful in the extreme. The level plane, stretching away for miles to the river on one hand and the mountains on the other, presents a site for a city as perfect as heart could desire; the blue outline of the mountains, looking north, with the green tint of those to the west, give a relief to the monotony of the plane without infringing upon its beauty; while the whole view presents a panorama of scenic loveliness that is almost indescribable, yet so pleasingly perceptible to the sense of sight. The stationhouse, hotel, and even *real estate offices*, seem to be inoculated with this beauty, and look differently from other buildings. The walk stretching away to the footbridge across the winding Shenandoah to the mountain containing the caverns looks like the footpath of fairies, who wend their way back and forth between the broad, lovely plateau and the weird, grand scenery underground; while the road ascending to the entrance of Weyer's Cave reflects the white and blue tints of cave marble and limestone. The eye never grows tired of resting upon this view, which is as startling and sublime after it has been seen for a dozen times as when first gazed upon.

The Grottoes of the Shenandoah would make Shendun a

place of resort and residence if there was not another attractive feature connected with the place. Already they have been instrumental in drawing thousands of people to the town, and will continue to increase in number as the beauty and grandeur of the caverns are made known. In many respects they are superior in cave scenery to any others that we have ever seen or heard of. While the Caverns of Luray are larger than these, and while the stalactites and stalagmites of the former are on a more massive scale than those of the latter, yet in Weyer's Cave there is a delicacy of texture in the formations and a purity in the whiteness of the carbon of lime which Luray does not possess. In passing through many of the apartments in Weyer's Cave we imagine that a class of elfins, fairies, and gnomes created these lovely, delicate draperies and folds, whose artistic touch was much more refined and cultured than those who carved the heavier but grander figures of Luray. From the entrance to the Pantheon, in passing through the Sentinel Chamber, Solomon's Temple, the Tapestried Chamber, the Armory, the Ball-room, the Senate Chamber, Robbers' Cave, Cathedral Hall, Lady Washington's Hall, Iceberg Hall, Glacier Hall, the Bridal Chamber, the Garden of Eden, the Cañons, the Pantheon, the scenery is exquisitely beautiful, from the heavily suspended shields to the delicately white folds of the drapery. One visit serves but to bewilder, two to delight, three to intoxicate, and half a dozen to take in or understand one-half of nature's wonders buried beneath the rugged soil of the overhanging mountain. And when you visit Weyer's Cave put yourself under Mr. Mohler's care, whose knowledge and ingenuity in unwinding the cause of these curious formations is beyond that of any geologist that has ever explained yet. Some of these apartments are wonderfully natural. Take the Bridal Chamber. This is about 60x40 and has numerous fissures opening into darkness all around. The old Tuck Comb is made of a stalagmite, while the Bridal Veil, hanging almost to the floor, is a stalactite of the most curious form and delicacy. Both comb and veil are natural, and have that appearance which impresses one as exquisite pieces of carving. To the left of the veil is a piece of statuary on a pedestal some six feet square, which is unique in appearance, while in front of the comb and veil is a couch with the recumbent figure of the bride resting peacefully, making the whole very natural in every way.

Nor is the Tapestried Chamber less remarkable. It is lovely in the extreme. The size is about 100x50 feet, and has every variety of formation, from the thinnest fold and drapery to the largest column. The fringed canopy hanging from the ceiling is one of the most peculiar sights one meets with, the upper fringe being white, while the lower is dark. Curtains and draperies hang midway between the ceiling and floor, in every conceivable variety of folds, from the most delicate wafer to the thickness of an inch. There is a hanging formation in this apartment like a chandelier with electric lights upon it, while in the shaded darkness of the distance folds of drapery and curtains can be seen until they fade away into unfathomable blackness. Here, on one side, is a perfectly-shaped stage-curtain, about eighteen feet high and twelve feet wide, the lower part being looped and drawn aside, while the dark shadows in the background distinctly recall to mind an unlighted stage.

One of the most unique and inexplicable passages among these wonders is the Armory. Ajax's shield is as perfect a representation of the real article as if it had been carved. It does not hang perpendicularly from the ceiling, but juts out at an angle of forty-five degrees. It is about five feet long and three and a half wide, with an edge about a quarter of an inch in thickness, while the base is some four inches. This peculiar freak, in its lateral extension straight out, without support, defies all laws of gravitation, and causes us to wonder how many mischievous elfins it took to play such a prank with nature. In this armory is a column some three feet high, leaning northward at an angle of some thirty-two and a half degrees, the solution of which is that this leaning was produced by the floor lowering itself. The cascade of frozen icicles, of purest white, presents another interesting feature in this apartment which is well worth seeing.

From beginning to end of this whole cavern the same brilliant, incomparable scenery is presented, and when we reach Cathedrall Hall, with its perfect representation of priest and altar, our admiration turns to awe, and we wonder why the Supreme Being should ever have given his handiwork to the creation of such things if, as the Protestants say, in them lie eternal damnation. The electric lights shining upon the altar are exact reproductions of the candles, and the statue in front the living image of a priest in his vestments ready for high mass. This hall eclipses anything in the way of cave scenery that is imaginable, and is some two hundred feet in length by forty in width.

These chambers, in and out, with their beautiful decorative hangings, are well worth a trip across the continent to see; and Fountain's Cave, just opened up, is equally as weird and sublime in scenery. Near here is Madison's Cave, of which Thomas Jefferson made a diagram, and which is far inferior to the other two in the way of cave scenery. Throughout Weyer's Cave the floor is perfectly dry and the temperature delightful; nor do we know of any spot in which two or three days can be spent with so much benefit and pleasure as in this place.

In addition to these beautiful natural productions in the way of over and underground scenery, Shendun has other resources, which are being developed and opened up by the capital and energy of the best citizens in the land, among whom may be mentioned Jed. Hotchkiss, the Catletts, the Bells, J. H. Bramwell, A. D. Wright, and others. In May, 1890, the Grottoes Company was organized with a capital stock of $3,000,000, with Jed. Hotchkiss as president. This gentleman is better known as the author of the "Virginias" and other productions, which, on account of their statistical information and topographical descriptions, have not only given him an enviable reputation, but conferred a positive benefit upon Virginia. He has made all this section a particular study, and understands the variety of resources and geological formations of the country with a minuteness almost puzzling. Mainly through his instrumentality the company was formed and purchased some thirty thousand acres of land, including mineral and timber, city site, and farm and park lands, lying within a boundary surrounding Shendun, formerly the Grottoes of the Shenandoah. The analyses made by Andrew S. McCreath, in his "Mineral Wealth of Virginia," from samples of ore gotten from this property, yielded from 43.700 to 46.200 per cent. of metallic iron; 0.124 to 0.242 of phosphorus. There are two grades of this ore, the lower being a red kidney ore found in a separate stratum, while the larger proportion of it is a rich limonite that, properly sorted, can be counted on for 50 per cent. of metallic iron. This company owns the Mount Vernon Iron-Works property, the great ore ranges of the Blue Ridge, and vast bodies of the finest timber lands in that section of the country. About one hundred and eighty blocks of city lots have been laid off by the company, located on the lovely plateau to which we have already alluded.

The result of this energy and capital has already impressed itself upon the place, for buildings and business plants are springing up all around. The Grottoes Hotel, kept by A. D. Wright, one of the most enterprising gentlemen in those parts, is a gem in every way, with appointments, *cuisine*, and a service second to none. A large plumbing concern, brick manufactories, and a sash, door, and blind factory have secured locations there, while stores, residences, and other buildings are going up, and although the place is but ten months old there is a progress and development that is wonderful in every way. The samples of ore on exhibition which were taken from the company's property show a vast resource, so far as minerals are concerned. The company has also matured plans for the erection of a large hotel on a commanding eminence overlooking the extensive plane, and which will be of great advantage to Shendun in every way; but it will never be kept better than Wright's.

From the agricultural and mineral resources surrounding this place it must be seen that it will become a business centre; yet so great are its facilities for a summer resort and a Mecca for pleasure-seekers, that the latter will have that just preference to which it is entitled, and which will necessarily become a source of great revenue to the company and Shendun itself. There is no place in Shenandoah Valley so fitted to make a town of this kind as the already famous Grottoes of the Shenandoah. They have already played a most material part in the development of the Valley by being the instrument of its introduction to thousands of people who would never have seen it except for the wide reputation spread abroad of their beauty and weird scenery.

CHAPTER V.

Clarke county—Date of formation—Its resources—Population and class of people—Berryville, the county-seat (formerly known as Battletown)—Growth of the place since the advent of the Shenandoah Valley railroad—The inhabitants of the place—Churches, schools, and social status—Many facilities and advantages of the town—Formation of the Berryville Land and Improvement Company—Some general remarks upon the town.

CLARKE county occupies part of the northern portion of Shenandoah Valley, and is second to none in Virginia for fertility of soil, healthfulness of climate, and fine agricultural resources. It was cut off from Frederick in the year 1835, and was duly organized in 1836. The soil is generally very rich, of a limestone character, and is noted for its productiveness as to cereals—wheat particularly. The great bulk of land lying west of Shenandoah river is a great wheat-producing country, often yielding from forty to forty-five bushels per acre.

In addition to the agricultural productions, this county has turned out to be possessor of a mineral wealth likely to add materially to its riches. Iron ore (brown hematite and specular) stratified on the slopes of mountains and in pockets on the course of the river, have been discovered in large quantities, and some have been worked for ten years—the products of these mines having been shipped to Sparrow Point, near Baltimore, Harrisburg and Carlisle, Pa., and the Shenandoah Iron Works, in Page county. Along the foot-hills of the Blue Ridge, in this county, fine specimens of copper and lead have been discovered east of the Shenandoah river, and tin has been reported to have been found on the Capon Springs' property by Mr. Bale, who shipped a cargo of the ore to Wales. A purchase of these lands has been negotiated for, including that part of the property on which satisfactory ore has been found. The ores of the county have been worked successfully, notwithstanding the fact that they had to be wagoned five or six miles to connect with railway facilities. There are many ore-bearing tracts which as yet have not been developed, nor can these mineral resources be with any reasonable certainty approximated until they are opened up.

Among the resources of this favored section may be mentioned its timber lands, including large quantities of oak, hickory, walnut, ash, poplar, chestnut, and other kinds of the best quality; and while much has been utilized already, there remain great bodies of it, especially along the foot-hills of the mountains. Stock-raising in the county is quite profitable, and sheep, cattle, horses, and swine are bred in large numbers. The horses of Clarke command a ready sale, on account of their superiority. There is a superabundance of vegetables, dairy products, and farm productions, which are advantageously disposed of by the citizens. The climate is admirable in every way, and the lands rolling and easy of tillage, producing vast quantities of every known product which the soil is capable of bringing forth.

The old family seats and estates of this county have preserved their original boundaries and owners with more tenacity than those of any other that we know of in Virginia. The Pages, Lewises, Clagetts, Taylors, Smiths, McCormicks, Whitings, and many others now occupy the houses of their ancestors, and they have kept them free from the inroads of unsanctified strangers with a care and prudence most commendable in every respect. Some of these are remarkably handsome in the way of architectural structure, while the lands of all are productive and fertile in the highest degree. Every evidence of comfort and contentment seems to surround them, and the social status and compact between these people still remains unimpaired and unshaken. Whether we take "Audley," the family seat of the Lewises, whose ancestors, the Washingtons, trod these same halls of the edifice, or "Page Brook," in the Millwood section, the family seat of the ancestors of Dr.

Page and John Y., all preserve the same family traditions and have that refined and conservative air which time alone can give, assisted by the adjuncts of culture and gentility.

The county-seat of Clarke, so fortunate in being the centre of the many advantages we have named, is Berryville, which lies upon the Norfolk and Western railroad (formerly known as the Shenandoah Valley road), forty miles south of Hagerstown and one hundred and ninety-nine miles north of Roanoke City. It is a very old place, and prior to the year 1798 was known as Battletown, taking this warlike title from the fights which old Daniel Morgan had at the place whenever he came to the town from his home, "Soldier's Rest," some three miles from the place. Saratoga was constructed by Mr. Daniel Morgan, who built the house with the Hessian prisoners, that even quarried the stone.

In 1798 Battletown was incorporated and called Berryville, in honor of Benjamin Berry, an honored citizen of the place at that time. Being the county-seat, it gradually increased until there were three or four hundred people, and it was supported by the trade from the surrounding agricultural region. It went through the ravages of the Civil war, and was the scene of several skirmishes during that period, in which its citizens played an important part, especially when it was shelled by a Maryland regiment. Subsequent to the war it recuperated, and in 1881, when the Shenandoah Valley railroad came through, had about five hundred people, but from that on the increase and growth quickened perceptibly until 1890, when the inhabitants numbered some eighteen hundred people.

No place in Virginia is blessed with a better and more charming people than Berryville. Whether we take them for honesty, uprightness, sobriety, or Christian principles, or whether they are viewed in a social way, they are all and everything that humanity can be. They are thrifty in a business way; they are just and righteous in all their dealings; they are thoroughly kind and hospitable in every conceivable manner, and genial and friendly to the stranger worthy of entering their gates.

There is a general air of good-feeling and fellowship, and unlike most small places everybody always has something good instead of bad to say of his neighbor. Enjoyment and innocent mirth rule the hour, and from the parents to the exquisitely lovely daughters who promenade the shaded sidewalks there is a desire and will to make everybody have a pleasant and enjoyable time.

The churches of almost every denomination are here—the Episcopal, Northern and Southern Methodist churches, Baptist church, Presbyterian—all of which have large and flourishing congregations and a fair average attendance, composed of respectable, orderly people, and the best material. The state of morality is exceptionally high, and a criminal charge is a rare thing, while drunkenness is almost unknown unless some strangers come in and indulge too freely. The place has ample educational facilities, which exert a fine influence over the town, and assists it in a material way as well. In addition to several good public graded schools, and private ones, too, Shenandoah Academy is here, with a fine roll of students, and the young Pages, Lewises, Taylors, Moores, McDonalds, Wheats, McCormicks, Castlemans, Deals, all learn the rudiments and higher branches of educational knowledge here. The natural result of all these advantages is a type of society of the best order imaginable, whether these people be taken as a church-going body, listening to the able discourses of Rev. P. P. Philips, Mr. Fitzwater, Rev. Mr. Wolf, Rev. Julius Broaddus, or be viewed as a whole attending the latest operatic representation of "Pauline, the Belle of Saratoga," so tastefully and ably acted by Miss Evelyn Page, Miss Lewis, supported by the talented operatic star of that country, the incomparable Sam Taylor, now one of the leading real estate men of Berryville and Front Royal. In fact, the social state of the town is all that could be desired in every way, and one well calculated not only to amuse and please, but to instruct also.

This place, which has been quiet so long, cannot remain so in the future in this onward age of development and progress.

The rich agricultural resources surrounding it, the vast body of timbered lands of superior quality, the mineral wealth throughout the county, the immediate delightful advantages of the town itself, will necessarily propel it forward in spite of internal schisms that in certain ways are not less contemptible than they are unwise. And Berryville has come forward to seek her own in this respect. The formation of the Berryville Land and Improvement Company, for the purpose of developing the resources of the town, is but the beginning of an end that will yet astonish the people of the place, who now have almost every nucleus for the founding of a town or the building of a city. If they fail to avail themselves of these wonderful resources and advantages pressing themselves upon the town, then the inhabitants should be buried beneath their own internal rendings and heresies, and have the epitaph "ignominious failure" carved upon their tombstones. But the people of this place as a whole can be depended upon, as well as those of the immediate surrounding neighborhood, who are largely interested in Berryville's welfare.

The town is well laid off, with broad streets, nicely shaded, and the adjacent country admirably suited for building sites—whether for manufacturing or residence purposes—and are being laid off and improved. Several manufactories are there, and the commercial interest is a good one, well supported by both town and country. Taking the town all in all, we know of no more advantageous place for business purposes, nor a more delightful one in which to reside.

CHAPTER VI.

Warren county—Formed in 1836—Character of its agricultural resources and mineral deposits—Front Royal, the county-seat—The twin cities, Front Royal and Riverton—Something of their past history—Growth of these places after the construction of the Shenandoah Valley railroad—Present number and character of the inhabitants of the twin cities—The Front Royal and Riverton Improvement Company—H. H. Downing—Manufacturing and commercial interests of the towns—The development companies—Churches, schools, and social state—One of the coming cities of Shenandoah Valley.

WARREN county, with a population of eight thousand people, was cut off from Frederick and Shenandoah counties in the year 1836, and is one of the best portions of this rich valley of which we have been writing. The lands are generally rolling, with about one-half composed of fertile river bottoms, and have the reputation of being fine agricultural lands as well as an unusually good grazing country, producing in abundance wheat, corn, oats, hay, rye, and barley, as well as the usual kinds of vegetables; and horses, cattle, sheep, and swine are bred in large numbers. The mineral deposits are good also, consisting of iron, manganese, kaolin, fire-clay, limestone, plumbago, ochre, and umber, all of which are found in sufficient quantities to meet the wants and demands of large manufacturing concerns. Specimens of these can be seen by application at the office of the Front Royal and Riverton Improvement Company, located at Front Royal, the county-seat of Warren.

The twin cities, Front Royal and Riverton, which are now virtually one place, are located on the line of the Shenandoah Valley division of the Norfolk and Western railroad, eighty-six miles from Washington by the Manassas Gap branch of the Richmond and Danville Railroad Company; sixty miles from Hagerstown, Maryland, and one hundred and seventy-nine miles from Roanoke, Virginia. Prior to the construction of the Shenandoah Valley road, Front Royal had some five hundred people, while Riverton boasted of three houses. The two places then were some three miles apart, but now, through the recent development, they have become a part and parcel of the same place. When the Shenandoah Valley railroad came, in 1879, both places began to improve—Riverton especially—until in 1890 Front Royal had increased to about two thousand and Riverton grown to seven hundred people. Then began a rapid growth, the end of which has by no means come, since it is really but in its infancy. But prior to the numerous industries which located in 1890, Front Royal and Riverton were by no means at a standstill; in fact, they underwent a steady growth between the years 1880 and 1890. The former place had two banks, a large tannery, a canning factory, cigar factory, flouring mills, Carson's lime works, horse-collar factory, wagon and buggy factory, marble yard, and harness factory. These industries represented a large amount of capital and employed a considerable number of operatives and laborers, who resided at the place. These industries came in after the Shenandoah Valley railroad, and gradually built up Front Royal and Riverton, until, in the year 1890, the places were a considerable nucleus for the development companies to work upon. These cities have had two great advantages ever since 1880—one of which was ample and sufficient water-power, and the best class of railway facilities by way of the Manassas Gap road and the Shenandoah Valley. The north fork and the south fork of the Shenandoah join here and make what is really the main valley of the Shenandoah, as Massanutten mountain—the floor of the valley raised—divides the north and south branches south of the twin cities, through a portion of Warren and Page counties. The position of the two towns of which we are writing is a peculiarly favorable one in a natural way, since all products and resources from both the north and south valley meet and join at this point to proceed northward.

From 1880 to 1890 the people who came to Front Royal and Riverton, together with the former inhabitants of the place, constituted a set of individuals who, though conservative, saw the advantage of manufacturing industries to build up a place, and inaugurated them as far as possible, and located those which we have already named. The banking facilities being fine, and the place enjoying a good surrounding trade from a rich agricultural country, improved rapidly. Whilst the citizens were very prudent and careful, they were not backward and timid, as many were in neighboring places; so when the great progressive move in 1888 and 1889 struck Shenandoah Valley, Front Royal and Riverton were ripe for it, and fell in with the advice and plans of strangers coming in readily, who, seeing the many natural advantages of the situation of the places, cast in their fortunes here. The result was the organization of the Front Royal and Riverton Improvement Company, which we venture to assert is one of the strongest developing companies in every way in Shenandoah Valley.

On the 5th day of June, 1890, this company was organized with a capital stock of $500,000, and H. H. Downing, of Fauquier, was made president. No man could have been selected to have filled this post with more capacity than this gentleman has done, as subsequent policy and success on his part has shown. Even before the charter was obtained he had every dollar of the stock placed, and was industriously at work securing industries for Front Royal and Riverton, consisting of various kinds both in wood and iron. The company purchased 1,700 acres of land in and around the twin cities, all available for building sites, either for manufacturing purposes or residences, and secured leases on 15,000 acres of mineral lands, including iron, copper, asbestos, fire-clay, galena, manganese, manganiferous ores, slate, and marble. It secured the mountain known as Green Hill—one solid mass of iron ore—and the opinion of an expert on the subject of these ores was "that they were sufficient to run the furnaces of Pennsylvania for some time. The company also let to contract the building of two bridges for the improvement of the two places, and all that body of land lying upon the eminence was laid off into squares, with broad, graded avenues, and lots cut off in the usual size. In fact, the policy and object of this company was the building up and improvement of these towns, and every consideration was sacrificed to that object. The result of the liberal donations and subscriptions made by the company was manifest in a short time by the location at Front Royal and Riverton of the following industries: A knitting factory, furniture factory, piano factory, two brick-manufacturing plants, wood-working company, patent machinery company, steam cracker factory, all of which necessarily would take a large number of operatives when in working trim. And H. H. Downing, upon securing a contract for these plants, next interested men of means like Strouse, Allemong, and Bowman, of Salem, Va., in these twin cities, and some of the largest capitalists in Roanoke responded to his urgent solicitation, and Front Royal and Riverton went ahead with wonderful strides, justly and honestly made in their behalf, based upon the situation of the places with reference to railway facilities and the agricultural and mineral resources of the surrounding country. The sale of lots held by the company in the fall of 1890 justified the hopes of the most sanguine, and was one of the most successful which took place in Shenandoah Valley during the year 1890. Large amounts were invested there, and the places have a bright future, toward which they may justly look forward with proper pride and pleasure.

From the time that the Front Royal and Riverton Improvement Company began its work of developing the resources and advantages of these towns and the surrounding country there has been a strenuous effort to locate and get in operation as many industries and manufactories in wood as possible. The object of this was a wise one—to utilize in every conceivable manner the great amount of material in the way of timber growing in the adjacent forests. Mr. Downing's policy—to engage and secure every industry in this respect possible—exhibited unusually good judgment, because it is mainly as much through a number of small manufactories that a city is built up as through larger ones. This manufacture of wood into every conceivable shape and form, for house-building as well as decorative architecture, is not only a nice industry, but an ornamental and useful one, too; and the boundless forests of poplar, oak, hickory, cherry, walnut, chestnut, and other woods furnish an almost endless supply of the best quality of material. From these varieties carriages, wagons, agricultural implements, furniture, buckets, tubs, barrel staves, and, indeed, almost every article made from wood, can be profitably manufactured here and be made a paying undertaking. And every facility will be given those desiring to locate by the companies so much interested in the future of these cities. The quantity and quality of this material has been fully examined, and before long these industries in this branch will re-echo all through Shenandoah Valley, and especially at places like these, where the raw material is abundant and railroad facilities render markets accessible.

In the manufacture of iron, too, Front Royal will take a prominent position, for three reasons: the accessibility of ores in the surrounding country, the cheap supply of coke and limestone, and the railroad facilities which the place must necessarily possess. We have already given an account of the ore regions around the twin cities, and it is unnecessary to revert to them; but in the way of limestone, the country is full of it, and the cost of placing it at the furnaces will be merely nominal. The facility of these places for obtaining coke will readily be seen the moment we unfold the railroad advantages connected with the towns now in existence and in prospective. The Shenandoah Valley branch of the Norfolk and Western Railroad Company places both the Flat Top coal regions and those of Connellsville, Pennsylvania, within reach of Front Royal and Riverton, from either of which she can draw her coke. But there is every prospect of a nearer field still. The Washington and Western railroad, whose charter extends from Washington to West Virginia, across the Shenandoah Valley railroad, and which will intersect that road between Luray and Front Royal, will place the coking fields of the coal regions of West Virginia almost at the furnaces of this section. Already the route of the road is being located, and Front Royal and Riverton have been named as a favorable point for intersection with the Shenandoah Valley railroad. The extension into West Virginia, which is almost a certainty, will be of infinite advantage to these towns, possessing already vast quantities of ores and limestone.

The Lexington and Front Royal Investment Company, by its policy, has taken a hand in the development of the twin cities. It is organized with a capital of $150,000, and has W. F. Pierson as president, with J. W. Ranke secretary and treasurer. The object of the company is necessarily a progressive one for any place in which it locates, for in addition to controlling some two hundred lots in Front Royal, the concern has secured the ground in Riverton on which to erect at least fifty thousand dollars' worth of buildings. No cause is so signally a developing one as that arising from building in a city, because the operation requires an expenditure of means for material and labor also. This undertaking should meet with success when it pursues a plan which benefits a whole community more or less, and we have no doubt of its reaching a high state of prosperity.

The West-End Land Company, organized September, 1890, with a capital stock of $300,000—one-half of which was at once issued—gave a signal progress towards that part of the town extending from the old portion to the Shenandoah Valley railroad. The company is composed of representative men, and purchased 111 acres, which were laid off into lots, with well-graded streets. Every inducement has been offered by this company to secure manufactories, and its policy is a liberal one in every way. In fact, the natural advantages of no place have been more extensively placed before the public than those of the twin cities, by the development companies within their borders, and success so far has repeatedly crowned their efforts.

Notwithstanding the fact that there is a rapid material development afoot, the moral, mental, and social state of the places have ample opportunities to progress. An Episcopal church, one Presbyterian, two Methodist, two Baptist, and one Roman Catholic throw open their doors of worship every Sabbath, and they are well attended and strongly supported. All have pastors of energy and talent, who guard zealously the moral welfare of the twin cities. The state of morality throughout the community is on a healthy basis—as in most places in this charming valley—and peace and contentment seem to be salient characteristics of the community. The educational facilities are undoubtedly good, there being a fine graded school, with good teachers and a fair curriculum, including the languages; yet the attendance in these places by the scholars is not so good as it should be. Socially, the towns are pleasant places, and some very nice people reside there, among whom may be mentioned the Clouds, the Bucks, the Turners, the Roys, the Millers, the Pettys, the Griffiths, the Downings, and others.

Front Royal and Riverton, with their agricultural and mineral resources, their manufacturing and commercial interests, their development companies, their resources in the way of ores and timber, and their railroad facilities, must in the course of a few years be numbered among the cities of the Shenandoah Valley. So far as we can judge the future by what has been accomplished in the past, there can be but little doubt of the reasonableness of such a conclusion, warranted by facts gathered from the soundest basis.

CHAPTER VII.

Augusta county—Once a part of Orange county—Cut off in 1738—This county once included all the country between the Blue Ridge mountains and Mississippi river—Its settlement and rapid growth—Population of same—Agricultural and mineral resources—Waynesboro—When laid off and origin of its name—Its original owners and celebrated tavern—Growth of the place, and the Civil War—Advent of the Shenandoah Valley railroad — Development of Waynesboro commenced by Basic City in 1889—The Waynesboro Company—The West Waynesboro Company — The Waynesboro and Basic City Land Company—Improvements—Manufacturing and commercial interests of the place—Churches, schools, and people of Waynesboro—This town obliged to become a part of Basic City.

AUGUSTA county, the home of civilization, refinement, and wealth, is one of the best counties within the domain of the fair Old Dominion, and on this account has always occupied a prominent part in everything connected with the State. Over a century ago her handful of citizens fought the Indians, and retraced their steps from these victorious fields to struggle for liberty against the encroachment of a parent country. When civil discord rose between the States this county went forth with its sons and gave their property and lives out of love to patriotism, and now she is taking a front place in this age of development, yielding her rich fields and embedded wealth as an assisting power to move the revolving wheels of progress. It is one of the oldest counties in the State, having been cut off from Orange in the year 1738, and was settled by an honest, worthy class of people from Eastern Virginia and Pennsylvania. At one time, by the treaty of Paris in 1763, its western boundary was limited by the Mississippi river, and it covered the vast territory now embracing all of the present State of Virginia west of the Blue Ridge, West Virginia, Kentucky, Ohio, Indiana, Illinois, Michigan, and Wisconsin. As years rolled on, and the people turned their faces westward, the country becoming thickly settled, Augusta was robbed of its vast area of territory, until the present limits were reached. From a handful of people tilling the fertile soil the county has grown until it has become a great manufacturing and commercial centre, with a population of almost forty thousand people, all engaged in lucrative pursuits, which more than supply the wants of its inhabitants. Nor are we in the least surprised at this, if we consider the rich resources lying within its borders.

The natural resources, both as to agriculture and minerals, are almost unlimited except by extent of territory and an imaginary boundary. The lands lie between the Blue Ridge and Alleghany mountains, and are a part of the justly celebrated Shenandoah Valley, and although in some portions of the county are mountainous, on the whole they may be said to be rolling, and are easily cultivated. They are extremely productive, yielding large crops of wheat, corn, hay, oats, and buckwheat, besides vegetables of every description, and have a justly celebrated reputation for the fine stock raised, including large numbers of horses, cattle, sheep, and swine. It is among the first counties in Shenandoah Valley for stock-breeding, having won an enviable reputation for its fine horses and cattle, large numbers of which are exported annually from its borders. Dairy farming is becoming a most important operation, and as the country develops the home consumption of the farm products will but increase its present agricultural wealth. Augusta hay has a State reputation and is eagerly sought after by almost every one who knows anything about this commodity. As far back as 1850 the county produced 419,006 bushels of wheat, 505,000 of Indian corn, 250,026 of oats, 15,225 tons of hay, and 275,483 pounds of butter. This county produces the largest quantity of hay of any other in the State except Rockingham, and leads all in the production of butter except Loudoun. As an agricultural country it has no superior.

Recent developments have likewise proven that the county is also rich in mineral wealth buried within its bowels, to be yet unearthed for the further enriching of its people. Almost all classes of mineral ores have been found, and near the towns of Waynesboro and Basic City the necessary ore for the mak- of basic steel crops out in vast quantities and of fine quality. Iron ore, manganese, ochre, glass sand, fire-clay, china-clay, and others abound throughout Augusta, ready to be mined and utilized for the benefit of mankind whenever it is necessary. No country South can show a better ore territory than this county, and Basic City derives its name from its being in the centre of the region of the South which is best suited, from the vast quantity of raw material, to the manufacture of basic steel. The value of this steel is too well known for an intelligent writer to comment upon. No place can show a better class of iron ores than the western range of the Blue Ridge contiguous to Basic City, and twenty miles west, by the Chesapeake and Ohio railroad, North Mountain range is reached, with brown hematite and Clinton ores in sufficient quantities to supply many furnaces for a long time. The celebrated Crimora manganese mines lie in this county, about nine miles north of Basic City, from which two-thirds of the manganese used in the United States is derived, and which has made the owners wealthy men. Nor is this the only point where this valuable ore is found in this country. With such material in the way of ores, it needs no prophet's eye to foresee that this country must at some day become a manufacturing centre of broad dimensions.

In the county of Augusta, on the Chesapeake and Ohio railroad, 125 miles from Richmond, 12 miles from Staunton, 143 miles from Hagerstown, and 96 miles from Roanoke, lies one of the oldest towns in this section of country, which has grown with scarcely a perceptible gait for the past fifty years, and known as Waynesboro at present—the same title it bore ninety-eight years ago. In 1798 the upper part of the town was laid off, while the lower part was mapped out four years later, in 1802, and the whole named after General Wayne, of Revolutionary fame. The original owners of the soil were jovial Virginians, and old Waynesboro Tavern was known as a place of social enjoyment, where a man was not excluded from "the set" if his love of the sparkling glass got the better of his judgment once in a while. Presidents, in wending their way from their native States, stopped within the rooms of this tavern. Jackson and Fillmore have dined from its festive board, while Benton and Calhoun, able statesmen, have spent the night there, and asked for "just one more glass before we retire."

Slowly this town grew as the centre of a rich agricultural country and rural trade until the year 1850, when there were some six hundred people, with two or three churches and an academy. When the Civil war broke out, in 1861, the town was the scene of carnage and blood, and from an eminence south can be plainly seen the points where the troops were stationed when hot shell waked up the quiet inhabitants of the place. Hunter passed through the place on his raid, and several lively skirmishes enlivened things considerably during this fearful period of death and destruction. Coming out of the war, it recuperated, and one or two manufactories located, when the Shenandoah Valley Railroad Company came in and Waynesboro then improved a trifle faster. A military academy was opened and a fine female school came into existence, while a few more industries made their appearance, and in 1889 the place had several schools, a flouring mill, two furniture factories, two planing, sash, door, and blind factories, a creamery, a machine factory for making rams, corn-shellers, and hay-cutters, with a population of some eleven hundred people.

But the latter part of the year 1889 was an era for this quiet country place, since it seemed all at once to seize a spirit of development, engendered doubtless by the formation of a developing company at Basic City, about three-quarters of a mile away. This place began its operations in December; Waynesboro followed suit, and in the same month the Waynesboro Company, with a capital stock of $100,000, was organized, and M. Erskine Miller elected president, with T. H. Antrim as vice-president and general manager. This organization gave a decided impetus to Waynesboro, which donned a garb of material growth at once that caused the older people to wonder what the world was coming to. The company purchased about 1,700 acres of land lying upon a beautiful plateau fronting on South river, sloping gently to the water, and looking east upon the beautiful valley of the Blue Ridge. Nice building lots, for manufacturing as well as business purposes, were laid off, and inducements offered for the location of plants. The West Waynesboro Company next organized, with General Rosser as president, and a capital stock of $200,000, which purchased a body of land and began using its capital and energy for the benefit of the place. The inauguration of the Waynesboro and Basic City Land Company was the conception of not only a wise plan for developing Waynesboro, but to give it a kind of communication with Basic City, so that the beating of the latter's arteries might throw blood into the former's veins, giving it new vital energy to stir up a sinking pulse. And this well-laid plan met with success, as has since been seen. The company purchased one hundred and thirty-four acres of land lying between and equi-distant from Waynesboro and Basic City, for residence purposes—especially villas. Realizing the importance of dwelling-houses for the manufacturing men locating at Basic City and Waynesboro, the company wisely purchased the land most accessible to both, and laid off its lots. The stock was eagerly taken and the land disposed of at most satisfactory prices. On this property is situated the lovely grove named "Ingall's Park," in honor of Mr. M. E. Ingalls, president of the Chesapeake and Ohio railroad. The company's capital stock was $100,000, and H. Webster Crowl was elected president.

The result of these developing causes was soon apparent in various ways. A large smelting plant for the reduction of tin was secured, and Hotel Brunswick placed under construction by the Waynesboro company—great acquisitions to the town. This hostelry, located on the south of the place, commands a lovely view of the surrounding country, and is built] on the Queen Anne style, with all modern appliances and improvements. Not only will it advance the interests of the place, but become, on account of the location and situation of the property, a famous summer resort. The manufacturing interests were greatly improved, and some new people came in, while the plan of construction of the block of buildings by Rosenburg & Co., brought on by this spirit of development, gave Waynesboro new life and a regenerated existence. There is an air of progress unmistakable about the place which indicates that it is fully alive to the age of material advancement. Improvements are going on, and plans mapped out to bring water from a spring half a mile south of the place, which is the finest in the Shenandoah Valley, and has a cooling draught unexcelled by any water percolating through stratas of purifying earth, thoroughly filtered and refreshed. The advantages of the place materially, with the assistance of these developing companies, and Basic City at hand, will cause Waynesboro to continue to improve and advance. The commercial interests of the town have always been good, since it has been a trading centre from times immemorial for the rich agricultural country around, while the pupils and boarders at the schools and colleges enhance this branch of the town's business in a marked manner.

Christian privileges and educational facilities in Waynesboro are unusually fine, giving the inhabitants of the place every opportunity for moral as well as mental training. There are Presbyterian, Methodist, and Baptist churches, which hold divine service and have the cordial support of the community, while the attendance is always good. Education can be obtained here in either a civil or military way, as both classes of schools exist at Waynesboro, conducted in the best possible manner. The Fishburne Military Academy, with over one hundred scholars and a full corps of instructors, academically as well as in the military department, is a good place at which a boy or young man can be both physically and mentally trained, besides being fitted for army service—by no means an unimportant item. The Waynesboro Female Academy, under Mrs. B. J. Winston, has a hundred and five scholars, and is well known everywhere as a school of the first order. Both are crowded to their full capacity, while the graded free school is admirably attended. The logical consequence of this Christian and mental training is a fine social and moral status in Waynesboro. We doubt if there is a more law-abiding and moral community anywhere than this, and the society is at once intelligent, cultivated, and refined. Certainly these are inducements second to none in the make-up of a place of residence, or one in which to locate with the responsibility of the moral and mental welfare of a family upon one's hands. The people are composed of the descendants of the best inhabitants of the Valley, whose staunch adherence to liberty, love of probity, honesty, and justice, render them pleasant to deal with, and always safe as guardians of the property, liberty, and lives of their fellow-creatures.

This place is destined to be one of the largest cities in the Shenandoah Valley, but not of its own exertions. It will become so through an eventual union with Basic City, only three-quarters of a mile away. Since the growth of both places—particularly Basic City—the two towns have become almost one, and there is a unity of time, interest, title and possession which will surely bring them into one city in a short time. Basic City will certainly absorb Waynesboro, and by so doing the former will gain a power and strength which cannot be calculated now. The two places should have become one in the start, and the feeling of petty jealousy which kept them apart cannot be too severely condemned, for these towns have a foundation for the largest city in that section of country, with every advantage surrounding them. We cannot wish either a more advantageous future than that they come under one head and make this basic steel section all that it should be, as they are fully capable of doing.

CHAPTER VIII.

Basic City—Location—On May 9th the junction of the Chesapeake and Ohio railroad and the Shenandoah Valley—Rapid growth—The cause—Centre of the basic steel section in the South—The Basic City Mining and Manufacturing Company—Policy of the company—Sam. Furrow—J. M. Quarles—Manufacturing and commercial interests of the place—Basic City and Waynesboro—Some general remarks upon the towns in Shenandoah Valley as to their present state and future progress.

WE come now to chronicle the history of a town which is at the same time more brief and marvellous in its wonderful growth and development than any other in Shenandoah Valley or Southwest Virginia. In January, 1890, there was no such place as Basic City in existence, so far as buildings and manufacturing plants go, while in January, 1891, the place has become a town of almost 1,200 people, with manufacturing industries enough completed, under construction, and secured to make a city of 5,000 or 6,000 people in less than another twelve months, provided no miracle of retrograding events occurs. This phenomenal place is located directly upon the line of the Chesapeake and Ohio railroad, at the point where the Shenandoah Valley railroad intersects the former, and on May 9, 1890, Basic City was composed of one hotel and stationhouse. The location had long been held in view as a point to found a city, owing to the situation being in the best portion of Augusta county, and the centre of not only the basic steel ore section, but unexcelled railroad facilities. Here, within a short distance, were the foot-hills of the Blue Ridge, filled with ore; limestone abounded on every side; the coking fields of the Chesapeake and Ohio system, as well as those of the Flat Top region, were within easy reach, and the climate being unexceptionably good, made this point a most favorable one at which to operate. The result was the formation of a development company on December 7, 1889, with a capital stock of $700,000, and the election of Samuel Furrow as president and J. M. Quarles vice-president and general manager of this enterprising concern. The policy of this company was undoubtedly the utilization of the many natural advantages of the place for the building of a city, and this company possessed every natural advantage necessary to operate successfully upon. This point is some 124 miles from Richmond, 12 miles from Staunton, 96 miles from Roanoke, and 143 miles from Hagerstown, Maryland. East and west, north and south, railroad facilities are unrivalled, while the ore region around is all that could be desired. Iron, sandstone, fire-clays, ochre, manganese, and other ores already named as belonging to Augusta county, abounded on all sides, and the agricultural country everything that heart could wish to supply twenty times the population with the necessaries and comforts of life. The town of Waynesboro, which hitherto had never thrown off its lethargy, began to stir after the move at Basic City, and it needed but the placing of these advantages before the public in order for Basic City to spring into existence as if by magic, and grow with great rapidity. This the company did through the great financiering abilities of Samuel Furrow, president, and J. M. Quarles, general manager.

Early in the year 1890 the company purchased all the land lying on both sides of the Chesapeake and Ohio and Shenandoah Valley railroads, and laid off its streets and lots. Mineral lands and rights were obtained, and the company secured the plant of the Basic City Car Works, with a working capital of $250,000, which would employ about two hundred and fifty men, and several smaller industries. The next step was preparation for a lot sale which would attract the attention and capital of people to the place, where natural advantages would speak for it strongly. On May 9, 1890, the first lot sale of the company was held and $150,000 worth sold, and, what was more to the point, the wonderful resources of the place were called to the attention of the public, and the consequences were, manufacturing plants not only came in rapidly, but began construction of their works at once, giving living and real security for the future of Basic City. In less than five months the town had the following industries secured, all of which began immediately to lay the foundation for future operations: The car works mentioned above; a paper mill, capital $50,000, to work 75 hands; hardware factory, capital stock $150,000, to work 250 hands; match factory, $50,000 capital, to employ 50 hands; cigar factory; lumber and coal company, capital $100,000, to employ 75 laborers; Myers' Brick Works, the Brinkel Brick Works, the Booker Steam Plant, the Ennis and Coyner Mill Works, the Lott Plant, the Basic City Iron Furnace, 100 tons capacity, to employ about three hundred hands at the works and mines both, which latter undertaking is a part and parcel of the Basic City Mining and Manufacturing Company. When the general manager, Mr. J. M. Quarles, first informed us of these numerous industries, secured in so short a time, our doubts were many; but as contract after contract was unfolded and the foundation for the works placed within our sight, every lingering doubt vanished and turned to admiration for the industry and energy of the men who had accomplished so great an undertaking. Nor did this enterprising concern halt upon the securing of these industries merely. It took the necessary steps to give them every aid, facility, and assistance possible that would benefit them and cause Basic City to progress.

The town was laid off with an eye to manufacturing purposes, for the broad, lovely plateau bounded north by South river, south by the Chesapeake and Ohio railroad, and east by Shenandoah Valley railroad was reserved solely for manufacturing and business purposes. The industries were located upon the river, and lots laid off especially for them, and in order to prevent any expense or trouble about handling freight, the company built a belt line of railroad track, extending for a mile, from the Chesapeake and Ohio railroad to the Shenandoah Valley railroad, giving these manufacturing concerns a line of road directly at their establishments, which was an undertaking fully appreciated in every way, and which added materially to the progress of Basic City. With this belt line completed, manufactories going up on all sides, residences and buildings of every class completed and under construction, this town has the appearance of a city, and the thriving, bustling, rushing air about the whole place is indicative of rapid progress in a material way. Water works were put under contract at once, which were constructed for the purpose of supplying the town, and brings the fluid from a spring south of the city unsurpassed in every way for coolness, purity, and quantity of water. In fact, this natural reservoir is an unusually fine one, and is another of the natural resources of the town.

After having laid the foundation for a manufacturing city, and done everything possible for its comfort and success, the company then turned its attention to the pleasure of guests desiring to visit Basic City, and placed under construction one of the finest hotels in the valley, now completed, and known as "Hotel Brandon." This structure, containing nearly a hundred rooms, was designed by the accomplished architect, Mr. Poindexter, of Washington, and is built in Queen Anne style, with all the appliances and comforts known now to hotel life. It was upholstered and furnished by Philip Brown, of Blue Ridge fame, and is one of the most elegant and comfortable hostelries that we know of anywhere. The view from the piazzas surrounding the hotel is lovely in the extreme, overlooking the growing city to the uplands beyond, and extending away westward to the ethereal blue of the everlasting mountains.

Another sensible move made by this company in the beginning was the establishment of a good journal for the purpose of having the many resources of the place put before the people in a judicious, prudent manner. The "Advance Steam Publishing Company," located in a handsome brick structure in the centre of the business part of the town, edits and publishes this paper, which has done so much for Basic City. It is a well-gotten-up newspaper edition, and gives the news of the day in addition to the advantages of Basic City. Journalism, well guarded and properly directed, has been one of the most powerful engines in the development of this country, and it should at all times receive the support and sanction of the people, and never be allowed to either suffer or transgress the bounds of domestic privacy or private character. We are happy to say that the journals of the country of which we are writing have ever held those rules inviolate.

Following this great industrial move of manufacturing enterprises into Basic City came a substantial mercantile interest, ever ready to be on hand to furnish supplies for the demands of any body of people. Stores have been erected and filled with the necessaries and comforts of life to meet the wants of the people, and banking facilities pursued the mercantile interest, which is nearly always the case. Thus, two buildings, existing all alone in May, 1890, grew into a thriving town of over a thousand people in eight months, eclipsing any other industrial city in this section, and laid the manufacturing plants necessary to bring in at least six thousand people in twelve months. The fact is startling even in relating it, yet not more so than the wonderful growth of this city, which has been managed with every possible advantage imaginable. Too much credit cannot be given to the projectors of this town.

Educational opportunities were not neglected, for the Normal College was removed from Harrisburg, Pa., here, and a fine building north of the town constructed for its use. The well-educated principal, Mr. Hounshell, has a roll of two hundred students and a full faculty of good teachers in attendance. This will be of material advantage to the town, and cast a potent influence over its mental and moral training so necessary to any place just beginning.

Basic City has before it another impetus which is forced to come in course of time. This place will include Waynesboro within its limits, upon the principle that the creator invariably takes care of the created. It was the industrial move on the part of this town which caused Waynesboro to wake from its long sleep of country quietude and don the cloak of enterprise and development, and this same spirit will move Basic City to take complete charge of Waynesboro in time to come, and develop, with the assistance of men like Antrim, the resources of this latter place. Another reason for the two places becoming one is the unity of interest, which will grow stronger and stronger each day. Waynesboro is as lovely a place for a residence as we know of, and many of the manufacturing people in Basic City will reside there with their families, which will soon cause both places to be as one, with the prospect of an ultimate union almost certain; and any spirit of opposition on the part of either cannot be too severely criticised, since both together, with their combined resources and capital, would make the two, at no long future day, one of the great cities of the Valley, not to be surpassed by any other.

Such is the brief history of Basic City, which now has far more than a sectional reputation.

There are other places along the line of this road, which we will not attempt a description of, for two reasons: Some are not within the scope of this work, and others have not played that part in the development of the section which entitles them to a consideration as one of the causes of the progress of the country, an inquiry into which is the origin and reason of this undertaking. Some of these places will be towns in course of time, and act an important role in the rapid growth of the country, but at present they have neither the natural advantages nor necessary stamina to cope with those we have been discussing. Many of those towns of which we have written are necessarily obliged to become cities, because every power that nature possesses, including her most prodigal gifts, have been showered upon them, and the very earth itself yields the wealth hid from sight to assist generous providence in playing its part under the canopy of showers and the genial rays of the sun. Shenanhoah Valley is as glorious a land as ever man saw, and no one can withhold his tribute of praise.

If Governor Spotswood really uttered the sentence, we cannot refrain from agreeing with him when he said that the Great Valley, including Southwest Virginia and Shenandoah Valley, was "God's country," in reference to its wonderful fertility, glorious climate, and sublime scenery.

THE END.

EVERYNAME INDEX

ACKERLY, J P 146
ADAIR, William 54
ADAMS, Mrs 161 Mrs R H 168 R H 168
ALLEMONG, 242 J W F 151-152 Mr 114
ALLEN, 4 201 George 151-153 Mr 114
ANTRIM, 258 T H 249
ARMES, Mr 227
BAILEY, James M 55
BAKER, 18
BALE, Mr 234
BARCLAY, 168 Capt 169
BARRIES, Casper 6
BATTE, Capt 3 Henry 3-4
BEATTY, D O 185
BECKWITH, 63 Harvey 59 68
BEELER, Christopher 198
BELL, 10 231
BENTON, 9 249
BERKELEY, Gov 4 William 3
BERRY, Benjamin 236
BEVERLY, 4
BLACKFORD, 129
BOCOCK, Thomas 61
BOHANON, 173
BOLLING, Daniel 57
BOSWELL, 142
BOTETOURT, Lord 9-10
BOTT, 38 156
BOUQUETTE, Col 10
BOWMAN, 4 242 A M 113-114 118 151-152 Mr 152
BOWYER, 9
BOYCES, 201
BOYD, William 10
BOYER, L S 206
BRADDOCK, 199 Gen 6 199
BRAMWELL, J H 231
BRAND, Alexander Y 215 221 Judge 222
BRECKENRIDGE, 9
BRIEDLER, W T 217
BROADDUS, Julius 237
BROCK, 155 Richard S 181
BROOKE, S S 146
BROWN, 142 178 H E 146 Philip 256
BUCHANAN, 9 Col 5 John 4
BUCK, 245
BUCKLAND, Jacob 57
BUERACHER, Samuel 217
BUFORD, Col 14
BURDEN, 4
BURKE, James 5-6 14
BURTON, Jesse 121
BURWELL, 196 201
BUTTON, George P 133
BYARS, James W 31
CALFEE, 178 L S 118 175-176 Lee S 175
CALHOUN, 249
CAMPBELL, 216 A A 183 A J

CAMPBELL (Cont.)
   216 Andrew W 216 Mr
   217 W B 216 W C 143
   Walter 221
CAMPER, 146 J W 146
CARR, 133 William 133
CARSON, 240
CARTER, 201 Col 196-197
   Robert 200
CASTLEMAN, 197 201 237
CATLETT, 231
CECIL, Maj 5
CHAPMAN, A A 54 F J 151
   155 Mr 155-156
CHAUVENET, S E 181
CHISWELL, Col 10 John 10
CHRISMAN, 4
CHRISTIAN, 4
CHUMBLEY, Joseph H 54
CLAGETT, 201 235
CLARK, 155 C H 81 Clarence
   H 71-72 79 81-83 136 209
   227 Clarence M 155 181
   Mr 82
CLARKE, 204 John 121
CLAYTON, 172
CLAYTOR, M H 146
CLOUD, 245
CLOYD, 9-10 David 9 Gordon
   9 Joseph 9 54 Thomas 9
COLLINS, E J 181
COOKE, 175
COON, J W 139
COWAN, 10 John T 54 57-58
   60 Mr 63
CRABTREE, J T 151 153
CRESAP, 17 Capt 11 17-18 Col
   17 Michael 11
CRITTENDEN, 9
CROCKET, 168
CROWL, H Webster 250
CULL, James 6 Mrs 6

CUMBERLAND, Duke Of 5
D'ARMOND, Mr 138
D'INVILLIER, 73
D'INVILLIERS, 35-36 86
DAVENPORT, J C 139
DAVIDSON, Mrs 16 Mrs
   Andrew 16
DAVIS, Mosby 57
DEAL, 237
DEAN, D H 57
DEFOARD, 220
DENNISTON, 155
DEPEW, Chauncey M 38 52 Mr
   52
DERR, Oscar D 146 Rush U
   145
DILLARD, Thomas 121
DINGES, Mr 176
DIXON, 36 148
DODDRIDGE, Dr 17
DOOLEY, W H 146
DOUGLAS, Achilles 121 John
   A 55
DOWNING, 245 H H 241-242
   Mr 242
DRAPER, 5 George 4 7 John 6
   Mary 6 Mrs 5 Mrs George
   6 Mrs John 6
DREHER, Dr 151 158
DREW, Mrs Thomas R 183
DUFF, 4
DUNMORE, Gov 12 Lord 12
   199
EASLEY, George W 57
ECHMAN, George 176
EDDY, C G 159 Charles G 155
   178 Col 172
EGGLESTON, William 54
ENGLISH, Mr 65 Sec 66 T B 59
   62 64-65
EVANS, Martha 15 Miss 16
FAIRFAX, Lord 197

FERGUSSON, S M 133
FIELD, Col 13 John 13
FILLMORE, 249
FITZWATER, Mr 237
FLANNAGAN, A H 54
FLEMING, William 13
FLICKWIR, D W 213 227
FLOYD, 9 177 John 173 John B 173
FOSTER, Fred E 169 177
FOWLER, 58 Elbert 55-56
FRANKLIN, Thomas 57
FREEMAN, Mr 223
FRENCH, Pole 53 W H 55
FRY, A L 57
FURROW, Samuel 254
GAMBILL, James M 133
GARDNER, Robert L 173
GEORGE II, King of ? 133
GEORGE III, King of ? 133
GEORGE III, King Of England 14
GILMER, Mrs 145
GLEANER, C H 57
GLOYD, Gov 173
GOOCH, A 55
GOODWYN, 168 Robert 169
GRAHAM, 58-59 63-65 67 71 83 Mr 60 Thomas 58-66 68
GRANT, 136
GREATHOUSE, 17-18 Daniel 11
GREEN, 4
GREY, 142
GRIFFIN, Dr 149
GRIFFITH, 245
GRIGG, Samuel 134
GRILLS, Eleanor 14
GUNN, Prof 168
HALE, John P 4 Mr 4
HALL, 201

HAMET, Col 160-161
HAMPTON, 9 Joseph 198
HARBISON, William 6
HARGROVE, Prof 222
HARMAN, Adam 5 Col 59
HARMON, Adam 8
HARPER, 4
HARRISON, J R 186
HART, 9
HARVEY, James A 54 Lewis K 57
HAUPT, Mr 138 S B 138
HERBERT, C E 146
HETH, 168 Capt 164-165 Stockton 161 164
HITE, Abraham 197 Joist 4
HIX, Joseph 15
HOGE, 168 Joseph H 54
HOLSTEIN, G M 174
HOOPAUGH, George 6
HOTCHKISS, 60 Jed 231 Mr 63
HOUNSHELL, Mr 257
HOWERTON, Mr 141 S W 141
HUGHES, Robert W 55
HUNTER, 249
IMBODEN, Gen 35
INDIAN, Bald Eagle 11 Black Wolf 15 Blue Jacket 13 Eliinipsico 13 Logan 13 16-17 Red Hawk 13
INGALLS, M E 250
INGLES, 5 8 160-161 168 Capt 9 Eleanor 14 Mary 6 160 Mrs 7-8 Mrs Thomas 15 Mrs William 6-7 Thomas 4-5 7 14-15 William 4 7 14-15 161 163
IRWIN, Chief 130
JACKSON, 205 249 Gen 228
JACOBSEN, Charles 135 Mr 136
JEFFERSON, Thomas 14 231

JEFFRESS, John J 57
JOHNSON, 9 David E 55 Dr 66
    Samuel 195 William 11
JOHNSTON, A N 55
JONES, 178 Thomas 174
KAGEY, D F 220-221
KEARSLEY, 168
KENT, 10 James G Mcg 133
KILLION, C M 153
KIMBALL, F J 227 Frederick J 209
KINNEAR, 134
KIRKPATRICK, 129
LANGHORNE, 178 J C 153
LARUE, 198 Isaac 198
LEE, 202 Col 223
LENARD, Henry 5-6
LEWIS, 13 200-201 235 237
    Andrew 8 12 14 132-133
    Charles 12-13 Col 13
    Edward 200 Gen 8 12-13
    H L D 200 Jane 14 133
    John 4 John E 129 Miss 237 Thomas 14
    Washington 200
LIGON, G J 153
LINDSEY, James 198 John 198
LITCHFIELD, 173
LOONEY, Absalom 15
LORRAINE, 215
LYBROOK, 6
LYNCH, John 121
MADISON, 9
MAHONE, Gen 78 William 54 78
MARSHALL, C G 220-221
MARTIN, 173 Robert 173
    Robert D 173 William 121
MASON, 36 148
MAXWELL, Capt 15
MAYES, Mr 178
MCCHANNAHAN, Capt 13

MCCONNELL, James A 143
MCCORMICK, 197 201 235 237
MCCREATH, 35-37 73 86 204
    Andrew S 206 232 Mr 38
MCDONALD, 237 August 12
MCDOWELL, 9 Mr 227
MCGAVOCK, 10
MCGILL, 178 James 85 Mr 85
MCGREGOR, 170
MCKAY, 4
MCNUTT, R B 55
MILLER, 245 J I 222 M Erskine 249 Mr 222 William 197
MILLS, 176 G T 40 George T 173 175-176
MILNES, 224
MOHLER, Mr 229
MONTGOMERY, Capt 8 John 173
MOOMAW, D C 141 W P 141
MOORE, 4 178 201 237 A Mason 204 I Q 57 James 15 James Jr 16 James Sr 15 John 16 Mary 16 Mr 66 Mrs 15-16 Rebecca 15 Sqr 66 W L 57 William 15
MOORMAN, Micajah 121
MORGAN, 4 Daniel 236
MORRISS, M M 185-186
MOSBY, 202
MURRAY, Capt 13
MURRELL, D G 121
NELSON, 66 196 201 M 151 W M 153
NICHOLSON, 142 H Q 146 148
NOLAN, C Powell 227
NORRIS, Septimus E 69
OPIE, Hierome L 197
OSBURN, 66
PACK, Capt 53-54
PAGE, 136 196 201 235 237

PAGE (Cont.)
  Brook 235 Dr 235-236
  Evelyn 237 John Y 200
  236 Mr 201
PALMER, Charles W 31
  George W 118 174 186-
  188 Mr 187
PARKER, Charles 63 J 57
  Richard E 197
PATTON, 4 9 Col 4 6 James 5
PECHIN, Edmund C 38 155
  172 181
PENDLETON, 201 Sgt 130
PENN, John 198
PERDUE, Daniel K 57
PETERS, Samuel 161
PETTY, 245
PEYTON, 9 William L 133
PHIL, Capt 141
PHILIPS, P P 237
PHIPPS, Park 69
PIERCE, 173 James N 173 Mr 173
PIERSON, W F 244
PLEASANTS, M F 79
POINDEXTER, Mr 256
POWELL, 142 Arthur T 153 D
  Lee 117 153 L L 117 153
PRESTON, 4 9 S R 183
  Susanna 9 William 8-9
PUGH, 142 J A 146 Mr 146
QUARLES, J M 254-255
RADFORD, 58 Dr 56 161 J
  Lawrence 118 161-162
  167-168 John B 54 56 118
  161 Mrs 168
RAINES, William 133
RAMEY, Lew 216 Lewis 215
RANKE, J W 244
RANSOM, W B 161
RAY, Lew 216
READ, Amos 57

REID, George 57
ROANE, 58-62 64-71 82 137
  209 Mr 61 66 69-71 R B
  58-61 64 68 Richard B 56-
  58 62 65-66 68 71 178
ROBERTSON, William Gordon 137
ROBINSON, 176-177 A 169 Mr 227
RODGERS, M M 153
RODMAN, 63 Lewis 59 68
RORER, 133 Ferdinand 133
ROSSER, Gen 250
ROY, 245
ROYER, O Howard 213
RUST, 204
RYAL, John W 136
SANDS, Jas 227
SEAY, Sgt 130
SERGEANT, 63-65 68-69 71
  82-83 J D 69-71 82 137 J
  Dickinson 59 63-64 66 68
  70 209 Mr 65 82
SHEPHARD, 4
SHICKEL, T J 151-152
SIMMONS, 142 James S 117
SIMPSON, John 15
SIMS, H A 143
SMITH, 235 John 57 Jonathan
  57 Ralph Jr 121 Richard
  121 Susanna 9 William P
  201
SNIDOW, John C 54
SPOTSWOOD, Alexander 195
  Gov 2 4 258
SPOTTS, A A 57 67 G W 57
  Mr 67
STARTZMAN, 134
STATHAM, Charles W 54
STEBBINS, B P 216 Mr 217
STEPHENS, 4 Widow 36
STOVER, Jacob 196

STRATTON, Joseph 121
STRAYER, E S 153
STROTHER, 58 P W 57 Philip W 54
STROUSE, 242 D B 113 151-152
STUART, A H 31 E S 118 H C 187 Henry C 31 W A 186-187
TABOR, George 57
TAYLOE, 132
TAYLOR, 178 201 235 237 Elizabeth 161 India 57 John Mccandless 118 160-161 Mr 176 Sam 237 Sarah 57
TERRY, 133 P L 227 Peyton L 133
THOMAS, Col 132-133
THOMPSON, 9 Arch 57
THROCKMORTON, 200
TINSLEY, B T 133
TOSH, 14 Jane 14 Miss 14 Mr Thomas 132 Thomas 14 132-133
TROUT, 134 John 133
TURNER, 245
TYLER, 168 George F 85 J Hoge 117 164 Sidney F 212
WALKER, Col 5 G C 60 Gilbert C 58 Gov 59 67 James A

WALKER (Cont.) 54 Thomas 5
WARDLE, 170
WARNE, Mr 38
WASHINGTON, 200 235 Col 8 Gen 13 197
WATSON, Dr 173
WAYNE, Gen 248
WELLS, C D 13
WHARTON, 56 58 G C 53-54 56-57 60 162 168 Gen 54-56 60 63 67-68 162 Mrs 162 Mrs G C 161
WHEAT, 201 237
WHEELWRIGHT, J F 227
WHITING, 200-201 235
WHITTEN, W H 57
WILLIAMS, Thomas N 129
WILLIS, 200
WILMER, 205
WILSON, Lizzie 138 Samuel 13
WINGFIELD, 142
WINSTON, Mrs B J 252
WOLF, Rev Mr 237
WOOD, 58-59 63 Abraham 2 Col 2-3 Mr 63 Richard 57 59 62 68 W W 59 67 Walter W 58
WOODRUM, R H 142 147
WORMLY, 197 Ralph 197
WRIGHT, A D 231-232
YANCEY, William T 54

www.ingramcontent.com/pod-product-compliance
Lightning Source LLC
Chambersburg PA
CBHW071425150426
43191CB00008B/1049